Ordinary Courage

For

Aunt Jane and Uncle Don McClelland

with Affection

Ordinary Courage

The Revolutionary War Adventures of Joseph Plumb Martin

Third Edition

Edited by

James Kirby Martin

Blackwell Publishing

Editorial material and organization © 2008 by Blackwell Publishing Ltd

BLACKWELL PUBLISHING
350 Main Street, Malden, MA 02148-5020, USA
9600 Garsington Road, Oxford OX4 2DQ, UK
550 Swanston Street, Carlton, Victoria 3053, Australia

The right of James Kirby Martin to be identified as the author of the editorial material in this work has been asserted in accordance with the UK Copyright, Designs, and Patents Act 1988.

First edition published 1993 by Brandywine Press
Second edition published 1999 by Brandywine Press
Third edition published 2008 by Blackwell Publishing Ltd

3   2011

Library of Congress Cataloging-in-Publication Data

Martin, Joseph Plumb, 1760–1850.
 Ordinary courage : the Revolutionary War adventures of Joseph Plumb Martin / edited by James Kirby Martin. – 3rd ed.
  p. cm.
 Rev. ed., with corrections and notes, of: Narrative of some of the adventures, dangers, and sufferings of a Revolutionary soldier. 1830.
 "First edition published 1993 by Brandywine Press. Second edition published 1999 by Brandywine Press"– T.p. verso.
 Includes bibliographical references and index.
 ISBN 978-1-4051-7706-1 (pbk. : alk. paper) 1. Martin, Joseph Plumb, 1760–1850. 2. United States–History–Revolution, 1775–1783–Personal narratives. 3. Soldiers–United States–Biography. I. Martin, James Kirby, 1943– II. Martin, Joseph Plumb, 1760–1850. Narrative of some of the adventures, dangers, and sufferings of a Revolutionary soldier. III. Title.

E275.M38 2008
973.3'8—dc22

                                    2007036379

A catalogue record for this title is available from the British Library.

Set in 10/12pt Sabon
by SPi Publisher Services, Pondicherry, India
Printed and bound in Singapore
by Ho Printing Singapore Pte Ltd

For further information on
Blackwell Publishing, visit our website at
www.blackwellpublishing.com

Contents

Introductory Comments

Etched on Joseph Plumb Martin's tombstone are the modest words, "A Soldier of the Revolution." He was born in 1760 just before the outbreak of the American Revolution. He lived for nearly 90 years, during which time the young United States established itself as a legitimate political entity, if not a potential rising star, among the nations of the world. He died in 1850, an "aged man" living in virtual poverty. Martin never commanded large bodies of troops in battle; he never held major political offices; he never engaged in vital diplomatic negotiations; he never invented anything of consequence or made a notable scientific discovery; and he never acquired great wealth to distribute as a renowned philanthropist. Martin was very much an ordinary person who in his youth served courageously in the Continental army and who in his adult years, according to one of his admirers, regularly displayed "a fund of knowledge, which, with his lively, social disposition, and ready wit, made him a highly entertaining and instructive companion."[1]

Martin grew to adulthood in times that were truly extraordinary. British North American colonists had begun to believe that their parent nation of Great Britain was attempting to subvert their fundamental liberties. When King and Parliament kept trying to tax

---

[1] Joseph Williamson, "Biographical Sketch of Joseph P. Martin, of Prospect, Maine, a Revolutionary Soldier," *The New England Historical and Genealogical Register*, 30 (1876): 330–31. Martin's remains are buried at the Sandy Point Cemetery in Sandy Point, Waldo County, Maine, close to where he lived from the mid-1780s to the time of his death in 1850.

them, the Americans vocalized such slogans as "no taxation without representation" and spoke anxiously about a plot by home government leaders to shackle them forever in the chains of imperial tyranny. They also protested defiantly, so much so that King George III during the summer of 1775 declared them to be in open rebellion. Four months earlier warfare had broken out when British regulars, looking for gunpowder and weapons, marched from Boston into the Massachusetts countryside and became entangled in a day of combat with resolute citizen-soldiers that began at the villages of Lexington and Concord.

Even after this initial shedding of blood, large numbers of colonists, including most patriot political leaders who gathered in Philadelphia during May 1775 to attend the Second Continental Congress, hoped and prayed for a peaceful resolution of grievances. More confrontational delegates, however, insisted upon making full provisions for defense. Their will prevailed. On June 14 Congress voted to establish a Continental army, initially to consist of the ten to fifteen thousand New England enthusiasts who had rallied together to challenge the King's troops and keep them entrapped in Boston. Soon thereafter the delegates selected general officers, and they named as commander in chief the highly regarded Virginia planter George Washington, then attending Congress and an experienced veteran of the French and Indian War.

These decisions had a lasting impact on the life of Joseph Plumb Martin, who was not yet 15 years old when Washington traveled northeast from Philadelphia to the vicinity of Boston to assume command of his newly adopted Continental force. Joseph was born on November 21, 1760, in the western Massachusetts town of Becket. His family lineage was certainly respectable. His father, the Reverend Ebenezer Martin, had graduated from Yale College in 1756. Two years later Ebenezer became the first Congregational minister in frontier Becket, where he moved with his wife Susanna. The daughter of a freehold farmer named Joseph Plumb, Susanna grew up in Milford, Connecticut, a few miles west of New Haven, the home of Yale. She wed Ebenezer while he was still in college. Joseph was one of seven children produced by their union.

Family life with Ebenezer was tumultuous. Throughout his checkered, largely unsuccessful ministerial career, he was continually quarrelsome, besides being enamored of his own opinions and careless in the handling of his personal finances. In late 1764 he lost his Becket pastorate because of an unpleasant disagreement with the town fathers over land ownership issues, this among other undefined "indiscretions." The latter likely related to his spendthrift habits.[2]

How Ebenezer provided for himself and his family during the next three and a half years remains unclear. Possibly Susanna's father gave them extended shelter in Milford. When Ebenezer finally secured another pastorate in June 1768 with the newly formed parish of Westford in the northeastern Connecticut town of Ashford, 7-year-old Joseph remained with his Plumb grandparents, who assumed permanent responsibility for his upbringing. Perhaps, among other reasons, they did so to help lighten the burden of family expenses as Ebenezer began anew his ministerial calling. Also, Susanna may have wanted to keep her young son away from his overbearing father.

Ebenezer Martin soon showed that he could not shed his imprudent ways. In 1772 he sidestepped debtors' prison by appearing before Connecticut's General Assembly and declaring his insolvency. Five years later his Westford congregants dismissed him for ongoing "complaints of unministerial conduct." Because he offered a public apology, he gained "a regular dismission." Ebenezer then migrated with his family to frontier New York and offered his pastoral services at various locations before his death in 1795. "His reputation" was never that of a saintly divine, wrote one Congregational church historian, but rather "of an able, but not always *wise* man—one who said smart things and *odd* things, that were remembered sometimes to his discredit and injury."[3]

While his father was ministering to his Westford parishioners, Joseph sprouted toward adulthood under the stern but benevolent nurturing of his grandparents. Grandfather Plumb was not "wealthy," as his grandson later described him, but he was a respectable, hardworking farmer. His desire was to teach his grandson how to make a satisfactory living from farming the land, but then Lexington and Concord intervened. Joseph found himself caught up in the *rage militaire* of 1775, or what seemed like a universal obsession to bear

[2] Joseph S. Clark, et al., "Churches and Ministers in Windham County, Connecticut," *The Congregational Quarterly*, 1 (1859): 268–69. For additional information, see the sketch of Ebenezer Martin in Franklin Bowditch Dexter, *Biographical Sketches of the Graduates of Yale College, 1701–1815* (6 vols., New York, 1885–1912), 2: 420–21; and "A Complete List of the Congregational and Presbyterian Ministers in Massachusetts, from Settlement of the Colonies to the Present Time," *The American Quarterly Register*, 7 (1834): 32, 35.
[3] Clark, et al., "Churches and Ministers," *Congregational Quarterly*, 269.

arms against the King's forces. Romantic images about the glories of marching off to war filled his youthful mind, a beguiling prospect in comparison to his tedious daily routine of farm chores. The life of a soldier was what Joseph was sure he most wanted, but he was not yet old enough to enlist without his grandparents' permission. The Plumbs refused to indulge his fancies, at least not during the first year of the Revolutionary War.

Joseph had no way of foreseeing that the *rage militaire* would not last. The patriot enthusiasts of 1775 found military service to be anything but glamorous. They had expected to fire a few musket shots at those damnable British "lobsterbacks," but they did not relish the rigorous training and discipline by which soldiers learn to function effectively in battle. Camp life was not only boring but very hazardous to personal health because of continuous exposure to the elements, rotten food, accumulated filth, and the ever lurking presence of such deadly diseases as smallpox. Combat, as some of these sunshine patriots soon learned, could result in permanent disablement or death from enemy gunfire and thrusting bayonets. For all of these reasons the patriot rush to arms of 1775 quickly waned. Washington's Continental force began the 1776 campaign season critically short of troop strength, which helped give Joseph his opening. When the Continental Congress called for special levies of state troops to serve for the remainder of the year, he was able to enlist without strong opposition from his grandparents.

As Martin explained, he thought he had formed "pretty correct ideas" regarding the reasons why the revolution was necessary. His romantic notions about war, however, did not prepare him for the terrible privations—he called them his "constant companions, Fatigue, Hunger, and Cold"—that he endured year after year as a Continental soldier. Repeatedly he risked life and limb as he fought in major engagements that in 1776 included the defense of Long Island and New York City and the Battle of White Plains; in 1777 the Battle of Germantown in Pennsylvania and the defense of the Delaware River forts; in 1778 the Battle of Monmouth in New Jersey; and in 1781 the siege of Yorktown in Virginia. Martin's length of service, his version of going to high school and college in making the passage to adulthood, made him a "duration" or long-term Continental enlistee, of whom there were very few, probably no more than 1 out of every 250 persons in the Revolutionary populace.

Only 22 years old at the war's end in 1783, Martin had to find some means to provide for himself in the days and years ahead. For a brief time he taught school among Dutch settlers in the Hudson Highlands region north of New York City. Even though the inhabitants encouraged Martin to remain with them, he had to reckon with his own academic shortcomings. Unlike his father, he had only the bare rudiments of a formal education. "I had never studied grammar an hour in my life," he admitted, then adding crisply: "When I ought to have been doing that, I was forced to be studying the rules and articles of war."

Farming was Martin's only real alternative. Before leaving the army, he had considered traveling with one of his comrades to western New York in search of tillable land. He did not make the trip. The most likely reason was that the Six Nations of Iroquois Indians still had not lost their long-standing claim to that region. Nor did Martin return to Milford. His Plumb grandparents had died during the war, and their farm holdings had likely passed to one or more of their sons—brothers of Joseph's mother—if not sold off for payment of debts.

Looking elsewhere for opportunity, Martin, like hundreds of other penniless veterans who mustered out of the service with little else except the clothes they were wearing, followed up on rumors that an abundance of decent land was available on easy terms in what would be the future state of Maine. In the spring of 1784 he traveled east with "no material halt" until he reached the mouth of the Penobscot River along the ruggedly beautiful mid-Maine coastline. Here in the vicinity of old, crumbling Fort Pownal, an important military post during the French and Indian War, he settled in and made his home for the remaining 66 years of his existence.[4]

Martin prospered at first, and he eventually moved from a rude cabin to a more impressive framed structure. In May 1794 he married Lucy, the 19-year-old daughter of Sara (Stimpson) and Isaac Clewley, a prominent local farmer and ship's carpenter. Over the years, Lucy bore several children, including Joseph (b. 1801), described in the records as "an idiot from birth"; twins Thomas and Nathan (b. 1805); James Sullivan (b. 1810); and Susan (b. 1814).[5]

---

[4]   Alan Taylor, *Liberty Men and Great Proprietors: The Revolutionary Settlement on the Maine Frontier, 1760–1820* (Chapel Hill, NC, 1990), 14–21. Taylor points out that the deceptive lure of cheap land was a major reason for the tripling of Maine's population to 100,000 people between 1775 and 1790.

[5]   Henry J. Martin, *Notices: Genealogical and Historical, of the Martin Family, of New England* (Boston, 1880), 289; Ethel Kenney Lord, "Isaac Clewley; Father and Son," *Daughters of the American Revolution Magazine*, 93 (1959): 235–36.

Martin gained the respect of his neighbors in the bustling little fishing and farming community that became the incorporated town of Prospect (now Stockton Springs) in the same year as his marriage. Seven times he won election to the town's board of selectmen. He was also a local justice of the peace and served in the Maine legislature. In 1818 he became Prospect's town clerk, a post he held for the next 25 years.[6]

Along the way something went awry for Martin and his growing family. When the United States Congress adopted the Revolutionary War Pension Act of 1818 to assist aging veterans who were subsisting in "reduced circumstances," a tactful way of referring to poverty, Martin quickly applied for relief. He testified under oath that "I have no real nor personal estate nor any income whatever[,] my necessary bedding and wearing apparel excepted— except two cows, six sheep, [and] one pig." He described himself as "a laborer" who "by reason of age and infirmity" was "unable to work" and reported that his wife Lucy was both "sickly and rheumatic." Without the proposed pension sum of $96.00 per year, he would, he declared, be "unable to support myself and family." The court, after establishing the estimated value of his whole estate at only $52.00, ruled that Martin should have "the assistance of his country."[7]

This portrait of destitution stands in stark contrast to the image of the enthusiastic young veteran who had tasted a modest level of affluence after first migrating to Maine. Clearly, something had gone drastically wrong. Martin may have inherited his father's spendthrift temperament, or perhaps his easygoing, affable disposition undercut his capacity to safeguard his own interests in business dealings. Still another possibility is that Martin, to comply with the terms of the Pension Act, purposely minimized the extent of his material assets. This explanation seems doubtful, however, since neighbors testified under oath about his more than humble if not desperate economic circumstances.

---

[6] Alice V. Ellis, *The Story of Stockton Springs, Maine* (Belfast, Me., 1955), 21, 73–75.

[7] Statement sworn before Judge William Crosby of the Court of Common Pleas, Third Eastern Circuit, Hancock County, Maine, July 7, 1820, contained in the Revolutionary War pension file of Joseph Plumb and Lucy Martin, Number W.1629, National Archives, Washington, DC (microfilm). For additional general information, see John P. Resch, "Politics and Public Culture: The Revolutionary War Pension Act of 1818," *Journal of the Early Republic*, 8 (1988): 139–58.

The most convincing explanation relates to the question of land ownership in mid-Maine. Hoping to obtain free land, Martin settled in the area of the Waldo Patent, which came under the control of Washington's Chief of Artillery, Henry Knox, after the Revolutionary War. Knox, now the Waldo Patent proprietor, expected to receive substantial payments from everyone, including Martin, for the land they had settled on in the Waldo Patent region. Having no choice, Martin agreed in 1797 to a payment schedule. In that year, he had finally received title to 100 acres of soldiers' bounty lands in the territory of Ohio, and he quickly assigned this grant to a land agent, hoping to use whatever cash he received to help pay for his 100-acre Waldo Patent farm. In 1801, he begged Knox for more time to meet his obligation but received no sympathy. Ten years later Martin owned only 50 acres, a small portion of which he farmed with no particular success. In the end, his $8.00 a month pension from the federal government, and for which he expressed much gratitude in his memoir, enabled him to live with his wife Lucy at a poor but dignified subsistence level for the rest of their lives.[8]

Advancing age, physical infirmities, and virtual impoverishment did nothing to blunt the workings of Martin's ever-curious mind. During his elderly years, noted one of his acquaintances, he regularly indulged his "taste for drawing, for poetry, and for composition." More than anything else, his diverse "intellectual pursuits contributed largely to the comfort of his old age."[9] Martin wrote lyrics for church hymns used by local Congregational churches and prepared illustrations of wild birds. He composed many verses of poetry and drafted a historical account of Fort Pownal, long since razed. His masterwork was his autobiographical reminiscence, the *Narrative of Some of the Adventures, Dangers and Sufferings of a Revolutionary Soldier*, which received virtually no public notice when first published in 1830 by a Hallowell, Maine, printer.[10]

---

[8] Taylor, *Liberty Men and Great Proprietors*, 247–49. Taylor suggests that Martin's less than flattering commentary in his memoir about Continental army officers, especially their self-indulgent behavior in providing for their own needs first, directly reflected his frustrating land patent dealings with Waldo Patent proprietor Henry Knox.

[9] Williamson, "Biographical Sketch," *New England Historical and Genealogical Register*, 331.

[10] Technically Martin's *Narrative* is not an autobiography, but rather a memoir, since the text focuses only on the years of his youth when he served as a Continental soldier, not his whole life.

Martin, like many an aging veteran of his much venerated generation, took pleasure in talking about his personal deeds and escapades in the martial struggle for American liberty. In turn, willing listeners encouraged him to record his wartime experiences. Setting aside concerns about his educational deficiencies, Martin started writing. At first he "thought a very few pages would contain" his recollections, but once under way he could not bring himself to cut short his writing. "As soon as I let one thought through my mind," he explained, "another would step up and ask for admittance." As he scribbled away, Martin felt the intoxicating pleasure of reliving the many memorable days of his youth. Unbeknown to him, he was crafting a priceless account of the Revolutionary era that in our own time has finally begun to receive long overdue and much deserved recognition as an authentic American classic. Certainly the *Narrative* deserves to stand in the company of another classic memoir of the era, Benjamin Franklin's *Autobiography*.

More than 500 diaries and recollections by soldiers who fought for independence are known to exist, but Martin's *Narrative* represents the most complete memoir by a common soldier. At its core is the highly entertaining story of a robust, fun-loving lad and his rite of passage to adulthood as a short- and long-term enlistee in the Continental army. Experiencing combat for the first time at the tender age of 15 served as the first crucial test of young Martin's personal fortitude. Since his initial venture in soldiering was anything but a pleasant experience, his decision to re-enlist for the duration of the war in 1777, he stated, was "against my inclination." Had he had some personal ambition, some clear goal for his life, or more capacity to fend off the self-serving solicitations of the so-called patriots who paid him to serve as their substitute, he would have said "no" to further campaigning. Having signed up again, however, Martin kept facing other examinations in "dangers and sufferings" that tested the depth of his capacity to put up with miserable living conditions along with the mayhem of war.[11]

In the end Martin took pride in having followed through on his long-term commitment, but at no point in describing his wartime journey into adulthood does he take himself too seriously or place himself on some larger-than-life heroic pedestal. Throughout his

---

[11] For a listing of diaries and recollections, see J. Todd White and Charles H. Lesser, eds., *Fighters for Independence: A Guide to Sources of Biographical Information on Soldiers and Sailors of the American Revolution* (Chicago, 1977).

account he stays within character by invariably presenting himself as a person of ordinary courage. Martin likewise shines a bright light on the ways in which he and other common persons demonstrated their agency as historical actors through their contributions to the hallowed events of the era. His memoir is anything but top down in its orientation; rather Martin presents history from the point of view of everyday persons like himself. "Alexander [the Great] never could have conquered the world without private soldiers," he wrote in his preface. Martin thus invites his readers to obtain a more rounded sense of historical reality by not just dwelling on the actions of great leaders but by also regarding the experiences of "one of the lowest in station in an army, a private soldier."

To assure greater breadth of focus in his *Narrative*, Martin embraced the thoughts and concerns of his rank-and-file comrades in arms. He depicted them not only as stout-hearted but as increasingly resentful of the civilian patriots for whom they were fighting. Their mounting anger reflected abysmal levels of material support, starting with such basics as food and clothing. Shortages could result in humorous situations, which Martin willingly describes. During the autumn of 1777, for example, a large Continental detachment, having failed after an exhausting march to engage enemy troops near Philadelphia, was returning to camp when the soldiers received a supply of whiskey but without food rations— they had not eaten for more than a day—to help absorb the alcohol. They became uproariously drunk, so much so, quips Martin, that "had the enemy come upon us at this time, there would have been an action worth recording."

No one guffawed, however, when various Continental brigades finally became mutinous in protesting their miserable circumstances. The two near uprisings of Martin's own Connecticut troops in January 1779 and May 1780 helped vent the anger of soldiers "exasperated beyond endurance," he wrote. From his perspective the blame lay with "their country sitting still and expecting the army to do notable things while fainting from sheer starvation."[12]

---

[12] On the subject of mounting soldier anger and forms of protest, see James Kirby Martin, "A 'Most Undisciplined, Profligate Crew': Protest and Defiance in the Continental Ranks, 1776–1783," in *Arms and Independence: The Military Character of the American Revolution*, eds. R. Hoffman and P. J. Albert (Charlottesville, Va., 1984), 119–40.

Having experienced the war and its dangers and sufferings firsthand, Martin had little tolerance for any romanticizing of the alleged virtuous character of the Revolutionary generation. As such, he would have dismissed the commentary of most historians of his day. Typical was the renowned work of George Bancroft, whose 10-volume history celebrated the establishment of a freedom-loving republic in America as part of a plan inspired by Providence to provide humanity with a safe haven from the debauched political and social systems of Europe. The colonists, wrote Bancroft, were avid participants in God's "grand design," and they eagerly left "behind ... their families and their all" and came forward "swift as a roe or a young hart over the mountains" to engage in combat against the tyrannical British. "The alacrity with which these troops were raised," declared Bancroft, "showed that the public mind heaved like the sea [for liberty] from New England to the Ohio and beyond the Blue Ridge."[13]

Martin's memoir does much more than just reject the lyrical chords of patriotic mythology. Through his personal memories so engagingly recalled in his memoir, he openly assaulted the rapidly forming public memory of the Revolution as a time of universal public virtue in which the colonists virtuously rose up as one and sacrificed their all to overcome the beastly British lion over eight long years of warfare. He knew how few persons had stayed out for the whole contest and how this small number had endured deep pangs of hunger if not near starvation, interminable marches in brutal weather, and the cheerless prospect of entering battle in ragged clothing if not half naked, all standard hallmarks of long-term Continental service. Had the civilian populace truly displayed such abiding selflessness, as later imagined by Bancroft and endless patriot-minded orators at July 4th celebrations, or had they willingly offered the army decent levels of material support, Martin and his comrades would not have suffered so much. They would not have had to endure the persistent shortages of so many necessities, even including straw and blankets that would have given warmth and helped sustain life itself during the long winter

[13] George Bancroft, *History of the United States from the Discovery of the American Continent* (10 vols., Boston, 1834–1874), 8: 62–64.

encampments at such sites of human suffering as Valley Forge and Jockey Hollow.[14]

With wit, charm, pathos, and an occasional dose of sarcasm, Martin thus framed his recollections in sharp contrast to the standard patriotic canon of his day. He did so because he still had not forgotten how he and his comrades, after so many years of faithful service, had been "turned adrift like old worn-out horses" at the war's end without receiving duly contracted forms of compensation, especially back wages. He did so because he did not like the "wiseacres" who were recasting reality by telling everyone what "an useless appendage" the Continental army apparently had been, relative to short-term militia units, in securing American independence. He did so because of the "hardhearted wretches" who were complaining about "poor old decrepit soldiers" like himself finally receiving pensions as long overdue compensation for their dedicated service. He did so, finally, because he felt a strong craving, if not compulsion, to present the truth of his experiences, no matter how much at odds with national mythology.

Martin's irreverence in regard to pronouncements about the Revolution's patriotic character bothered many of his early readers. One contemporary commentator described the *Narrative* as "a lively view of the privations and sufferings of the common soldiery in the mighty conflict for liberty and independence," but he also felt compelled to mention its many "defects," which he left unspecified. He obviously meant matters of content in addition to grammar and punctuation, especially since he "regretted" that Martin, "before sending his book to the press, ... had not placed it in the hands of some judicious friend for revisal."[15] This person, like so many other nineteenth-century Americans, would have preferred to have his

---

[14] On Revolutionary realities in comparison to patriotic mythologies, see James Kirby Martin and Mark Edward Lender, *A Respectable Army: The Military Origins of the Republic, 1763–1789*, 2nd edition (Wheeling, Ill., 2006), passim. On public memories and celebrations of the Revolution in comparison to personal memories shared by Martin and others, see Alfred F. Young, *The Shoemaker and the Tea Party* (Boston, 1999), passim; Alfred F. Young, *Liberty Tree: Ordinary People and the American Revolution* (New York, 2006), 1–23; Sarah J. Purcell, *Sealed with Blood: War, Sacrifice, and Memory in Revolutionary America* (Philadelphia, 2002), passim.

[15] Williamson, "Biographical Sketch," *New England Historical and Genealogical Register*, 330–31.

history laced through with great heroes and patriotic lore. A "judicious friend" thus might have shown Martin how to modify his words to make them fit more correctly with the mythologized public memories of the Revolution.

No one, however, could have persuaded Martin to abandon his point of view, quite simply because he had developed a sense of history at variance with the conventions of his own time. Martin's wartime experiences had taught him the importance of studying the lives of ordinary persons. In his prefatory remarks, he invited his readers to consider what famous military commanders could have accomplished without their soldiers. "Nothing at all," he concluded emphatically. After describing his modest part in the defense of the Delaware River forts during the campaign of 1777, Martin commented on what "little notice" writers had accorded that valiant but futile effort. The reason, he stated, is that "there was no Washington, Putnam, or Wayne there. Had there been, the affair would have been extolled to the skies." The fundamental problem lay with the way in which his generation preferred to record history: "Great men get great praise, little men nothing. But it always was so and always will be."

Martin, who died on May 2, 1850, some 67 years after his military service came to an end, was not prophetic on the latter count. Many historians of our own era are devoting countless hours to reconstructing the lives of ordinary persons. They do so in an effort to comprehend more fully the contributions of the lowly, the forgotten, and the unnoticed in history. More specifically, modern-day historians have come to appreciate that George Washington, for whom Martin held abiding respect, could never have achieved the exalted stature of a great military captain without the services and sacrifices of the ordinary soldiers who so courageously stood by him during the Revolutionary War. Each was as necessary and essential as the other in their mutual triumph of securing American liberties. That was Joseph Plumb Martin's insightful message over 175 years ago, as his masterful *Narrative* so engagingly makes clear.

Editorial Method

Martin had a natural ability to express himself clearly in vigorous prose. What he needed was an editor to help him overcome his lack of training in the fundamental rules of grammar and punctuation.

Apparently he did not have access to such a person, so I have defined my editor's role as that of proffering assistance to him as well as to his modern readers. Martin, for instance, occasionally made grammatical errors. He would "sat" out on a journey, rather than "set" out. I have silently corrected these slips along with a handful of minor spelling errors. With respect to punctuation, Martin had a particular fascination with commas. He seemed to think that every good sentence required several of them. I have adjusted or eliminated his extraneous punctuation, especially commas, with an eye toward sharpening the intended meaning of his words. Very occasionally I have added commas for the same reason. In almost all instances I have eliminated the period and dash combination [.—] that he sometimes employed to separate sentences, a standard form of punctuation in Martin's era but no longer in fashion today. In those instances in which his words have fallen into disuse, changed in meaning, or lost resonance to our modern ear, I have added clarifying terms in brackets. An example would be mauger [notwithstanding].

Serving as Martin's surrogate editor, I concluded that brief portions of the *Narrative* repeat points already well established or divert readers from the main story line. Like any prideful writer, Martin probably would have objected to any tampering with his text. Like any worthwhile editor, I would have reminded him of the need to maintain a crisp pacing to assure an engaging presentation of his many adventures. Since copies of the original 1830 edition have become extremely scarce, those seeking the full text should consult George F. Scheer's 1962 edition of the *Narrative*, which bears the title *Private Yankee Doodle*.

I have prepared a series of notes to help amplify the historical setting of Martin's adventures. He did not dwell on the larger ramifications of the wartime events in which he participated. His battle descriptions, for example, have a tactical emphasis but rarely make reference to broader matters of strategy. The notes provide supplemental information about the sweep of issues, personalities, and events during the Revolutionary era. They also offer information about the many geographic sites mentioned by Martin during his seven years of military campaigning. As an additional aid to readers, I have included five maps originally prepared by the respected nineteenth-century cartographer Colonel Henry B. Carrington. The complete set of these maps may be found in Carrington's *Battle Maps and Charts of the American Revolution*, originally published in 1881.

Acknowledgments

I owe a special debt of gratitude to those individuals who so kindly extended me assistance in the preparation of this volume through its various editions. James L. Kochan and Alan Stein, at one time associated with the Morristown National Historical Park in New Jersey, provided guidance in locating a microfiche version of the 1830 edition of Martin's memoir. A rare original copy of the *Narrative* may be found in the Park's renowned Lloyd W. Smith Collection of Early Americana. The Morristown site encompasses the Jockey Hollow camp site where Washington's Continentals suffered through the unusually harsh winter of 1779–80. David J. Fowler, former Research Director of the David Library of the American Revolution in Washington Crossing, Pennsylvania, graciously answered numerous queries and furnished a copy of Martin's Revolutionary War pension file. Dave Fowler and the late Ezra Stone, for many years the David Library's president, were always hospitable and supportive colleagues and friends. Karen Guenther, Leigh Fought, and Karen Martin made substantial contributions in matters relating to research and editing. Historian David Burner regularly offered his encouragement and infectious enthusiasm. At Blackwell Publishing, Peter Coveney, Executive Editor in History, and Deirdre Ilkson, Editorial Assistant, have been indispensable participants in the development of this new, updated edition. Joseph Plumb Martin, I am sure, would have heartily endorsed the dedication of this volume to my aunt and uncle, Jane and Donald McClelland. He would have also taken great pleasure in their company and friendship, as has this Martin of a later generation.

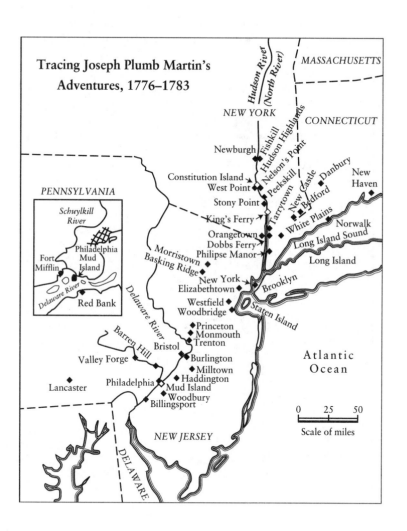

Tracing Joseph Plumb Martin's
Adventures, 1776–1783

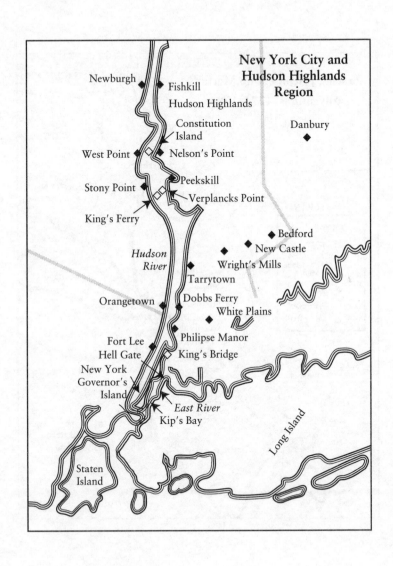

New York City and Hudson Highlands Region

Newburgh

Fishkill

Hudson Highlands

Constitution Island

Danbury

West Point

Nelson's Point

Stony Point

Peekskill

Verplancks Point

King's Ferry

Bedford

New Castle

Hudson River

Wright's Mills

Tarrytown

Orangetown

Dobbs Ferry

White Plains

Fort Lee

Philipse Manor

Hell Gate

King's Bridge

New York

Governor's Island

East River

Kip's Bay

Long Island

Staten Island

NARRATIVE

of some of the

ADVENTURES, DANGERS AND SUFFERINGS

of a

REVOLUTIONARY SOLDIER;

interspersed with

Anecdotes or Incidents that Occurred within his

own Observation

WRITTEN BY HIMSELF

[Joseph Plumb Martin]

"Long sleepless nights in heavy arms I've stood;
And spent laborious days in dust and blood."

Pope's Homer

Preface

Joseph Plumb Martin [JPM] contends that ordinary persons too often get virtually no credit for their contributions to their times and that they should receive just as much attention as that bestowed on great leaders in the construction of historical memories.

I have somewhere read of a limner, who, when he had daubed a representation of some animal, was always compelled, for the information of the observer, to write under it what he intended it to represent: As, "this is a goose, this is a dog," &c. So, many books, and mine in particular among the rest, would perhaps be quite unintelligible as to the drift of them, unless the reader was informed beforehand what the author intended.

I shall, therefore, by way of preface, inform the reader that my intention is to give a succinct account of some of my adventures, dangers, and sufferings during my several campaigns in the Revolutionary army. My readers (who, by the by, will, I hope, none of them be beyond the pale of my own neighborhood) must not expect any great transactions to be exhibited to their notice. "No alpine wonders thunder through my tale," but they are here, once for all, requested to bear it in mind, that they are not the achievements of an officer of high grade which they are perusing, but the common transactions of one of the lowest in station in an army, a private soldier.

Should the reader chance to ask himself this question (and I think it very natural for him to do so) how could any man of common sense ever spend his precious time in writing such a rhapsody of nonsense? To satisfy his inquiring mind, I would inform him, that, as the adage says, "every crow thinks her own young the whitest," so every private soldier in an army thinks his particular services as essential to carry on the war he is engaged in, as the services of the most influential general: And why not? What could officers do without such men? Nothing at all. Alexander never could have conquered the world without private soldiers.

But, says the reader, this is low; the author gives us nothing but everyday occurrences; I could tell as good a story myself. Very true, Mr. Reader, everyone can tell what he has done in his lifetime, but everyone has not been a soldier, and consequently can know but little or nothing of the sufferings and fatigues incident to an army. All know everyday occurrences, but few know the hardships of the "tented field." I wish to have a better opinion of my readers, whoever they may be, than even to think that any of them would wish me to stretch the truth to furnish them with wonders that I never saw, or acts or deeds I never performed. I can give them no more than I have to give, and if they are dissatisfied after all, I must say I am sorry for them and myself too; for them, that they expect more than I can do, and myself, that I am so unlucky as not to have it in my power to please them....

The critical grammarian may find enough to feed his spleen upon if he peruses the following pages; but I can inform him beforehand, I do not regard his sneers; if I cannot write grammatically, I can think, talk, and feel like other men. Besides, if the common readers can understand it, it is all I desire; and to give them an idea, though but a faint one, of what the army suffered that gained and secured our independence, is all I wish. I never studied grammar an hour in my life. When I ought to have been doing that, I was forced to be studying the rules and articles of war....

A note of interrogation: Why we were made to suffer so much in so good and just a cause; and a note of admiration to all the world, that an army voluntarily engaged to serve their country, when starved, and naked, and suffering everything short of death (and thousands even that), should be able to persevere through an eight years war, and come off conquerors at last!

But lest I should make my preface longer than my story, I will here bring it to a close.

Chapter I

Introductory

JPM recalls his childhood while living with his grandparents. Reflects on the outbreak of the Revolutionary War and his romantic notions about becoming a soldier.

> Have patience just to hear me out;
> And I'll tell you what I've been about.

The heroes of all Histories, Narratives, Adventures, Novels, and Romances have, or are supposed to have ancestors, or some root from which they sprang. I conclude, then, that it is not altogether inconsistent to suppose that I had parents too. I shall not undertake to trace my pedigree (like the Welsh) some thousand years beyond the creation; but just observe that my father was the son of a "substantial New England farmer," (as we Yankees say) in the then colony, but now state of Connecticut, and county of Windham. When my father arrived at puberty he found his constitution too feeble to endure manual labor; he therefore directed his views to gaining a livelihood by some other means. He, accordingly, fitted himself for and entered as a student in Yale College, some time between the years 1750 and '55.

My mother was likewise a "farmer's daughter"; her native place was in the county of New Haven, in the same state. She had a sister, married and settled in the vicinity of the college, who often boarded the students when sick. My father being once in that condition, and being at board at this aunt's, my mother happened to be there on a visit: My father seeing her, it seems, like a great many others in like circumstances, took a fancy to her, followed up his courtship, and very possibly obtained her consent as well as her parents—married her a year and a half before his collegial studies were ended, which (if known at the time) would have been cause of his expulsion from college; but it seems it never was known there, and he, of course, escaped a keelhauling.

After my father left college, he studied divinity, had "a call," accepted it, and was settled in the county of Berkshire, in the (now) Commonwealth of Massachusetts, as a gospel minister of the Congregational order; in which county of Berkshire, I, the redoubtable hero of this Narrative, first made my appearance in this crooked, fretful world, upon the 21st day of November in the year 1760. I have been told that the day on which I was born was a thanksgiving day, which day is, generally, celebrated with good cheer. One might have thought it a little ominous being born on such a day, but I can assure the reader it was no omen of good to me, especially for the seven or eight years I was in the army—nor, indeed, ever since.

My grandsire, on my mother's side, having at this time no other daughter but my mother (my aunt, mentioned above being dead), she of course became the darling, for which reason, I suppose, I was his favorite grandson and received his Christian and surnames as my given name.

I lived with my parents until I was upwards of seven years old, when I went to live with this good old grandsire; for good he was, particularly to me. He was wealthy, and I had everything that was necessary for life, and as many superfluities as was consistent with my age and station. There were none belonging to the family, as constant residents, except the old gentleman, lady, and myself. It is true my grandsire kept me pretty busily employed, but he was kind to me in every respect, always gave me a playday when convenient, and was indulgent to me almost to a fault. Ah! I ought not to have left him while he lived; I fouled my own nest most sadly when I did it; but children "are full of notions."

I remember the stir in the country occasioned by the Stamp Act, but I was so young that I did not understand the meaning of it; I likewise remember the disturbances that followed the repeal of the Stamp Act, until the destruction of the tea at Boston and elsewhere. I was then 13 or 14 years old and began to understand something of the works going on. I used...to inquire a deal about the French War, as it was called, which had not been long ended; my grandsire would talk with me about it while working in the fields, perhaps as much to beguile his own time as to gratify my curiosity. I thought then, nothing should induce me to get caught in the toils of an army. "I am well, so I'll keep," was my motto then, and it would have been well for me if I had ever retained it.

Time passed smoothly on with me till the year 1774 arrived. The smell of war began to be pretty strong, but I was determined to have no hand in it, happen when it might; I felt myself to be a real coward. What—venture my carcass where bullets fly! That will never do for me. Stay at home out of harm's way, thought I, it will be as much to your health as credit to do so. But the pinch of the game had not arrived yet; I had seen nothing of war affairs, and consequently was but a poor judge in such matters.

One little circumstance that happened in the autumn of this year will exhibit my military prowess, at this time, in a high point of view. In the afternoon, one Sabbath day, while the people were assembled at meeting, word was brought that the British (regulars, as the good people then called them) were advancing from Boston, spreading death and desolation in their route in every direction. What was the intent of spreading this rumor, I know not, unless it was to see how the people would stand affected; be it what it would, it caused me a terrible fright.[1] I went out of the house in the dusk of the evening, when I heard the sound of a carriage on the road in the direction of Boston. I thought they were coming as sure as a gun; I shall be dead or a captive before tomorrow morning. However, I went to bed late in the evening, dreamed of "fire and sword," I suppose, waked in the morning, found myself alive, and the house standing just where it did the evening before.

The winter of this year passed off without any very frightening alarms, and the spring of 1775 arrived. Expectation of some fatal event seemed to fill the minds of most of the considerate people throughout the country. I was ploughing in the field about half a mile from home, about the 21st day of April, when all of a sudden the bells fell to ringing and three guns were repeatedly fired in succession down in the village; what the cause was we could not conjecture. I had some fearful forebodings that something more than

---

[1] The story was only partially rumor. British regulars did indeed advance from Boston on September 1, 1774, to seize patriot artillery at Cambridge and a public store of gunpowder at Charlestown. Local citizens threatened armed resistance but did not engage the regulars. Still, word spread widely of a bloody encounter, causing some New Englanders to rush momentarily to arms.

the sound of a carriage wheel was in the wind. The regulars are coming in good earnest, thought I.

My grandsire sighed, he "smelt the rat." He immediately turned out the team and repaired homeward. I set off to see what the cause of the commotion was. I found most of the male kind of the people together; soldiers for Boston were in requisition. A dollar deposited upon the drumhead was taken up by someone as soon as placed there and the holder's name taken, and he enrolled with orders to equip himself as quick as possible. My spirits began to revive at the sight of the money offered; the seeds of courage began to sprout; for, contrary to my knowledge, there was a scattering of them sowed, but they had not as yet germinated; I felt a strong inclination, when I found I had them, to cultivate them. O, thought I, if I were but old enough to put myself forward, I would be the possessor of one dollar, the dangers of war to the contrary notwithstanding; but I durst not put myself up for a soldier for fear of being refused, and that would have quite upset all the courage I had drawn forth.

The men that had engaged "to go to war" went as far as the next town, where they received orders to return, as there was a sufficiency of men already engaged, so that I should have had but a short campaign had I have gone.

This year there were troops raised both for Boston and New York. Some from the back towns were billeted at my grandsire's; their company and conversation began to warm my courage to such a degree that I resolved at all events to "go a sogering."[2] Accordingly, I used to pump my grandsire in a roundabout manner to know how he stood affected respecting it. For a long time he appeared to take but little notice of it. At length, one day I pushed the matter so hard upon him, he was compelled to give me a direct answer, which was that he should never give his consent for me to go into the army unless I had the previous consent of my parents. And now I was completely graveled [perplexed]; my parents were too far off to obtain their consent before it would be too late for the present campaign. What was I to do? Why, I must give up the idea, and that was

[2] In the wake of Lexington and Concord, patriot leaders in Massachusetts quickly called for troop support from other New England colonies. The Connecticut Assembly responded decisively before the end of April by ordering the formation of six regiments, each to enlist 1,000 soldiers, and added two more in July. The *rage militaire* was on, and in the summer and autumn of 1775, as observed by young Martin, it seemed as if everyone wanted to be a "soger."

hard; for I was as earnest now to call myself, and be called a soldier, as I had been a year before *not* to be called one. I thought over many things and formed many plans, but they all fell through, and poor disconsolate I was forced to sit down and gnaw my fingernails in silence.

I said but little more about "soldiering" until the troops raised in and near the town in which I resided came to march off for New York. Then I felt bitterly again; I accompanied them as far as the town line, and it was hard parting with them then. Many of my young associates were with them; my heart and soul went with them, but my mortal part must stay behind. By and by they will come swaggering back, thought I, and tell me of all their exploits, all their "hairbreadth 'scapes," and poor Huff will not have a single sentence to advance. O, that was too much to be borne with by me.

The thoughts of the service still haunted me after the troops were gone, and the town clear of them; but what plan to form to get the consent of all, parents and grandparents, that I might procure thereby to myself the (to me then) bewitching name of a soldier, I could not devise. Sometimes I thought I would enlist at all hazards, let the consequences be what they would; then again, I would think how kind my grandparents were to me, and ever had been, my grandsire in particular: I could not bear to hurt their feelings so much. I did sincerely love my grandsire; my grandma'am I did not love so well, and I feared her less. At length a thought struck my mind: Should they affront me grossly, I would make that a plea with my conscience to settle the controversy with. Accordingly, I wished nothing more than to have them, or either of them, give "His Honor" a high affront, that I might thereby form an excuse to engage in the service *without* their consent, leave, or approbation.

It happened that in the early part of the autumn of this year, I was gratified in my wishes; for I thought I had received provocation enough to justify me in engaging in the army during life, little thinking that I was inflicting the punishment on myself that I fancied I was laying on my grandparents for their (as I thought) willful obstinacy. And as this affair was one and the chief cause of my leaving those kind people and their hospitable house, and precipitating myself into an ocean of distress, I will minutely describe the affair.

My grandsire, as I have before observed, often gave me playdays, especially after the spring and fall sowing, when I went where I pleased, a gunning, or fishing, or to whatever recreation took my fancy. "This fall," said the old gentleman to me one day, "come, spring to it, and let us get the winter grain in as soon as possible, and you shall have a playday after the work is done." Accordingly, I did do the best I could to forward the business, and I believe I gave him satisfaction, for he repeated his promise to me often. Just before we had done sowing, I told him that all my young associates were going to New Haven to commencement this season.[3] "Well," said he, "you shall go too, if you choose, and you shall have one of the horses; you shall have your choice of them, and I will give you some pocket money."...

My grandsire had a piece of salt marsh about three miles from home, which he had mowed three or four days before the day arrived which was to make me completely happy, at least for a time. Two days previous he sent me to rake up the hay; I buffeted heat and mosquitoes and got the hay all up; and as that sort of hay is not easily injured by the weather, I thought there was nothing to prevent my promised happiness.

Well, the day arrived. I got up early, did all the little jobs about the place, that my grandsire might have nothing to accuse me of. He had gone out during the morning and did not return till breakfast time. I was waiting with impatience for his coming in, that I might prepare for my excursion, when, lo, he did come—much to my sorrow; for the first words I heard were, "Come, get up the team, I have gotten such a one," naming a neighbor's boy somewhat older than myself, "to go with us and cart home the salt hay." Had thunder and lightning fallen upon the four corners of the house, it would not have struck me with worse feelings than these words of his did. Shame, grief, spite, revenge, all took immediate possession of me. What could I do; go I must, that was certain, there was no remedy; and go I did, but with a full determination that the old gentleman should know that I had feelings of some sort or other, let him think of me as he would.

I, according to his orders, prepared the team, he undertook to act teamster, and I set off before them for the marsh alone that I might indulge myself in my grief without molestation. The way to the marsh lay about a mile and a half on the highway to the college.

---

[3]   Yale College, founded in 1701, was the third oldest institution of higher learning in the colonies. The college held its annual commencement on the second Wednesday of each September. Although the graduation ceremony may have been solemn, much revelry surrounded the occasion, including everything from fireworks displays to town-and-gown fisticuffs between students and the likes of Martin's young friends.

I had hardly got into the highway before I was overtaken by a troop of my young mates, all rigged off for commencement, swaggering like nabobs. The first compliment was, "Hallo, where are you going? We thought you was one of the foremost in the party; your grandsire never intended to let you go, and you was a fool to believe him." I did not believe *them*; my grandsire had never deceived me in such circumstances before, and I was willing even then, vexed as I was, to attribute it to forgetfulness or to anything but willfulness. However, I…considered myself as much injured as though it had been done ever so designedly.

I, however, went to the marsh; my grandsire, team, and boy arrived soon after me. We put a load of hay upon the cart, and, as it was getting rather late in the day, the old gentleman concluded to go home with the team and left the other youngster and me to pole the rest of the hay off the marsh to the upland, as it was dangerous going upon the lower part of it, being in many places soft and miry. He told us to go to some of the fences and cut a pair of sassafras poles, those being light, and have the remainder of the hay in readiness by his return.

And now comes the catastrophe of the play. I concluded now was the time for me to show my spunk; we went up to the upland where was plenty of fruit; I lay down under an apple tree and fell to eating. The other boy ate too, but still urged me to obey my orders; I was resolved to disobey, let the consequences be what they would. However, he by his importunity at length got me down upon the marsh; we poled one cock [a small pile] of hay off the marsh, when we saw the old gentleman coming full drive, Jehu-like.[4] Down he came, when lo and behold we had gotten one cock of hay only in a condition to be taken upon the cart; what was to be done. To go on to the marsh was dangerous in the extreme; to stop then to pole it off would not do; the time would not allow it.

O, my grandsire was in a woeful passion. I stood aloof. Whose fault was it, he inquired; the blame was quickly laid to my account, and justly too, for I was the only culprit. The old gentleman came at me hammer and tongs with his six-feet cartwhip. Ah, thought I to myself, good legs, do your duty now if ever; I houghed [hoofed] the gravel, or rather the marsh, in good earnest. There were 20 people or more near us at work; they all suspended their labor to see the

---

[4] Jehu was a king of Israel in the ninth century BC who was known for his furious driving of chariots. See II Kings 9:20.

race. But I was too light-footed for the old gentleman, and the people on the marsh setting up a laugh, it rather disconcerted him; he, however, chased me about 30 or 40 rods[5] when he gave over the pursuit and returned. I ran as much further before I dared to look back; but hearing no sound of footsteps behind me, I at last ventured to look over my shoulder and saw him almost back to his team; I followed him in my turn, but not quite so nimble as I went from him. He endeavored to spit a little of his spite upon the other youngster, but he *stepped* up close to him so that he could not use his whip; and then pled his own cause so well that the old gentleman said no more to him.

He then had to venture upon the marsh at all events. I took a rake and raked after the cart, but took especial care to keep out of harm's way till the hay was all upon the cart. I was then called upon to help bind the load; I complied, but I kept on tiptoe all the time, ready to start in case I saw any symptoms of war; but all passed off. We got off the marsh safe and without any hindrance; and it was well for me, after all, that we met with no disaster.

And here ends my Introductory Chapter. If the reader thinks that some passages in it record incidents not altogether to my credit as a boy, I can tell him that I thought at the time I did right, and to tell the truth I have not materially altered my opinion respecting them since. One thing I am certain of and that is, reader, if you had been me, you would have done just as I did. What reason have you then to cavil?

---

[5] One rod equals 5.5 yards or 16.5 feet. Throughout his memoir Martin uses the rod as a standard unit for measuring distances. In this situation, he estimated the length of the chase at 165 to 220 yards, or roughly the length of two football fields.

Chapter II

Campaign of 1776

Young JPM enlists in the Continental service for six months and quickly learns about the horrors of war as he engages in combat against British forces in the defense of New York City and environs. Musters out of the service at the end of the year.

> At Uncle Joe's I liv'd at ease;
> Had cider and good bread and cheese;
> But while I stay'd at Uncle Sam's
> I'd nought to eat but—"faith and clams."

During the winter of 1775–76, by hearing the conversation and disputes of the good old farmer politicians of the times, I collected pretty correct ideas of the contest between this country and the mother country (as it was then called). I thought I was as warm a patriot as the best of them; the war was waged; we had joined issue, and it would not do to "put the hand to the plough and look back." I felt more anxious than ever, if possible, to be called a defender of my country. I had not forgot the commencement affair that still stuck in my crop; and it would not do for me to forget it, for that affront was to be my passport to the army.

One evening, very early in the spring of this year, I chanced to overhear my grandma'am telling my grandsire that I had threatened to engage on board a man-of-war. I had told her that I would enter on board a privateer then fitting out in our neighborhood; the good old lady thought it a man-of-war, that and privateer being synonymous terms with her.[1] She said she could not bear the thought of my being on board of a man-of-war; my grandsire told her that he supposed I was resolved to go into the service in some way or other, and he had rather I would engage in the land service if I must engage in any. This I thought to be a sort of tacit consent for me to go, and I determined to take advantage of it as quick as possible.

Soldiers were at this time enlisting for a year's service. I did not like that; it was too long a time for me at the first trial. I wished only to take a priming before I took upon me the whole coat of paint for a soldier. However, the time soon arrived that gratified all my wishes. In the month of June, this year, orders came out for enlisting men for six months from the 25th of this month. The troops were styled new levies; they were to go to New York.[2] And notwithstanding

[1]   The terms were not synonymous. Men-of-war, or warships, were heavily armed naval vessels. In the pages that follow, Martin references a number of warships belonging to the British Royal Navy. Privateering vessels, by comparison, were privately owned and operated by special commissions, or letters of marque, normally granted by the Continental Congress. So long as the war continued, such commissions permitted privateers to run down and capture enemy craft, especially merchant ships carrying supplies to British land forces in America. As such, privateering represented legalized piracy, since captured vessels and goods could be sold as prizes, in turn netting handsome profits for owners, captains, and crews. The lure of quick wealth caused many a young person like Martin to consider becoming a privateering crew member, and more than 10,000 patriots did so before the war was over.

[2]   Recruiting for the Continental army had gone poorly in late 1775 and early 1776, evidence that initial popular enthusiasm about military service was quickly passing. For a fleeting moment numbers did not seem to matter, especially when British regulars under General William Howe succumbed to the pressure of George Washington's Continentals surrounding Boston and sailed away in mid-March 1776. Soon, however, all signs pointed toward a new, huge massing of the king's troops in the vicinity of New York City.

Responding to pleas from Washington for more soldiers, the Continental Congress sanctioned the "new levies" of troops, who were to serve for no more than six months. Congress asked Connecticut to fill seven regiments. Although soon incorporated into the Continental army, these "new levies" were defined as state troops. Connecticut was to outfit its regiments and pay wages, even though the troops were to serve beyond that colony's borders.

The new levy state regiments of 1776 were not some conglomeration of local militia companies. In Connecticut, as in the other rebellious colonies, virtually all able-bodied males between the ages of 16 and 60 belonged to militia units for the purpose of providing home defense. No one expected militiamen to perform service beyond their colony's borders. As the war progressed, the distinction between state troops and militia blurred. State troops more often came to represent detachments of militiamen called up for short-term Continental service. Their purpose was to augment the fighting strength of long-term, hard-core regulars who formed the backbone of Continental forces.

I was told that the British army at that place was reinforced by 15,000 men, it made no alteration in my mind; I did not care if there had been 15 times 15,000, I should have gone just as soon as if there had been but 1,500. I never spent a thought about numbers; the Americans were invincible in my opinion. If anything affected me, it was a stronger desire to see them.

Well, as I have said, enlisting orders were out. I used frequently to go to the rendezvous, where I saw many of my young associates enlist, had repeated banterings to engage with them, but still when it came "case in hand," I had my misgivings. If I once undertake, thought I, I must stick to it; there will be no receding. Thoughts like these would, at times, almost overset my resolutions.

But mauger [notwithstanding] all these "doleful ideas," I one evening went off with a full determination to enlist at all hazards. When I arrived at the place of rendezvous I found a number of young men of my acquaintance there. The old bantering began— come, if you will enlist I will, says one; you have long been talking about it, says another—come, now is the time. "Thinks I to myself," I will not be laughed into it or out of it, at any rate; I will act my own pleasure after all. But what did I come here for tonight? Why, to enlist; then enlist I will. So seating myself at the table, enlisting orders were immediately presented to me; I took up the pen, loaded it with the fatal charge, made several mimic imitations of writing my name, but took especial care not to touch the paper with the pen until an unlucky wight who was leaning over my shoulder gave my hand a stroke, which caused the pen to make a woeful scratch on the paper. "O, he has enlisted," said he. "He has made his mark; he is fast enough now." Well, thought I, I may as well go through with the business now as not. So I wrote my name fairly upon the indentures [enlistment papers]. And now I was a *soldier*, in name at least, if not in practice.[3]

But I had now to go home after performing this, my heroic action. How shall I be received there? But the report of my adventure had reached there before I did. In the morning when I first saw my grandparents, I felt considerably of the sheepish order. The old gentleman first accosted me with, "Well, you are going a soldiering then, are you ?" I had nothing to answer; I would much rather he

---

[3] Martin's date of enlistment was July 6, 1776. He joined the 5th regiment under the command of Colonel William Douglas and was assigned to Captain Samuel Peck's 3rd company.

had not asked me the question. I saw that the circumstance hurt him and the old lady too; but it was too late now to repent. The old gentleman proceeded, "I suppose you must be fitted out for the expedition, since it is so." Accordingly, they did "fit me out" ... with arms and accouterments, clothing, and cake, and cheese in plenty, not forgetting to put my pocket Bible into my knapsack. Good old people! They wished me well, soul and body; I sincerely thank them for their kindness and love to me, from the first time I came to live with them to the last parting hour....

I was now what I had long wished to be, a soldier. I had obtained my heart's desire; it was now my business to prove myself equal to my profession. Well, to be short, I went with several others of the company on board a sloop bound to New York; had a pleasant though protracted passage; passed through the straight called Hell Gate ... ; arrived at New York; marched up into the city, and joined the rest of the regiment that were already there.

And now I had left my good old grandsire's house as a constant resident forever, and had to commence exercising my function [drilling]. I was called out every morning at reveille beating, which was at daybreak, to go to our regimental parade in Broad Street, and there practice the manual exercise, which was the most that was known in our new levies, if they knew even that. I was brought to an allowance of provisions which, while we lay in New York, was not bad: If there was any deficiency it could in some measure be supplied by procuring some kind of sauce, but I was a stranger to such living; I began soon to miss grandsire's table and cellar. However, I reconciled myself to my condition as well as I could....

I would here, once for all, remark that as I write altogether from memory, the reader must not expect to have an exact account of dates, I mean of days and weeks; as to years and months I shall not be wide from the mark.

And as I have entitled my book "The Adventures, &c., of a Revolutionary Soldier," it is possible the reader may expect to have a minute detail of all my adventures. I have not *promised* any such thing; it was what belonged to me and what transpired in my line of duty that I proposed to narrate.... I never wished to do anyone an injury through malice in my life; nor did I ever do anyone an intentional injury while I was in the army, unless it was when sheer necessity drove me to it, and my conscience bears me witness that innumerable times I have suffered rather than take from anyone what belonged of right to them, even to satisfy the cravings of nature. But I cannot say so much in favor of my levity that would often get the upper hand of me, do what I would; and sometimes it would run riot with me; but still I did not mean to do harm, only recreation, reader, recreation. I wanted often to recreate myself, to keep the blood from stagnating....

I remained in New York two or three months, in which time several things occurred, but so trifling that I shall not mention them; when, sometime in the latter part of the month of August, I was ordered upon a fatigue party. We had scarcely reached the grand parade when I saw our sergeant major directing his course up Broadway toward us in rather an unusual step for him. He soon arrived and informed us, and then the commanding officer of the party, that he had orders to take off all belonging to our regiment and march us to our quarters, as the regiment was ordered to Long Island, the British having landed in force there.[4] Although this was not unexpected to me, yet it gave me rather a disagreeable feeling, as I was pretty well assured I should have to sniff a little gunpowder. However, I kept my cogitations to myself, went to my quarters, packed up my clothes, and got myself in readiness for the expedition as soon as possible. I then went to the top of the house where I had a full view of that part of the Island; I distinctly saw the smoke

[4] Having fared poorly in the early days of the war, England's leaders planned a gigantic campaign effort for 1776. The goal was to crush the rebellion in one campaign season. Besides sending about 10,000 troops to Quebec Province in Canada to drive off a patriot invasion force, the king's ministers provided for a massive concentration of troops in the vicinity of New York City. The bivouac point was Staten Island, where General William Howe, having retreated to Halifax, Nova Scotia, arrived with nearly 10,000 troops in mid-June. Two months later the British had 32,000 well-trained soldiers ready to strike at the patriots, besides 13,000 sailors who manned 70 naval vessels and 370 transport ships.

By comparison, Washington had 28,000 troops on his muster rolls but only 19,000 actually present and fit for duty, and most of them were untrained amateurs like Martin. Just as bad, because of its many waterways New York was virtually indefensible, especially since the British could use their vast naval resources to strike wherever they pleased. To protect New York City, Washington divided his forces by placing roughly 7,000 troops, along with batteries of artillery, at Brooklyn Heights on Long Island, which commanded the city to the southeast across the East River.

General Howe recognized the weakness of an army divided by a river as well as the opportunity to destroy the patriot force at Brooklyn Heights. On August 22 he began landing thousands of troops at Gravesend, Long Island, and he launched a multi-pronged assault at daybreak on August 27. As the Battle of Long Island raged that morning, Martin's regiment crossed the East River to Brooklyn Heights to help reinforce the beleaguered patriot force.

of the field artillery, but the distance and the unfavorableness of the wind prevented my hearing their report, at least but faintly. The horrors of battle then presented themselves to my mind in all their hideousness; I must come to it now, thought I. Well, I will endeavor to do my duty as well as I am able and leave the event with Providence.

We were soon ordered to our regimental parade, from which, as soon as the regiment was formed, we were marched off for the ferry. At the lower end of the street were placed several casks of sea bread, ... nearly hard enough for musket flints; the casks were unheaded and each man was allowed to take as many as he could as he marched by. As my good luck would have it, there was a momentary halt made; I improved the opportunity thus offered me, as every good soldier should upon all important occasions, to get as many of the biscuits as I possibly could; no one said anything to me, and I filled my bosom and took as many as I could hold in my hand, a dozen or more in all, and when we arrived at the ferry stairs I stowed them away in my knapsack. We quickly embarked on board the boats. As each boat started, three cheers were given by those on board, which was returned by the numerous spectators who thronged the wharves; they all wished us good luck, apparently, although it was with most of them perhaps nothing more than ceremony.

We soon landed at Brooklyn, upon the Island, marched up the ascent from the ferry to the plain. We now began to meet the wounded men, another sight I was unacquainted with, some with broken arms, some with broken legs, and some with broken heads. The sight of these a little daunted me, and made me think of home, but the sight and thought vanished together. We marched a short distance, when we halted to refresh ourselves. Whether we had any other victuals besides the hard bread I do not remember, but I remember my gnawing at them; they were hard enough to break the teeth of a rat. One of the soldiers complaining of thirst to his officer, "Look at that man," said he, pointing to me, "he is not thirsty, I will warrant it." I felt a little elevated to be styled a man.[5]

While resting here, which was not more than 20 minutes or half an hour, the Americans and British were warmly engaged within sight of us. What were the feelings of most or all the young soldiers at this time, I know not, but I know what were mine. But let mine

---

[5] Only 15 years old when he first entered combat, Martin recalled these words as a great compliment.

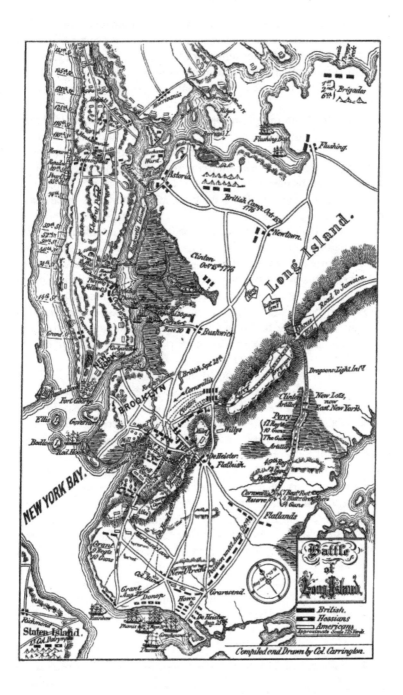

or theirs be what they might, I saw a lieutenant who appeared to have feelings not very enviable; whether he was actuated by fear or the canteen I cannot determine now. I thought it fear at the time, for he ran round among the men of his company, sniveling and blubbering, praying each one if he had aught against him, or if *he* had injured anyone that they would forgive him, declaring at the same time that he, from his heart, forgave them if they had offended him, and I gave him full credit for his assertion; for had he been at the gallows with a halter about his neck, he could not have shown more fear or penitence. A fine soldier you are, I thought, a fine officer, an exemplary man for young soldiers! I would have then suffered anything short of death rather than have made such an exhibition of myself....

The officers of the new levies wore cockades of different colors to distinguish them from the standing forces, as they were called; the field officers wore red, the captains white, and the subaltern officers green. While we were resting here our lieutenant colonel and major (our colonel not being with us) took their cockades from their hats; being asked the reason, the lieutenant colonel replied that he was willing to risk his life in the cause of his country, but unwilling to stand a particular mark for the enemy to fire at. He was a fine officer and a brave soldier.[6]

We were soon called upon to fall in and proceed. We had not gone far, about half a mile, when I heard one in the rear ask another where his musket was. I looked round and saw one of the soldiers stemming off without his gun, having left it where we last halted; he was inspecting his side as if undetermined whether he had it or not; he then fell out of the ranks to go in search of it. One of the company, who had brought it on (wishing to see how far he would go before he missed it) gave it to him. The reader will naturally enough conclude that he was a brave soldier. Well, he was a brave fellow for all this accident, and received two severe wounds by musket balls while fearlessly fighting for his country at the battle of White Plains. So true is the proverb, "A singed cat may make a good mouser." ...

We overtook a small party of the artillery here, dragging a heavy 12-pounder upon a field carriage, sinking halfway to the naves in the sandy soil. They pled hard for some of us to assist them to get

---

[6] Martin's lieutenant colonel was James Arnold, and Phineas Porter served the regiment as major.

on their piece; our officers, however, paid no attention to their entreaties, but pressed forward toward a creek, where a large party of Americans and British were engaged. By the time we arrived, the enemy had driven our men into the creek, or rather millpond (the tide being up), where such as could swim got across; those that could not swim, and could not procure anything to buoy them up, sank. The British, having several fieldpieces stationed by a brick house, were pouring the canister and grape upon the Americans like a shower of hail. They would doubtless have done them much more damage than they did, but for the 12-pounder mentioned above; the men having gotten it within sufficient distance to reach them, and opening a fire upon them, soon obliged them to shift their quarters. There was in this action a regiment of Maryland troops (volunteers), all young gentlemen. When they came out of the water and mud to us, looking like water rats, it was a truly pitiful sight. Many of them were killed in the pond, and more were drowned. Some of us went into the water after the fall of the tide, and took out a number of corpses and a great many arms that were sunk in the pond and creek.[7]

Our regiment lay on the ground we then occupied the following night. The next day in the afternoon we had a considerable tight scratch with about an equal number of the British, which began rather unexpectedly, and a little whimsically. A few of our men (I mean of our regiment) went over the creek upon business that usually employed us, that is in search of something to eat. There was a field of Indian corn at a short distance from the creek, with several cocks [piles] of hay about halfway from the creek to the cornfield; the men purposed to get some of the corn, or anything else that was eatable. When they got up with the haycocks, they were fired upon by about an equal number of the British from the cornfield; our people took to the hay, and the others to the fence, where they

[7] Defending the patriot right wing closest to the shoreline were Delaware and Maryland troops under Brigadier General William Alexander, the pretended Lord Stirling. The brunt of the battle fell on them after Howe's troops smashed through other portions of the extended rebel line in advance of Brooklyn Heights. Stirling with some 250 Marylanders held off the hard-pressing enemy as their comrades retreated through treacherous swampland surrounding Gowanus Creek to reach Brooklyn Heights. Of the valiant Maryland band, only ten escaped. The other "young gentlemen" were shot down or captured. Overall American casualties that day amounted to an estimated 200 killed and 1,097 captured; the British suffered only 367 casualties.

exchanged a number of shots at each other, neither side inclining to give back. A number, say 40 or 50 more of our men, went over and drove the British from the fence; they were by this time reinforced in their turn, and drove us back. The two parties kept thus alternately reinforcing until we had the most of our regiment in the action. After the officers came to command, the English were soon routed from the place, but we dare not follow them for fear of falling into some snare, as the whole British army was in the vicinity of us; I do not recollect that we had anyone killed outright, but we had several severely wounded, and some, I believe, mortally.

Our regiment was alone, no other troops being near where we were lying. We were upon a rising ground, covered with a young growth of trees; we felled a fence of trees around us to prevent the approach of the enemies' horse. We lay there a day longer. In the latter part of the afternoon there fell a very heavy shower of rain which wet us all to the skin and much damaged our ammunition. About sunset, when the shower had passed over, we were ordered to parade and discharge our pieces. We attempted to fire by platoons for improvement, but we made blundering work of it; it was more like a running fire than firing by divisions. However, we got our muskets as empty as our stomachs, and with half the trouble, nor was it half the trouble to have reloaded them, for we had wherewithal to do that, but not so with our stomachs.

Just at dusk, I, with one or two others of our company, went off to a barn about half a mile distant with intent to get some straw to lodge upon, the ground and leaves being drenched in water, and we as wet as they. It was quite dark in the barn, and while I was fumbling about the floor someone called to me from the top of the mow [hay stack], inquiring where I was from; I told him. He asked me if we had not had an engagement there, having heard us discharging our guns, I told him we had, and a severe one, too; he asked if many were killed; I told him that I saw none killed, nor any very badly wounded. I then heard several others, as it appeared, speaking on the mow. Poor fellows, they had better have been at their posts than skulking in a barn on account of a little wet, for I have not the least doubt but that the British had possession of their mortal parts before the noon of the next day.

I could not find any straw, but I found some wheat in the sheaf, standing by the side of the floor. I took a sheaf or two and returned as fast as I could to the regiment. When I arrived the men were all paraded to march off the ground; I left my wheat, seized my musket and fell into the ranks. We were strictly enjoined not to speak, or

even cough, while on the march. All orders were given from officer
to officer, and communicated to the men in whispers. What such
secrecy could mean we could not divine. We marched off in the
same way that we had come on to the Island, forming various conjectures among ourselves as to our destination. Some were of opinion that we were to endeavor to get on the flank, or in the rear of
the enemy. Others, that we were going up the East River to attack
them in that quarter; but none, it seems, knew the right of the
matter. We marched on, however, until we arrived at the ferry,
where we immediately embarked on board the bateaux[8] and were
conveyed safely to New York, where we were landed about three
o'clock in the morning, nothing against our inclinations.[9]

The next day the British showed themselves to be in possession
of our works upon the Island by firing upon some of our boats
passing to and from Governors Island.[10] Our regiment was employed
during this day in throwing up a sort of breastwork at their alarm
post upon the wharves (facing the enemy), composed of spars and
logs and filling the space between with the materials of which the
wharves were composed—old broken junk bottles, flint stones,
&c., which, had a cannon ball passed through, would have chanced
to kill five men where the ball would one. But the enemy did not see
fit to molest us.

We stayed several days longer in the city, when one morning we
discovered that a small frigate had advanced up and was lying
above Governors Island, close under the Long Island shore. Several
other ships had come up and were lying just below the town. They
seemed to portend evil. In the evening, just at dark, our regiment was
ordered to march to Turtle Bay,[11] a place about four miles distant on
the East River, where were a large warehouse or two, called (then)
the King's stores, built for the storing of marine stores belonging to

---

[8]   Flat-bottomed boats used to carry small numbers of troops and supplies on
inland waterways.
[9]   Various factors facilitated the American withdrawal. On the land side, invariably
dilatory General Howe chose not to press his advantage and assault the rebel lines
on Brooklyn Heights. Meanwhile, contrary northeasterly winds on August 28 and
29 kept British naval vessels from sailing into the East River and sealing off the
only avenue of escape. Under cover of a heavy fog more than 9,000 troops thus
glided away and were back on Manhattan Island by the early morning hours of
August 30.
[10]   An advanced post for patriot troops before the battle, the island lies in the upper
part of New York Bay just off Brooklyn Heights near the mouth of the East River.
[11]   Very much in the country then, but at today's 46th and 47th streets.

the government before the war. There was at this time about 2,500 barrels of flour in those storehouses, and it was conjectured that the design of the fore-mentioned frigate, or rather the officers and crew of her, was to seize on this flour; we were, therefore, ordered to secure it before the British should have an opportunity to lay their unhallowed hands upon it. We arrived at the place about midnight, and by sunrise or a little after had secured the whole of it by rolling it up a steep bank and piling it behind a ledge of rocks....

We continued here some days to guard the flour. We were forbidden by our officers to use any of it, except our daily allowance; we used, however, to purloin some of it to eat and exchange with the inhabitants for milk, sauce, and such small matters as we could get for it of them.

While we lay here I saw a piece of American workmanship that was (as I thought) rather remarkable. Going one evening upon a picket guard in a subaltern officer's command a mile or two farther up the river, we had to march through the enclosures close upon the bank of the river. There was a small party of British upon an island in the river.... These British soldiers seemed to be very busy in chasing some scattering sheep that happened to be so unlucky as to fall in their way. One of the soldiers, however, thinking perhaps he could do more mischief by killing some of us, had posted himself on a point of rocks at the southern extremity of the island and kept firing at us as we passed along the bank. Several of his shots passed between our files, but we took little notice of him, thinking he was so far off that he could do us but little hurt, and that we could do him none at all, until one of the guard asked the officer if he might discharge his piece at him. As it was charged and would not hinder us long, the officer gave his consent. He rested his old six-feet barrel across a fence and sent an express to him. The man dropped, but as we then thought it was only to amuse us, we took no further notice of it but passed on. In the morning upon our return, we saw the brick-colored coat still lying in the same position we had left it in the evening before. It was a long distance to hit a single man with a musket; it was certainly over half a mile.[12]

---

[12]   Even at less than 100 yards, muskets were inaccurate weapons, and balls fired by muskets generally lost any lethal velocity after 300 yards. Since Martin's comrade took careful aim (muskets lacked sights), he must have fired a long rifle, a weapon capable of greater accuracy at substantial distances, but certainly not half a mile (880 yards). A killing shot at that range had nothing to do with much vaunted and mythologized American marksmanship. It was a lucky shot at best, except for the British soldier.

One evening while lying here, we heard a heavy cannonade at the city, and before dark saw four of the enemy's ships that had passed the town and were coming up the East River. They anchored just below us. These ships were the *Phoenix* of 44 guns; the *Roebuck* of 44; the *Rose* of 32; and another, the name of which I have forgotten.[13] Half of our regiment was sent off under the command of our major to man something that were called "lines," although they were nothing more than a ditch dug along on the bank of the river, with the dirt thrown out toward the water. They stayed in these lines during the night and returned to the camp in the morning unmolested.

The other half of the regiment went the next night under the command of the lieutenant colonel upon the like errand. We arrived at the lines about dark and were ordered to leave our packs in a copse wood,[14] under a guard, and go into the lines without them. What was the cause of this piece of *wise* policy I never knew, but I knew the effects of it, which was that I never saw my knapsack from that day to this, nor did any of the rest of our party unless they came across them by accident in our retreat. We "manned the lines" and lay quite ... unmolested during the whole night.... We had a chain of sentinels quite up the river, for four or five miles in length. At an interval of every half hour they passed the watchword to each other, "All is well." I heard the British on board their shipping answer, "We will alter your tune before tomorrow night"; and they were as good as their word for once.

It was quite a dark night, and at daybreak the first thing that "saluted our eyes" was all the four ships at anchor, with springs upon their cables, and within musket shot of us. The *Phoenix* lying a little quartering and her stern toward me, I could read her name as distinctly as though I had been directly under her stern. What is the meaning of all this, thought I, what is coming forward now? They appeared to be very busy on shipboard, but we lay still and showed our good breeding by not interfering with them, as they were strangers, and we knew not but they were bashful withal. As soon as it was fairly light, we saw their boats coming out of a creek or cove on the Long Island side of the water, filled with British soldiers. When they came to the edge of the tide, they formed their boats in line. They continued to augment their forces from the Island until they

[13] The *Rose* had ascended the East River on September 3. The other two war vessels were the frigates *Orpheus* (32 guns) and *Carysfort* (28 guns).

[14] A dense thicket of brush or small trees.

appeared like a large clover field in full bloom. And now was coming on the famous Kip's Bay affair, which has been criticized so much by the historians of the Revolution. I was there and will give a true statement of all that *I* saw during that day.[15]

It was on a Sabbath morning, the day in which the British were always employed about their deviltry, if possible, because, they said, they had the prayers of the church on that day. We lay very quiet in our ditch waiting their motions, till the sun was an hour or two high; we heard a cannonade at the city, but our attention was drawn toward our own guests. But they being a little dilatory in their operations, I stepped into an old warehouse which stood close by me, with the door open inviting me in, and sat down upon a stool. The floor was strewed with papers which had in some former period been used in the concerns of the house but were then lying in "woeful confusion." I was very demurely perusing these papers when all of a sudden there came such a peal of thunder from the British shipping that I thought my head would go with the sound. I made a frog's leap for the ditch, and lay as still as I possibly could, and began to consider which part of my carcass was to go first. The British played their parts well; indeed, they had nothing to hinder them. We kept the lines till they were almost leveled upon us, when our officers, seeing we could make no resistance, and no orders coming from any superior officer, and that we must soon be entirely exposed to the rake of their guns, gave the order to leave the lines.

In retreating we had to cross a level clear spot of ground 40 or 50 rods wide, exposed to the whole of the enemy's fire; and they gave it to us in prime order. The grapeshot and langrage flew merrily, which served to quicken our motions.[16] When I had gotten a little out of the reach of their combustibles, I found myself in company with one who was a neighbor of mine when at home and one

---

[15] Kip's Bay is at today's East 34th Street and represents the geographical point in the East River from which General Howe launched his invasion of Manhattan Island on Sunday, September 15, 1776. Martin's regiment happened to be on duty at Kip's Bay and took the brunt of the criticism for the precipitous flight of troops.

[16] Grapeshot consisted of racks or bags of iron balls fired from cannon; langrage was irregularly shaped shot most often employed in naval encounters to rip apart enemy sails and rigging. More than 70 large artillery pieces bombarded the shoreline for nearly two hours and easily cleared the way for the landing of some 9,000 British and Hessian troops, representing the first major step in driving the patriots off Manhattan Island and securing New York City as the primary North American base for British military operations against the American rebels.

other man belonging to our regiment; where the rest of them were I knew not. We went into a house by the highway in which were two women and some small children, all crying most bitterly. We asked the women if they had any spirits in the house; they placed a case bottle of rum upon the table and bid us help ourselves. We each of us drank a glass and bidding them good-bye betook ourselves to the highway again.

We had not gone far before we saw a party of men, apparently hurrying on in the same direction with ourselves. We endeavored hard to overtake them, but on approaching them we found that they were not of our way of thinking; they were Hessians. We immediately altered our course and took the main road leading to King's Bridge.[17] We had not long been on this road before we saw another party just ahead of us, whom we knew to be Americans. Just as we overtook these, they were fired upon by a party of British from a cornfield, and all was immediately in confusion again.

I believe the enemy's party was small; but our people were all militia, and the demons of fear and disorder seemed to take full possession of all and everything on that day. When I came to the spot where the militia were fired upon, the ground was literally covered with arms, knapsacks, staves, coats, hats, and old oil flasks.... All I picked up of the plunder was a block-tin syringe, which afterwards helped to procure me a thanksgiving dinner.[18] Myself and the man whom I mentioned as belonging to our company were all who were in company at this time, the other man having gone on with those who were fired upon; they did not tarry to let the grass grow much under their feet.

We had to advance slowly, for my comrade having been sometime unwell was now so overcome by heat, hunger, and fatigue that he became suddenly and violently sick. I took his musket and endeavored to encourage him on. He was, as I before observed, a nigh [near] neighbor of mine when at home, and I was loath to leave him behind, although I was anxious to find the main part of the regiment,

[17] King's Bridge, sometimes rendered Kingsbridge, was at the northern end of Manhattan Island (today's West 230th Street and Marble Hill Avenue), where the post road to New England crossed over Spuyten Duyvil Creek and passed through the Bronx. By day's end Martin and his fleeing comrades reached the lines that Washington had earlier formed on the rise of land known as Harlem Heights (running north of today's 125th Street).

[18] Martin uses this term not in reference to the November holiday celebrated by modern Americans but to bountiful meals.

if possible before night, for I thought that that part of it which was not in the lines was in a body somewhere.

We soon came in sight of a large party of Americans ahead of us who appeared to have come into this road by some other route; we were within sight of them when they were fired upon by another party of the enemy; they returned but a very few shots and then scampered off as fast as their legs would carry them. When we came to the ground they had occupied, the same display of lumber presented itself as at the other place. We here found a wounded man and some of his comrades endeavoring to get him off. I stopped to assist them in constructing a sort of litter to lay him upon, when my sick companion growing impatient moved on, and as soon as we had placed the wounded man upon the litter I followed him.

While I was here one or two of our regiment came up and we went on together. We had proceeded but a short distance, however, before we found our retreat cut off by a party of the enemy, stretched across the Island. I immediately quitted the road and went into the fields, where there happened to be a small spot of boggy land covered with low bushes and weeds; into these I ran and squatting down concealed myself from their sight. Several of the British came so near to me that I could see the buttons on their clothes. They, however, soon withdrew and left the coast clear for me again. I then came out of my covert and went on, but what had become of my sick comrade or the rest of my companions I knew not. I still kept the sick man's musket; I was unwilling to leave it, for it was his own property, and I knew he valued it highly, and I had a great esteem for him. I had indeed enough to do to take care of my own concerns; it was exceeding hot weather, and I was faint, having slept but very little the preceding night, nor had I eaten a mouthful of victuals for more than 24 hours.

I waddled on as well and as fast as I could, and ... directly came to a foul place in the road, where the soldiers had taken down the fence to pass into the fields. I passed across the corner of one field and through a gap in a cross fence into another; here I found a number of men resting under the trees and bushes in the fences. Almost the first I saw, after passing the gap in the fence, was my sick friend. I was exceeding glad to find him, for I had but little hope of ever seeing him again; he was sitting near the fence with his head between his knees. I tapped him upon the shoulder and asked him to get up and go on with me. "No," said he (at the same time regarding me with a most pitiful look), "I must die here." I endeavored to argue the case with him, but all to no purpose; he insisted upon dying there. I told him he should not die there nor anywhere else that day, if I could help it; and at length with more persuasion and some force I succeeded in getting him upon his feet again and to moving on.

There happened just at this instant a considerable shower of rain, which wet us all to the skin, being very thinly clad. We, however, continued to move forward, although but slowly. After proceeding about half a mile we came to a place where our people had begun to make a stand. A number, say 200 or 300, had collected here, having been stopped by the artillery officers; they had two or three fieldpieces fixed and fitted for action, in case the British came on, which was momentarily expected. I and my comrades (for I had found another of our company when I found my sick man) were stopped here, a sentinel being placed in the road to prevent our going any further. I felt very much chagrined to be thus hindered from proceeding, as I felt confident that our regiment, or some considerable part of it, was not far ahead, unless they had been more unlucky than I had. I remonstrated with the officer who detained us. I told him that our regiment was just ahead; he asked me how I knew that. I could not tell him, but I told him I had a sick man with me who was wet and would die if exposed all night to the damp cold air, hoping by this to move his compassion; but it would not do. He was inexorable. I shall not soon forget the answer he gave me when I made the last-mentioned observation respecting the sick man. "Well," said he, "if he dies the country will be rid of one who can do it no good." Pretty fellow! thought I, a very compassionate gentleman! When a man has got his bane in his country's cause, let him die like an old horse or dog, because he can do no more! The *only wish* I would wish such men would be to let them have exactly the same treatment which they would give to others.

I saw but little chance of escaping from this very humane gentleman by fair means, so I told my two comrades to stick by me and keep together, and we would get from them by some means or other during the evening. It was now almost sundown and the air quite chilly after the shower, and we were as wet as water could make us. I was really afraid my sick man would die in earnest. I had not stayed there long after this entertaining dialogue with my obliging friend, the officer, waiting for an opportunity to escape, before one offered. There came to the sentinel, I suppose, an old acquaintance of his, with a canteen containing some sort of spirits; after drinking himself, he gave it to the sentinel, who took a large pull upon it. They then fell into conversation together, but soon taking a hare from the same hound, it put them into quite "a talkative mood"; I

kept my eyes upon them and when I thought I saw a chance of getting from them, I gave my companions a wink, and we passed by
the sentinel without his noticing us at all. A walk of a very few rods
concealed us from his view by a turn in the road and some bushes,
and thus we escaped from prison....

We went on a little distance when we overtook another man
belonging to our company. He had just been refreshing himself with
some bread and dry salt fish and was putting "the fragments" into
his knapsack. I longed for a bite, but I felt too bashful to ask him,
and he was too thoughtless or stingy to offer it. We still proceeded,
but had not gone far when we came up with the regiment, resting
themselves on the "cold ground" after the fatigues of the day. Our
company all *appeared* to rejoice to see us, thinking we were killed
or prisoners. I was *sincerely* glad to see them, for I was once more
among friends or at least acquaintances. Several of the regiment
were missing, among whom was our major. He was a fine man, and
his loss was much regretted by the men of the regiment.[19] We were
the last who came up; all the others who were missing were either
killed or taken prisoners.

And here ends the "Kip's Bay" affair, which caused at the time
and has since caused much "inkshed." ... One anecdote which I have
seen more than once in print, I will notice. A certain man, or the
friends of a certain man, have said that this certain man was sitting
by the highway side when the Commander in Chief passed by and
asked him why he sat there. His answer, as he or they say, was, "That
he had rather be killed or taken by the enemy than trodden to death
by cowards." A brave man he! I doubt whether there was such
another there that day, and I much doubt whether he himself was
there under such circumstances as he or his friends relate. Every man
that I saw was endeavoring by all sober means to escape from death
or captivity, which at that period of the war was almost certain death.
The men were confused, being without officers to command them.[20]

---

[19]   The advancing British had captured Major Phineas Porter. Eventually he obtained
his freedom and served as a major and colonel of Connecticut militia before the war
ended. He died in 1804.
[20]   The panicky retreat appalled Washington, who reputedly brandished his riding
cane and pistols in attempting to regain control of fleeing soldiers and officers alike.
The day's only good news was that General Howe was slow to push across Manhattan
Island to the Hudson River. Because of his dilatoriness 3,000 patriot troops posted
in New York City were able to elude his forces by scampering up the west side of the
island to Harlem Heights.

I do not recollect of seeing a commissioned officer from the time I left the lines on the banks of the East River in the morning until I met with the *gentlemanly* one in the evening. How could the men fight without officers? ...

We lay that night upon the ground which the regiment occupied when I came up with it. The next day in the forenoon the enemy, as we expected, followed us "hard up" and were advancing through a level field. Our rangers and some few other light troops under the command of Colonel Knowlton of Connecticut, and Major Leitch of, I believe, Virginia, were in waiting for them. Seeing them advancing, the rangers, &c. concealed themselves in a deep gully overgrown with bushes; upon the western verge of this defile was a post and rail fence, and over that the afore-mentioned field. Our people let the enemy advance until they arrived at the fence, when they arose and poured in a volley upon them. How many of the enemy were killed and wounded could not be known, as the British were always as careful as Indians to conceal their losses. There were doubtless some killed, as I myself counted 19 ball-holes through a single rail of the fence at which the enemy were standing when the action began.[21]

The British gave back and our people advanced into the field. The action soon became warm. Colonel Knowlton, a brave man and commander of the detachment, fell in the early part of the engagement. It was said by those who saw it that he lost his valuable life by unadvisedly exposing himself singly to the enemy. In my boyhood I had been acquainted with him; he was a brave man and an excellent citizen. Major Leitch fell soon after, and the troops who were then engaged were left with no higher commanders than their captains, but they still kept the enemy retreating.

---

[21] Martin had only a fuzzy understanding of the beginnings of the Harlem Heights engagement of September 16. Washington wanted to reconnoiter British lines, hidden by heavy woods about two miles to the south, to determine whether the enemy was preparing to advance that day. Before dawn Lieutenant Colonel Thomas Knowlton and his rangers went out to gather what information they could, which resulted in a skirmish with British light infantry. As the morning progressed the fighting increased as each side committed more troops. Both Knowlton and Major Andrew Leitch, who was leading a flanking party, fell mortally wounded within a few minutes of each other, but junior-grade officers refused to abandon the field. Martin's regiment eventually joined the battle, which at its peak involved about 5,000 troops from each side before Washington decided to disengage at around 2 p.m. This encounter showed the Americans that they could hold their own against British and Hessian regulars, a real morale booster for an army that had suffered through so embarrassing a flight the previous day.

Our regiment was now ordered into the field, and we arrived on the ground just as the retreating enemy were entering a thick wood, a circumstance as disagreeable to them as it was agreeable to us at that period of the war. We soon came to action with them. The troops engaged, being reinforced by our regiment, kept them still retreating until they found shelter under the cannon of some of their shipping lying in the North [Hudson] River. We remained on the battleground till nearly sunset, expecting the enemy to attack us again, but they showed no such inclination that day. The men were very much fatigued and faint, having had nothing to eat for 48 hours. At least the greater part were in this condition, and I among the rest. While standing on the field after the action had ceased, one of the men near the lieutenant colonel complained of being hungry; the colonel, putting his hand into his coat pocket, took out a piece of an ear of Indian corn burnt as black as a coal. "Here," said he to the man complaining, "eat this and learn to be a soldier." ...

We had 8 or 10 of our regiment killed in the action, and a number wounded, but none of them belonged to our company. Our lieutenant colonel was hit by a grapeshot, which went through his coat, waistcoat, and shirt to the skin on his shoulder, without doing any other damage than cutting up his epaulet.[22]

A circumstance occurred on the evening after this action which, although trifling in its nature, excited in me feelings which I shall never forget. When we came off the field we brought away a man who had been shot dead upon the spot, and after we had refreshed ourselves we proceeded to bury him. Having provided a grave, which was near a gentleman's country seat (at that time occupied by the Commander in Chief),[23] we proceeded, just in the dusk of evening, to commit the poor man, then far from friends and relatives, to the bosom of his Mother Earth.

Just as we had laid him in the grave in as decent a posture as existing circumstances would admit, there came from the house

---

[22] Harlem Heights cost the British an estimated 168 casualties, not counting Hessian losses, in comparison to about 60 patriot casualties. Martin's wounded colonel, James Arnold, did not rejoin the Continental service but did serve as a major of Connecticut militia after 1776.

[23] The mansion of alleged tory Roger Morris, formerly a British military officer who had married one of New York's wealthiest heiresses, Mary Philipse, daughter of Frederic, the second lord of Philipse Manor. This residence later passed to merchant Stephen Jumel and is today known as the Jumel Mansion.

toward the grave two young ladies, who appeared to be sisters. As they approached the grave, the soldiers immediately made way for them with those feelings of respect which beauty and modesty combined seldom fail to produce, more especially when, as in this instance, accompanied by piety. Upon arriving at the head of the grave, they stopped and with their arms around each other's neck stooped forward and looked into it, and with a sweet pensiveness of countenance which might have warmed the heart of a misogynist, asked if we were going to put the earth upon his naked face. Being answered in the affirmative, one of them took a fine white gauze handkerchief from her neck and desired that it might be spread upon his face, tears at the same time flowing down their cheeks. After the grave was filled up they retired to the house in the same manner they came. Although the dead soldier had no acquaintance present (for there were none at his burial who knew him), yet he had mourners and females too. Worthy young ladies! ...

Another affair which transpired during and after the above-mentioned engagement deserves to be recorded by me, as no one else has to my knowledge ever mentioned it. A sergeant belonging to the Connecticut forces, being sent by his officers in the heat of the action to procure ammunition, was met by a superior officer, an aide-de-camp to some general officer (I believe), who accused him of deserting his post in time of action. He remonstrated with the officer and informed him of the absolute necessity there was of his obeying the orders of his own officers; that the failure of his procuring a supply of ammunition might endanger the success of the day, but all to no purpose. The officer would not allow himself to believe him, but drew his sword and threatened to take his life on the spot if he did not immediately return to his corps. The sergeant, fired with just indignation at hearing and seeing his life threatened, cocked his musket, and stood in his own defense. He was, however, taken, confined and tried for mutiny, and condemned to be shot.

The sentence of the court martial was approved by the Commander in Chief, and the day for his execution set. When it arrived, an embankment was thrown up to prevent the shot fired at him from doing other damage, and all things requisite on such occasions were in readiness. The Connecticut troops were then drawn out and formed in a square, and the prisoner brought forth; after being blindfolded and pinioned, he knelt upon the ground. The corporal with his six executioners were then brought up before him, ready at the fatal word of command to send a brave soldier into the eternal world because he persisted in doing his duty and obeying the lawful and urgent orders of his superior officers, the failure of which might, for aught the officer who stopped him knew, have caused the loss of hundreds of lives. But the sergeant was reprieved, and I believe it was well that he was, for his blood would not have been the only blood that would have been spilt.[24]

The troops were greatly exasperated, and they showed what their feelings were by their lively and repeated cheerings after the reprieve, but more so by their secret and open threats before it. The reprieve was read by one of the chaplains of the army after a long harangue to the soldiers setting forth the enormity of the crime charged upon the prisoner, repeatedly using this sentence, "crimes for which men ought to die," which did much to further the resentment of the troops already raised to a high pitch. But, as I said before, it was well that it ended as it did, both on account of the honor of the soldiers and the safety of some others....

We remained here till sometime in the month of October without anything very material transpiring, excepting starvation, and *that* had by this time become quite a secondary matter. Hard duty and nakedness were considered the prime evils, for the reader will recollect that we lost all our clothing in the Kip's Bay affair. The British were quite indulgent to us, not having interrupted our happiness since the check they received in the action before mentioned, but left us at our leisure to see that they did not get among us before we were apprized of their approach, and that, in all its bearings, was enough.

It now began to be cool weather, especially the nights. To have to lie as I did almost every other night (for our duty required it) on the cold and often wet ground, without a blanket and with nothing but thin summer clothing, was tedious. I have often while upon guard lain on one side until the upper side smarted with cold, then turned that side down to the place warmed by my body and let the other take its turn at smarting, while the one on the ground warmed; thus alternately turning for four or six hours till called upon to go on sentry, as the soldiers term it; and when relieved from a tour of two long hours at that business and returned to the guard again, have

---

[24] Colonel Joseph Reed of Pennsylvania, Washington's talented but quirky adjutant general and the officer in question, demanded the court martial of the sergeant, Ebenezer Leffingwell of Colonel John Durkee's 20th Continental regiment, originally organized in Connecticut. On September 22 a hearing board condemned Leffingwell to die, but he won this dramatic reprieve because Reed, having mused about the incident, implored Washington to pardon the sergeant.

had to go through the operation of freezing and thawing for four or six hours more—in the morning the ground as white as snow with hoar frost. Or perhaps it would rain all night like a flood; all that could be done in that case was to lie down (if one could lie down), take our musket in our arms and place the lock between our thighs, and "weather it out."

A simple affair happened, while I was upon guard at a time while we were here, which made [a] considerable disturbance ... and caused me some extra hours of fatigue at the time. As I was the cause of it at first, I will relate it. The guard consisted of nearly 200 men, commanded by a field officer. We kept a long chain of sentinels placed almost within speaking distance of each other, and being in close neighborhood with the enemy we were necessitated to be pretty alert. I was upon my post as sentinel about the middle of the night; thinking we had overgone the time in which we ought to have been relieved, I stepped a little off my post toward one of the next sentries, it being quite dark, and asked him in a low voice how long he had been on sentry. He started as if attacked by the enemy and roared out, "Who comes there?" I saw I had alarmed him and stole back to my post as quick as possible.

He still kept up his cry, "Who comes there?" and receiving no answer, he discharged his piece, which alarmed the whole guard, who immediately formed and prepared for action and sent off a non-commissioned officer and file of men to ascertain the cause of alarm. They came first to the man who had fired and asked him what was the matter; he said that someone had made an abrupt advance upon his premises and demanded, "How comes you on, sentry?" They next came to me, inquiring what I had seen; I told them that I had not seen or heard anything to alarm me but what the other sentinel had caused. The men returned to the guard, and we were soon relieved, which was all I had wanted.

Upon our return to the guard, I found, as was to be expected, that the alarm was the subject of general conversation.... They were confident that a spy or something worse had been among us, and consequently greater vigilance was necessary. We were accordingly kept the rest of the night under arms, and I cursed my indiscretion for causing the disturbance, as I could get no more rest during the night. I could have set all to rights by speaking a word, but it would not do for me to betray my own secret. But it was diverting to me to see how much the story gained by being carried about, both among the guard and after its arrival in the camp....

Sometime in October the British landed at Frog's Neck, or Point, and by their motions seemed to threaten to cut off our retreat to York Island.[25] We were thereupon ordered to leave the Island. We crossed King's Bridge and directed our course toward the White Plains. We saw parties of the enemy foraging in the country, but they were generally too alert for us. We encamped on the heights called Valentine's Hill,[26] where we continued some days, keeping up the old system of starving. A sheep's head which I begged of the butchers, who were killing some for the "gentlemen officers," was all the provisions I had for two or three days....

We marched from Valentine's Hill for the White Plains in the night.... We arrived at the White Plains just at dawn of day, tired and faint—encamped on the plains a few days and then removed to the hills in the rear of the plains. Nothing remarkable transpired while lying here for some time. One day after roll call, one of my messmates with me set off upon a little jaunt into the country to get some sauce of some kind or other. We soon came to a field of English turnips; but the owner was there, and we could not get any of them without paying for them in some way or other. We soon agreed with the man to pull and cut off the tops of the turnips at the halves, until we got as many as we needed. After the good man had set us to work and chatted with us a few minutes, he went off and left us. After he was gone, and we had pulled and cut as many as we wanted, we packed them up and decamped, leaving the owner of the turnips to pull his share himself.

When we arrived at the camp, the troops were all parading. Upon inquiry we found that the British were advancing upon us. We flung our turnip plunder into the tent, packed up our things, which was easily done, for we had but a trifle to pack, and fell into

---

[25]   More often called Throg's Neck. General Howe remained inactive for nearly a month after the Harlem Heights engagement. Then he launched a daring amphibious maneuver late on October 12 to outflank Washington's strong Harlem Heights defenses. Howe's objective was to get behind the Americans and entrap them at the northern end of Manhattan Island. Sending troops on transport vessels from the East River through Hell Gate and then to Throg's Neck, Howe's force had reached a tangled swampland. Slight American resistance convinced the British commander to look for a safer landing site, which turned out to be Pell's Point three miles farther into Long Island Sound. Advance British units reached Pell's Point on October 18. Meanwhile, to avoid entrapment Washington struck northward from his Harlem Heights defenses, moving his force across King's Bridge before reconcentrating in the village of White Plains about 15 miles to the north.
[26]   Just north of King's Bridge and Spuyten Duyvil Creek.

the ranks. Before we were ready to march, the battle had begun. Our regiment then marched off, crossed a considerable stream of water which crosses the plain, and formed behind a stone wall in company with several other regiments and waited the approach of the enemy.[27]

They were not far distant, at least that part of them with which we were quickly after engaged. They were constructing a sort of bridge to convey their artillery, &c. across the before-mentioned stream. They, however, soon made their appearance in our neighborhood. There was in our front about 10 rods distant an orchard of apple trees. The ground on which the orchard stood was lower than the ground that we occupied, but was level from our post to the verge of the orchard, when it fell off so abruptly that we could not see the lower parts of the trees.

A party of Hessian troops and some English soon took possession of this ground. They would advance so far as just to show themselves above the rising ground, fire, and fall back and reload their muskets. Our chance upon them was, as soon as they showed themselves above the level ground, or when they fired, to aim at the flashes of their guns; their position was as advantageous to them as a breastwork. We were engaged in this manner for some time, when, finding ourselves flanked and in danger of being surrounded, we were compelled to make a hasty retreat from the stone wall. We lost, comparatively speaking, very few at the fence, but when forced to retreat we lost in killed and wounded a considerable number. One man who belonged to our company, when we marched from the parade, said, "Now I am going out to the field to be killed," and he said more than once afterwards that he should be killed; and he was. He was shot dead on the field. I never saw a man so prepossessed with the idea of any mishap as he was....[28]

[27] Washington had deployed his troops along a three-mile line running through the village of White Plains. To their right across the Bronx River was unfortified Chatterton's Hill. When General Howe's force of 13,000 bore down on White Plains on the morning of October 28, the necessity of controlling Chatterton's Hill was obvious. Ordering troops onto the hill, Washington also sent a column of 1,500, including Martin's regiment, across the Bronx and over a mile in front of the slope to delay the oncoming British. The Battle of White Plains ensued. By the end of the day the British controlled Chatterton's Hill, thereby forcing Washington to pull his line back from White Plains.

[28] The British should have had a greater premonition of death. Their casualties at White Plains were an estimated 313 killed and wounded, as compared to about 175 for the Americans.

We did not come in contact with the enemy again that day, and just at night we fell back to our encampment. In the course of the afternoon the British took possession of a hill on the right of our encampment, which had in the early part of the day been occupied by some of the New York troops. This hill overlooked the one upon which we were and was not more than half or three fourths of a mile distant. The enemy had several pieces of field artillery upon this hill, and, as might be expected, entertained us with their music all the evening. We entrenched ourselves where we now lay, expecting another attack. But the British were very civil, and indeed they generally were, after they had received a check ... for any of their rude actions; they seldom repeated them, at least not till the affair that caused the reprimand had ceased in some measure to be remembered.

During the night we remained in our new made trenches, the ground of which was in many parts springy. In that part where I happened to be stationed, the water before morning was nearly over shoes, which caused many of us to take violent colds by being exposed upon the wet ground after a profuse perspiration. I was one who felt the effects of it and was the next day sent back to the baggage to get well again, if I could, for it was left to my own exertions to do it, and no other assistance was afforded me. I was not alone in misery; there were a number in the same circumstances. When I arrived at the baggage, which was not more than a mile or two, I had the canopy of heaven for my hospital and the ground for my hammock; I found a spot where the dry leaves had collected between the knolls [higher ground]. I made up a bed of these and nestled in it, having no other friend present but the sun to smile upon me. I had nothing to eat or drink, not even water, and was unable to go after any myself, for I was sick indeed. In the evening one of my mess-mates found me out and soon after brought me some boiled hog's flesh (it was not pork) and turnips, without either bread or salt. I could not eat it, but I felt obliged to him notwithstanding. He did all he could do. He gave me the best he had to give, and had to steal that, poor fellow. Necessity drove him to do it to satisfy the cravings of his own hunger as well as to assist a fellow sufferer.

The British soon after this left the White Plains and passed the Hudson into New Jersey. We, likewise, fell back to New [North] Castle and Wright's Mills. Here a number of our sick were sent off to Norwalk in Connecticut[29] to recruit [rest]. I was sent with them as a nurse. We were billeted among the inhabitants. I had in my ward seven or eight *sick soldiers*, who were (at least soon after their arrival there) as well in health as I was. All they wanted was a cook and something for a cook to exercise his functions upon. The inhabitants here were almost entirely what were in those days termed tories. An old lady, of whom I often procured milk, used always when I went to her house to give me a lecture on my opposition to our good King George. She had always said (she told me) that the regulars would make us fly like pigeons....

The man of the house where I was quartered had a smart-looking Negro man, a great politician. I chanced one day to go into the barn where he was threshing. He quickly began to upbraid me with my opposition to the British. The king of England was a very powerful prince, he said—a very powerful prince; and it was a pity that the colonists had fallen out with him; but as we had, we must abide by the consequences. I had no inclination to waste the shafts of my rhetoric upon a Negro slave. I concluded he had heard his betters say so. As the old cock crows, so crows the young one; and I thought, as the white cock crows, so crows the black one. He ran away from his master before I left there, and went to Long Island to assist King George; but it seems the King of Terrors was more potent than King George, for his master had certain intelligence that poor Cuff was laid flat on his back.

This man had likewise a Negress who (as he was a widower) kept his house. She was as great a doctress as Cuff was a politician, and she wished to be a surgeon. There was an annual thanksgiving while we were here. The *sick* men of my ward had procured a fine roasting pig, and the old Negro woman having seen the syringe that I picked up in the retreat from Kip's Bay, fell violently in love with it and offered me a number of pies of one sort or other for it. Of the pig and the pies we made an excellent thanksgiving dinner, the best meal I had eaten since I left my grandsire's table.

Our surgeon came among us soon after this and packed us all off to camp, save two or three who were discharged. I arrived at camp

[29] North Castle and Wright's Mills, now Kensico, were more secure positions in rugged terrain north of White Plains. Norwalk, a western coastal town on Long Island Sound, was later plundered and burned by British raiders during July 1779 in alleged retaliation for supporting privateering activity.

with the rest, where we remained, moving from place to place as occasion required, undergoing hunger, cold, and fatigue until the 25th day of December, 1776, when I was discharged (my term of service having expired) at Philipse Manor, in the state of New York near Hudson's River.[30]

Here ends my first campaign. I had learned something of a soldier's life, enough I thought to keep me at home for the future. Indeed, I was then fully determined to rest easy with the knowledge I had acquired in the affairs of the army. But the reader will find ... that the ease of a winter spent at home caused me to alter my mind. I had several *kind* invitations to enlist into the standing army then about to be raised, especially a very pressing one to engage in a regiment of horse, but I concluded to try a short journey on foot first. Accordingly, I set off for my good old grandsire's, where I arrived, I think, on the 27th, two days after my discharge, and found my friends all alive and well. They appeared to be glad to see me, and I am sure I was *really* glad to see them.

[30] Philipse Manor was the huge estate of loyalist Frederick Philipse III, located along the Hudson River just north of King's Bridge. The imposing main residence, Manor Hall, remains the oldest standing building in Westchester County and functions as a state-supported museum in modern-day Yonkers, New York.

The official war records of William Douglas's regiment indicate that Martin received his discharge on December 15, perhaps a clerical error. Whatever the case, by going home to Connecticut the venturesome young soldier, now turned 16 years old, missed participating in Washington's brilliant tactical victory over Hessian forces at Trenton on December 26, 1776.

Chapter III

Campaign of 1777

JPM rejoins the Continental army, this time making a long-term commitment as a duration substitute for others buying their way out of the service. Engages in combat around Philadelphia and the bloody defense of the Delaware River forts. Ends the year by going into winter camp at Valley Forge.

> When troubles fall within your dish,
> And things don't tally with your wish:
> It's just as well to laugh as cry—
> To sing and joke, as moan and sigh:—
> For a pound of sorrow never yet
> Cancel'd a single ounce of debt.

The spring of 1777 arrived. I had got recruited [rested] during the winter and began to think again about the army. In the month of April, as the weather warmed, the young men began to enlist. Orders were out for enlisting men for three years, or during the war. The general opinion of the people was that the war would not continue three years longer; what reasons they had for making such conjectures I cannot imagine, but so it was. Perhaps it was their wish that it *might* be so, induced them to think that it *would* be so.[1]

---

[1] In the autumn of 1776 the Continental Congress had to reckon with contradictory forms of reality. To respond effectively to the massive British military counterthrust, Washington needed large numbers of long-term, well-trained, highly disciplined soldiers. Congress proceeded to authorize a new army, which had a projected strength of 75,000, to consist of soldiers who were to serve for either

One of my mates, and my most familiar associate, who had been out ever since the war commenced, and who had been with me the last campaign, had enlisted for the term of the war in the capacity of sergeant. He had enlisting orders, and was every time he saw me, which was often, harassing me with temptations to engage in the service again. At length he so far overcame my resolution as to get me into the scrape again, although it was at this time against my inclination, for I had not fully determined with myself, that if I did engage again, into what corps I should enter. But I would here just inform the reader, that that little insignificant monosyllable—No— was the hardest word in the language for me to pronounce, especially when solicited to do a thing which was in the least degree indifferent to me; I could say Yes, with half the trouble.

But I had enlisted. However, when I was alone and had time to reflect, I began sorely to repent. The next day I met the sergeant and told him that I repented my bargain; he endeavored to persuade me to stick to it, but I could then say—No. He told me that he would speak to his captain about the matter, and as I had taken no bounty money, he thought that he would dismiss me. Accordingly, he told the captain of my unwillingness to be held, and he let me run at large once more; I then determined to wait my own time before I engaged again.

The inhabitants of the town were about this time put into what were called squads, according to their ratable property. Of some of the most opulent, one formed a squad—of others, two or three, and of the lower sort of the people, several formed a squad. Each of these squads were to furnish a man for the army, either by hiring or by sending one of their own number.

I had an elbow relation, a sort of (as the Irishman said) cousin-in-law, who had been in the army the two preceding campaigns, and now had a lieutenant's commission in the standing [Continental] army. He was continually urging my grandparents to give their consent for me to go with him. He told the old gentleman a power of fine stories, and made him promises respecting his behavior to me,

---

three years or for the duration of the war, if the contest was not over sooner. At the same time unfortunately, the immense British campaign effort had all but obliterated the *rage militaire*. The patriot enthusiasts of 1775 had learned that making war was fraught with risks to life and limb. Virtually no one now wanted to be a Continental long-termer. In Connecticut, for example, intensive recruiting during the first three months of 1777 produced only a handful of enlistees for the state's designated quota of eight Continental regiments.

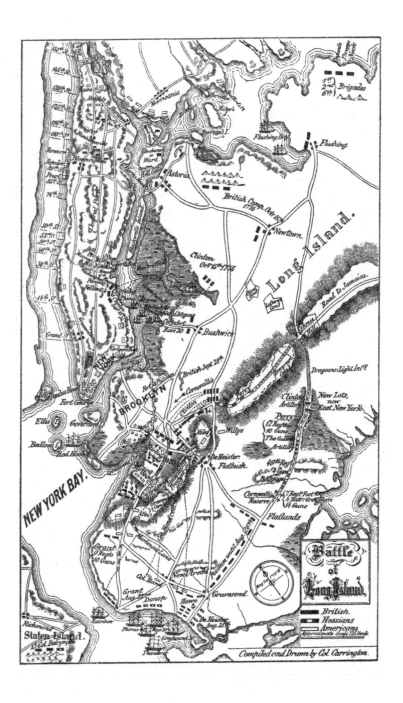

our arms and equipment. Uncle Sam was always careful to supply us with these articles, even if he could not give us anything to eat, drink, or wear. We stayed but a short time here, ... then marched to Peekskill[4] on the Hudson River, and encamped in the edge of the Highlands at a place called Old Orchard. Here we were tormented by the whippoorwills. A potent enemy! says the reader. Well, a potent enemy they were, particularly to our rest at night; they would begin their imposing music in the twilight and continue it till 10 or 11 o'clock, and commence again before the dawn, when they would be in a continual roar. No man, unless he were stupefied, could get a wink of sleep during the serenade, which in the short nights in the month of May was almost the whole of the night.

I was one day, while lying here, upon what was called a camp guard. We kept a considerable chain of sentinels. In the night there came what in military phrase is called the visiting rounds, which is an officer attended by a small escort to inspect the condition of the guards and see that they do their duty. The officer ... went to the extreme end of the line of sentinels and began his examination. One sentry, he found, who had stowed himself away snugly in an old papermill; another had left his post to procure a draught of milk from the cows in a farmer's yard, and others were found, here and there, neglecting their duty. He brought off all the delinquents to deliver them up to the *righteous* sentence of a court martial. In his progress he came to me, I being at the time on sentry duty too. I hailed him and demanded of him the countersign, which he regularly gave me and passed on. I did not expect to hear anything further about it, as I concluded that I had done my duty to perfection.

In the morning before guard relieving, I happened to be posted at the colonel's marquee door, when the above-mentioned officer came into the tent, and was telling some of our officers the consequences of his last night's expedition. I listened attentively to his recital. "At last," said he, "I came to a sentinel who challenged me like a man. I thought I had found a soldier after detecting so many scoundrels, but what think ye! As soon as I had given him the countersign, the puppy shouldered his piece, and had I been an enemy

---

[4] Peekskill was the site of a major Continental army supply depot on the east side of the Hudson River in the Hudson Highlands about 30 miles north of Manhattan Island. On March 23, 1777, a British raiding force of 500 mounted a surprise assault on Peekskill and destroyed patriot supplies there.

I could have knocked his brains out." At the first part of his recital, I grew a foot in my own estimation in a minute, and I shrunk as much and as fast at the latter part of it. I was confident he did not know me, and I as well knew it was me he had reference to. Aha! thought I, this admonition shall not lose its effect upon me; nor did it so long as I remained in the army.

I was soon after this transaction ordered off, in company with about 400 others of the Connecticut forces, to a set of old barracks a mile or two distant in the Highlands to be inoculated with the smallpox. We arrived at and cleaned out the barracks, and after two or three days received the infection, which was on the last day of May....[5] Our hospital stores were deposited in a farmer's barn in the vicinity of our quarters.

One day, about noon, the farmer's house took fire and was totally consumed with every article of household stuff it contained, although there were 500 men within 50 rods of it, and many of them within 5 when the fire was discovered, which was not till the roof had fallen in. Our officers would not let any of the inoculated men go near the fire, and the guard had enough to do to save the barn, the fire frequently catching in the yard and on the roof, which was covered with thatch or straw....

I had the smallpox favorably as did the rest, generally. We lost none, but it was more by good luck, or rather a kind Providence interfering, than by my good conduct that I escaped with life. There was a considerable large rivulet which ran directly in front of the barracks; in this rivulet were many deep places and plenty of a species of fish called suckers. One of my roommates, with myself, went off one day, the very day on which the pock began to turn upon me. We went up the brook until we were out of sight of the people at the barracks, when we undressed ourselves and went into the water, where it was often to our shoulders, to catch suckers by means of a fishhook fastened to the end of a rod; we continued at this business

---

[5] During 1776 the spread of virulent epidemic diseases like smallpox among patriot soldiers caused hundreds of deaths—and was another reason why enthusiasm for patriot military service had waned so dramatically. To combat the smallpox problem, Washington finally agreed to have all new troops inoculated. The process, known as variolation, involved cutting open the skin and rubbing in puss drawn from smallpox pustules. The purpose was to induce mild cases, thereby assuring immunity. The numbers who died from variolation were few in comparison to those who contracted the disease naturally.

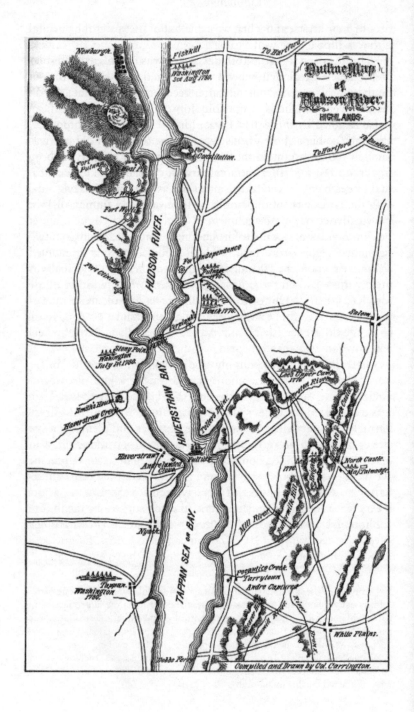

three or four hours, and when we came out of the water the pustules of the smallpox were well cleansed....

I left the hospital on the 16th day after I was inoculated and soon after joined the regiment, when I was attacked with a severe turn of the dysentery, and immediately after recovering from that I broke out all over with boils. Good old Job could scarcely have been worse handled by them than I was; I had 11 at one time upon my arm, each as big as half a hen's egg, and the rest of my carcass was much in the same condition. I attributed it to my not having been properly physicked after the smallpox, in consequence of our hospital stores being in about the same state as the commissary's.

In the latter part of the month of June or the beginning of July, I was ordered off in a detachment of about a hundred men, under the command of a captain, to the lines near King's Bridge to join two regiments of New York troops which belonged to our brigade.... We arrived upon the lines and joined the other corps which was already there. No one who has never been upon such duty as those advanced parties have to perform, can form any adequate idea of the trouble, fatigue, and dangers which they have to encounter. Their whole time is spent in marches (especially night marches) watching, starving, and in cold weather freezing and sickness. If they get any chance to rest, it must be in the woods or fields, under the side of a fence, in an orchard or in any other place but a comfortable one, lying down on the cold and often wet ground, and, perhaps, before the eyes can be closed with a moment's sleep, alarmed and compelled to stand under arms an hour or two, or to receive an attack from the enemy; and when permitted again to endeavor to rest, called upon immediately to remove some four or five miles to seek some other place, to go through the same maneuvering as before; for it was dangerous to remain any length of time in one place for fear of being informed of by some tory inhabitant (for there were a plenty of this sort of savage beast during the Revolutionary War) and 10,000 other causes to harass, fatigue, and perplex, which time and room will not permit me to enumerate.

We were once on one of those night marches, advancing toward the enemy and not far from them, when toward the latter part of the night there came on a heavy thundershower. We were ordered into some barns near by, the officers as usual ordering themselves into the houses. I thought I might get a nap if it did storm, but hardly had I sunk into a slumber when we were informed that we were discovered by the enemy, and that two or three thousand Hessians were advancing upon and very near us. We were immediately hurried out, the shower then being at its height, and the night as dark as Egypt, except when it lightened, which when passed only served to render it, if possible, still darker. We were then marched across fields and fences, pastures and brooks, swamps and ravines, a distance of two or three miles, and stationed upon a hill, or rather a ledge of rocks, which was as completely fortified by nature with a breastwork of rocks as it could have been by art. Here we waited for Mynheer[6] till the sun was two hours high, but no one coming to visit us we marched off and left the enemy to do the same, if they had not already done it.

We remained on this hard and fatiguing duty about six weeks.... We [then] marched to Peekskill and rejoined our regiments sometime in the fore part of the month of August. A short time after my arrival at Peekskill, I was sent off to King's Ferry (about five miles below) to take some bateaux that were there and carry them to Fort Montgomery in the edge of the Highlands.[7]

While upon this tour of duty, an accident happened to me which caused me much trouble and pain. After we had arrived at the fort with the boats, we tarried an hour or two to rest ourselves, after which we were ordered to take a couple of the boats and return again to King's Ferry. Wishing to be the first in the boat, I ran down [to] the wharf and jumped into it. There happened to be the butt part of an oar lying on the bottom of the boat, and my right foot, on which the whole weight of my body bore, alighted in my leap directly upon it lengthwise; it rolled over and turned my foot almost up to my ankle—so much so that my foot lay nearly in a right angle with my leg. I had then to go to the ferry where I was landed, and having no acquaintance with any of the party, most of whom were New Yorkers, and consequently at that time no great friends to the Yankees, I was obliged to hop on one foot all the way (upwards of

---

[6] A mocking term for Hessians, which in the Dutch language was a polite expression of greeting meaning "my lord."

[7] With the British occupying New York City and environs, King's Ferry (about 25 miles north of Manhattan Island) represented the southernmost crossing point used by the rebels in moving back and forth over the Hudson River. King's Ferry connected Verplancks Point on the east side of the Hudson with Stony Point on the west side. About 10 miles farther north overlooking the river's west bank were forts Montgomery and Clinton, integral bastions in the rebels' elaborate but lightly-manned Highlands defensive network that was designed to keep the British from gaining control of the whole of the Hudson River corridor—with the potentially disastrous effect of severing New England from the rest of the rebellious colonies.

five miles), not being able in the whole distance to procure a stick to assist me, although I often hobbled to the fences on each side of the road in hopes to obtain one. It was dark when I was landed at the ferry, and it was quite late before I arrived at the camp. Some of my messmates went immediately for the surgeon, but he was at a game of backgammon and could not attend to minor affairs; however, in about an hour he arrived, bathed my foot, which was swelled like a bladder, fumbled about it for some time when he gave it a wrench, which made me ... "merely yawl out."

The next day, as I was sitting under the shade before my tent, my foot lying upon a bench, swelled like a puffball, my captain passed by and must needs have a peep at it. I indulged his curiosity, upon which he said it was not set right, and taking hold of it he gave it a twist, which put it nearly in the same condition it was at first. I had then to send for Mr. Surgeon again, but he was not to be found. There was a corporal in our company who professed to act the surgeon in such cases, and he happening at the time to be present, undertook the job and accomplished it, but it was attended with more difficulty than at the first time, and with more pain to me. It was a long time before it got well and strong again; indeed it never has been entirely so well as it was before the accident happened....

Our troops, not long after this, marched to join the main army in Pennsylvania.[8] The heavy baggage was left to come on after them, and I, being an invalid, was left as one of the guard to conduct it. The baggage soon followed the troops, and I underwent not a little trouble on the march in consequence of my lame foot. When I joined the regiment the baggage was immediately sent back to Bethlehem,[9] nearly 50 miles in the country, and I was again sent

---

[8] In planning for the 1777 campaign, General Howe decided not to work in coordinated fashion with the army of General John Burgoyne that dropped out of Canada. Rather than focusing on reconquering the Hudson River corridor in concert with Burgoyne and cutting New England off from the rest of the states, Howe concluded that the quickest way to end the rebellion was to destroy Washington's army. Failing during June to bait the American commander into a climactic battle in New Jersey, Howe next loaded some 15,000 troops onto transport ships and moved them by sea up through Chesapeake Bay, where they landed on August 25 at Head of Elk, Maryland, some 50 miles southwest of Philadelphia. In response, Washington rushed his army south through the rebel capital to challenge the British force, only to take a beating at the Battle of Brandywine Creek on September 11. In the wake of Brandywine, Washington called for reinforcements. Led by General Alexander McDougall, four regiments stationed at Peekskill, including Martin's, thus made haste to join the main army.

[9] Located in Pennsylvania's Lehigh Valley.

with it as a guard. It was much against my inclination to go on this business, for I had for some time past been under the command of other officers than my own, and now I must continue longer under them. Soldiers always like to be under the command of their own officers; they are generally bad enough, but strangers are worse. I was obliged to obey my officers' orders and go on this duty, but when I was away they could not hinder me from coming back again. I was resolved not to stay at Bethlehem, and as soon as we arrived there I contrived to get the permission of the officers of the guard to return to camp again immediately. I arrived at camp the second day after leaving the baggage. My officers inquired of me why I had returned? If I was able to do hard duty, they said they were glad that I had joined the company again; if not, they were sorry. I endeavored to appear to be as well as possible, for I had no notion of being sent away from my officers and old messmates again, if I could avoid it.

When I arrived at camp it was just dark; the troops were all preparing for a march.[10] Their provisions (what they had) were all cooked, and their arms and ammunition strictly inspected and all deficiencies supplied. Early in the evening we marched in the direction of Philadelphia. We naturally concluded there was something serious in the wind. We marched slowly all night. In the morning there was a low vapor lying on the land which made it very difficult to distinguish objects at any considerable distance. About daybreak our advanced guard and the British outposts came in contact. The curs began to bark first and then the bulldogs. Our brigade moved off to the right into the fields. We saw a body of the enemy drawn up behind a rail fence on our right flank; we immediately formed in

[10] What follows is Martin's brief description of the Battle of Germantown that occurred on October 4. The British had marched triumphantly into Philadelphia on September 26, and General Howe stationed about 9,000 of his troops just north of the city in Germantown. Washington saw an opportunity to catch his adversary off guard, but his battle plan, which involved four separate columns converging on the encamped British, was too complex. The regiments under General McDougall, including Martin's, were part of General Nathanael Greene's column; and because of dense morning fog and the distance they had to travel, they got into position late. Meanwhile, other American units, which began the day fighting well, became entangled and started firing at one another. The result was both panic and a precipitous stampede back into the countryside. The Americans suffered nearly 1,100 casualties that day, including 438 troops captured (British losses have been estimated at 550), but they had fought well enough in the battle's early stages to believe that a great victory had almost been theirs, a curious form of a morale booster.

line and advanced upon them. Our orders were not to fire till we could see the buttons upon their clothes, but they were so coy that they would not give us an opportunity to be so curious, for they hid their clothes in fire and smoke before we had either time or leisure to examine their buttons.

They soon fell back and we advanced, when the action became general. The enemy were driven quite through their camp. They left their kettles in which they were cooking their breakfasts on the fires, and some of their garments were lying on the ground, which the owners had not time to put on. Affairs went on well for some time. The enemy were retreating before us until the first division that was engaged had expended their ammunition. Some of the men unadvisedly calling out that their ammunition was spent, the enemy were so near that they overheard them, when they first made a stand and then returned upon our people, who, for want of ammunition and reinforcements, were obliged in their turn to retreat, which ultimately resulted in the rout of the whole army.

There were several other circumstances which contributed to the defeat of our army on that day, but as I am narrating my own adventures, and not a history of the war, I shall omit to mention them. Those who wish to know more may consult any or all the authors who have given the history of the Revolutionary War.

I had now to travel the rest of the day, after marching all the day and night before and fighting all the morning. I had eaten nothing since the noon of the preceding day, nor did I eat a morsel till the forenoon of the next day, and I needed rest as much as victuals. I could have procured that if I had had time to seek it, but victuals was not to be found. I was tormented with thirst all the morning (fighting being warm work), but after the retreat commenced I found ample means to satisfy my thirst. "I could drink at the brook," but I could not "bite at the bank."

There was one thing in such cases as I have just mentioned (I mean, in retreating from an enemy) that always galled my feelings, and that was whenever I was forced to a quick retreat to be obliged to run till I was worried [wearied] down. The Yankees are generally very nimble of foot and in those cases are very apt to practice what they have the ability of performing. Some of our men at this time seemed to think that they could never run fast or far enough. I never wanted to run, if I was forced to run, further than to be beyond the reach of the enemy's shot, after which I had no more fear of their overtaking me than I should have of an army of lobsters doing it, unless it were their horsemen, and they *dared* not do it.

After the army had collected again and recovered from their panic, we were kept marching and countermarching, starving and freezing, nothing else happening, although that was enough, until we encamped at a place called the White Marsh, about 12 miles to the northward of Philadelphia. While we lay here, there was a spell of soft still weather, there not being wind enough for several days to dispel the smoke caused by the fires in camp. My eyes were so affected by it that I was not able to open them for hours together; the ground, which was soft and loamy, was converted into mortar, and so dirty was it that any hogsty was preferable to our tents to sleep in; and to cap the climax of our misery, we had nothing to eat, nor scarcely anything to wear.

Being pinched with hunger, I one day strolled to a place where sometime before some cattle had been slaughtered. Here I had the good luck (or rather bad luck, as it turned out in the end) to find an ox's milt,[11] which had escaped the hogs and dogs. With this prize I steered off to my tent, threw it upon the fire and broiled it, and then sat down to eat it without either bread or salt. I had not had it long in my stomach before it began to make strong remonstrances and to manifest a great inclination to be set at liberty again. I was very willing to listen to its requests, and with eyes overflowing with tears at parting with what I had thought to be a friend, I gave it a discharge. But the very thoughts of it would for some time after almost make me think that I had another milt in my stomach.

About this time information was received at headquarters that a considerable body of British troops were advanced and encamped on the western side of the river Schuylkill, near the lower bridge two or three miles from Philadelphia. Forces were immediately put in requisition to rout them from thence. Our brigade was ordered off with some detachments from other parts of the army. We marched from camp just before night as light troops, light in everything, especially in eatables. We marched to a place called Barren Hill,[12] about 12 or 15 miles from the city. From here, about 10 o'clock in the evening, we forded the Schuylkill where the river (including a bare gravelly island, or flat, which we crossed) was

[11] Apparently the ox's spleen.
[12] A small crossroads community located on the east side of the Schuylkill River and the site of a battle with British forces in which Martin participated on May 20, 1778.

about 40 rods wide, as near as I could judge, and the water about to the waist. It was quite a cool night in the month of October; the water which spattered on to our clothes froze as we passed the river. Many of the young and small soldiers fell while in the water and were completely drenched; we, however, got over and marched two or three miles on a dreary road (for that part of the country), surrounded by high hills and thick woods. All of a sudden we were ordered to halt; we were to appearance in an unfrequented road, cold and wet to our middles, and half starved: We were sorry to be stopped from traveling, as exercise kept us warm in some degree. We endeavored to kindle fires, but were ordered by the officers immediately to extinguish them, which was done by all except one, which having been kindled in a hollow tree could not be put out. I got so near to this that I could just see it between the men's legs, which was all the benefit that I derived from it.

We lay there freezing about two hours, and then were ordered to fall in and march back again. About an hour before day we dashed through the river again, at the same place at which we had crossed the preceding evening, and I can assure the reader that neither the water nor weather had become one degree warmer than it was then.

We went on to Barren Hill again, where we lay all the day, waiting as it appeared for reinforcements.... Just at dark, the reinforcements having arrived and all things being put in order, we marched again, and about 9 or 10 o'clock we tried the waters of the Schuylkill once more at the same place where we crossed the preceding night. It was not so cold as it was then, and the crossing was not so tedious, but it was bad enough at this time.

We marched slowly the remainder of the night. At the dawn of day we found ourselves in the neighborhood of the enemy. I mean in the neighborhood of where they *had* been, for when we were about to spring the net, we discovered that the birds had flown.... There was a British guard at a little distance from the bridge, upon the opposite side of the river; they turned out to do us honor and sent off an express to the city to inform their friends that the Yankees had come to pay them a visit, but they were so unmannerly as to take no notice of us. After we had taken so much pains and been at so much trouble to come to see them, they might have shown a little more politeness, considering that it would not have cost them half the trouble to meet us as we had been at to meet them. But perhaps they thought that as we had undergone so much fatigue and vexation on our journey, we might feel cross and peevish, and perchance some unlucky accidents might have happened. The British were politic, and it is good to be cautious and discreet.

We had nothing to do now but to return as we came. Accordingly, we marched off slowly, hoping that the enemy would think better of it and follow us, for we were loath to return without seeing them; however, they kept to themselves, and we went on. I was hungry, tired, and sleepy. About noon we halted an hour or two, and I went a little way into the fields, where I found a black walnut tree with a plenty of nuts under it; these nuts are very nutritious, and I cracked and ate of them till I was satisfied.

We marched again.... About sunsetting we again waded the Schuylkill, at a ford a little higher up the river. The river was not so wide here as at the former place, but the water was deeper; it was to the breast. When we had crossed, and it had become dark, we met the quartermasters, who had come out to meet us with wagons and hogsheads of whiskey! (thinking perhaps that we might take cold by being so much exposed in the cold water). They had better have brought us something more substantial, but we thought that better than nothing. The casks were unheaded, and the quartermaster sergeants stood in the wagons and dealt out the liquor to the platoons, each platoon halting as it came up till served. The intention of the quartermaster sergeants was to give each man a gill of liquor, but as measuring it out by gills was tedious, it was dealt out to us in pint measures with directions to divide a pint between four men. But as it was dark and the actions of the men could not be well seen by those who served out the liquor, each one drank as much as he pleased; some perhaps half a gill, some a gill, and as many as chose it drained the pint.

We again moved on for the camp, distant about five miles. We had not proceeded far before we entered a lane fenced on either side with rails.... Here was fun. We had been on the march since we had drunk the whiskey, just long enough for the liquor to assume its height of operation; our stomachs being empty the whiskey took rank hold, and the poor brain fared accordingly. When the men came to the fence, not being able, many or most of them, to keep a regular balance between head and heels, they would pile themselves up on each side of the fence, swearing and hallooing, some losing their arms, some their hats, some their shoes, and some themselves. Had the enemy come upon us at this time, there would have been an action worth recording; but they did not, and we, that is such as could, arrived at camp about midnight, where "those who had remained with the stuff" had made up some comfortable fires for our accommodation. Poor fellows! It was all they could do; as to victuals, they had none for themselves. I had then been nearly 30 hours without a mouthful of anything to eat, excepting the walnuts, having been the whole time on my feet (unless I happened to fall over the fence, which I do not remember to have done) and wading in and being wet with the water of the river. I ... rolled myself up in my innocency, lay down on the leaves, and forgot my misery till morning.

Soon after this affair our two Connecticut regiments (they being the only troops of that state then with the main army) were ordered off to defend the forts on the Delaware River, below the city.[13] We marched about dark, hungry and cold, and kept on till we could proceed no further from sheer hunger and fatigue. We halted about one o'clock at night in a village and were put into houses of the inhabitants, much I suppose to their contentment, especially at that time of night. Sleep took such strong hold of me and most of the others that we soon forgot our wants.

Not so with some five or six of our company, who were determined not to die of hunger that night.... They, therefore, as soon as all was still, sallied out on an expedition. They could not find anything eatable but the contents of a beehive, which they took the liberty to remove from the beehouse.... I had no hand in the battle and consequently no share in the spoil. One man who belonged to this foraging party had rather an uncouth visage; he had very thick lips, especially the upper one, a large flat nose, and quite a wide mouth, which gave him, as the Irishman said, really an open

[13] The forts were part of a patriot defensive network designed to prevent enemy ships from making passage up the Delaware River to Philadelphia. Once in control of the rebel capital, General Howe had to knock out the Delaware forts to assure his army a secure and easily accessible supply line back to New York City and England. His only other alternative was to keep hauling vital goods over the cumbersome land passage from Head of Elk, Maryland, a route the rebels could more easily disrupt. Howe's intentions became clear on October 2 when a British force overran the small patriot fort at Billingsport, New Jersey, that guarded the southernmost line of the Delaware's defenses. Here in the river's main channel the patriots had positioned below the water line two rows of chevaux-de-frise (bulky wooden crates with huge, outward-projecting iron hooks that could tear open the hulls of ships). In response to this loss, Washington detached John Durkee's 4th Connecticut and Martin's regiment, Chandler's 8th Connecticut, to reinforce the more elaborate main line of defense some five miles north of Billingsport. Since Howe controlled the landside below Philadelphia, Martin and his comrades had to cross over the Delaware River to New Jersey before marching south to reach their destination.

countenance. One of the inhabitants of the city he had helped to sack, not quite forgetting his resentment for the ill usage he had received from this paragon of beauty and his associates in the outrage, gave him a severe wound directly in the middle of the upper lip, which added very much to its dimensions. In the morning when we came to march off, Oh! the woeful figure the poor fellow exhibited! ... To see him on the parade endeavoring to conceal his face from the men, and especially from the officers, was ludicrous in the extreme, and as long as it lasted it diverted our thoughts from resting on our own calamities.

We crossed the Delaware between the town of Bristol in Pennsylvania, and the city of Burlington in New Jersey.[14] We halted for the night at the latter place, where we procured some carrion beef[15] (for it was no better); we cooked it and ate some, and carried the remainder away with us.... We halted ... the [next] night at a village called Haddington [Haddonfield]....[16] We were put into the houses for quarters during the night. Myself and about a dozen more of the company were put into a chamber where there was a fireplace but no fire nor anything to make one with; it looked as if there had been no fire there for several years. We, however, soon procured wherewithal to make a fire with and were thus enabled to keep the outside comfortable, let the inside do as it would.

There was no other furniture in the room excepting an old quill wheel and an old chair frame. We procured a thick board and placed the ends upon the wheel and chair and all sat down to regale ourselves with the warmth, when the cat happening to come under the bench to partake of the bounty, the board bending by the weight upon it, both ends slipped off at once and brought us all slap to the floor; upon taking up the board to replace it again we found the poor cat, pressed as flat as a pancake with her eyes started out two inches from her head. We did not eat her, although my appetite was sharp enough to have eaten almost anything that could be eaten.

After we had got regulated again, we began to contrive how we were to behave in our present circumstances, as it regarded belly timber. At length after several plans had been devised, many

---

[14] About 20 miles northeast of Philadelphia.

[15] Decayed or rotting meat, quite often supplied to the army by unscrupulous, profiteering patriot merchants.

[16] To get to Haddonfield, the two Connecticut regiments marched some 20 miles to the south that day, which would have brought them to within about 10 miles of their destination.

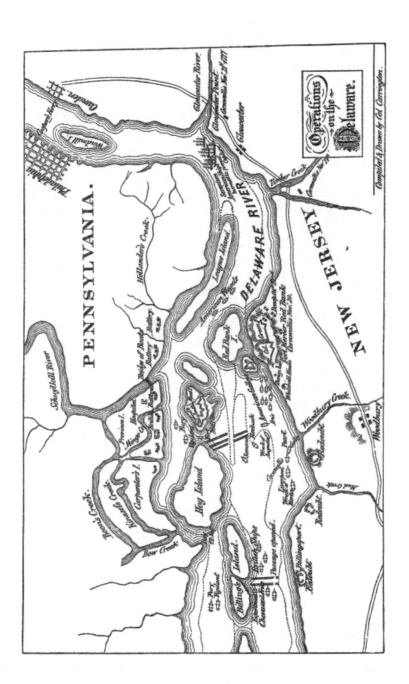

"resolves proposed and all refused a passage," it was finally determined that two or three of the most expert at the business should
sally forth and endeavor to procure something by foraging.
Accordingly, two of the club went out and shortly after returned
with a Hissian, a cant word with the soldiers for a goose. The next
difficulty was, how to pluck it; we were in a chamber and had nothing to contain the feathers. However, we concluded at last to pick
her over the fire and let that take care of the feathers. We dressed
her and then divided her among us; if I remember rightly, I got *one
wing*…. After this sumptuous repast I lay down and slept as well as
a gnawing stomach would permit.

In the morning we found a sad witness of our overnight's adventure to testify against us; the whole funnel of the chimney was stuck
full of feathers from top to bottom, and it being a very calm night
the street opposite the house was as full of them as the chimney. We
would have set the chimney on fire, but having nothing to do it with
we concluded to let chimney and street unite in their testimony
against us if they pleased; but as we marched off early in the morning we heard no more about the goose….

This day we arrived at Woodbury, New Jersey, which was the
end of our present journey. We encamped near the village, planted
our artillery in the road at each end of it, placed our guards, and
prepared to go into Fort Mifflin on Mud Island….[17]

Immediately after our arrival at Woodbury, I was ordered upon
an advanced guard, about half a mile in advance of a bridge which
lay across a large creek into which the tide flowed. The enemy's
shipping lay in the river a little below us. They had also a fortification on the shore opposite to their shipping, at a place called
Billingsport. There was a guard of the Jersey militia in advance of
us. We used to make excursions in parties of three or four from our
guard into the neighborhood of the enemy, and often picked up
stragglers from their post and shipping.

I was soon relieved from this guard, and with those who were able
of our two regiments sent to reinforce those in the fort, which was
then besieged by the British. Here I endured hardships sufficient to

[17]   Fort Mifflin was actually on Port Island contiguous to Mud Island. The fort lay
close to the marshy Pennsylvania shoreline below Philadelphia, a little south of the
point where the Schuylkill River empties into the Delaware River. About a mile away
along the New Jersey shoreline was Fort Mercer at Red Bank. Woodbury was a
small hamlet just to the east of Red Bank.

kill half a dozen horses. Let the reader only consider for a moment, and he will be satisfied if not sickened. In the cold month of November without provisions, without clothing, not a scrap of either shoes or stockings to my feet or legs, and in this condition to endure a siege in such a place as that, was appalling in the highest degree.

In confirmation of what I have here said, I will give the reader a short description of the pen that I was confined in. Confined I was, for it was next to impossible to have got away from it, if I had been so disposed. Well, the island, as it is called, is nothing more than a mud flat in the Delaware, lying upon the west side of the channel. It is diked around the fort with sluices so constructed that the fort can be laid under water at pleasure (at least it *was* so when I was there, and I presume it has not grown much higher since). On the eastern side, next [to] the main river, was a zig zag wall built of hewn stone, built as I was informed before the Revolution at the king's cost. At the southeastern part of the fortification (for fort it could not with propriety be called) was a battery of several long 18-pounders. At the southwestern angle was another battery with four or five 12- and 18-pounders and one 32-pounder. At the north-western corner was another small battery with three 12-pounders. There were also three blockhouses in different parts of the enclo-sure, but no cannon mounted upon them, nor were they of any use whatever to us while I was there. On the western side between the batteries was a high embankment, within which was a tier of pali-sades. In front of the stone wall for about half its length was another embankment, with palisades on the inside of it and a narrow ditch between them and the stone wall.

On the western side of the fortification was a row of barracks, extending from the northern part of the works to about half the length of the fort. On the northern end was another block of bar-racks, which reached nearly across the fort from east to west. In front of these was a large square two-story house for the accom-modation of the officers of the garrison; neither this house nor the barracks were of much use at this time, for it was as much as a man's life was worth to enter them, the enemy often directing their shot at them in particular. In front of the barracks and other neces-sary places were parades and walks; the rest of the ground was soft mud. I have seen the enemy's shells fall upon it and sink so low that their report could not be heard when they burst, and I could only feel a tremulous motion of the earth at the time. At other times, when they burst near the surface of the ground, they would throw the mud 50 feet in the air.

The British had erected five batteries with six heavy guns in each and a bomb battery with three long mortars in it on the opposite side of the water, which separated the island from the main on the west, and which was but a short distance across. They had also a battery of six guns a little higher up the river, at a place called the Hospital Point.[18] This is a short description of the place which I was destined with a few others to defend against whatever force, land or marine, the enemy might see fit to bring against it.

The first attempt the British made against the place after I entered it was by the *Augusta*, a 64-gun ship. While maneuvering one dark night she got on the *chevaux-de-frise*[19] which had been sunk in the channel of the river. As soon as she was discovered in the morning we plied her so well with hot shot that she was soon in flames. Boats were sent from the shipping below to her assistance, but our shot proving too hot for them, they were obliged to leave her to her fate; in an hour or two she blew up with an explosion which seemed to shake the earth to its center, leaving a volume of smoke like a thundercloud, which, as the air was calm, remained an hour or two. A 20-gun ship which had come to the assistance of the *Augusta* in her distress shared her fate soon after.[20]

Our batteries were nothing more than old spars and timber laid up in parallel lines and filled between with mud and dirt. The British batteries in the course of the day would nearly level our works; and we were, like the beaver, obliged to repair our dams in

[18]   Once in control of the landside south of Philadelphia, the British established a number of artillery batteries along the shoreline, including the one at Hospital Point. Their purpose was to cannonade Fort Mifflin into oblivion.

[19]   An elaborate network of metal-tipped poles, up to 40 feet in length, secured to a base and designed in this case to entangle or puncture holes in enemy craft trying to reach Philadelphia through this portion of the Delaware River.

[20]   Martin's memory rarely failed him, but in this instance he confused names and events. On October 22, even as the two Connecticut regiments were on the march to Woodbury, the British launched an elaborate but unsuccessful land and water assault against Fort Mercer. Among the British warships engaged, the *Augusta* and the *Merlin*, the latter carrying 20 guns, either ran aground or struck a line of chevaux-de-frise and were destroyed. The next day two British men-of-war attacked Fort Mifflin, only to catch on fire and sink under withering patriot fire—they could also have suffered damage by getting caught up in the triple line of chevaux-de-frise protecting the downstream side of the fort. Martin may have been ferried over to Fort Mifflin on the 23rd, and he could have been recalling the action of this date or possibly one of the British naval strikes against the fort between November 10 and 15. The former seems most likely.

the night. During the whole night at intervals of a quarter or half an hour, the enemy would let off all their pieces, and although we had sentinels to watch them and at every flash of their guns to cry, "a shot," upon hearing which everyone endeavored to take care of himself, yet they would ever and anon, in spite of all our precautions, cut up some of us.

The engineer in the fort was a French officer by the name of Fleury....[21] He was a very austere man and kept us constantly employed day and night; there was no chance of escaping from his vigilance.

Between the stone wall and the palisades was a kind of yard or pen, at the southern end of which was a narrow entrance not more than 8 or 10 feet wide, with a ditch about 4 feet wide in the middle, extending the whole length of the pen. Here on the eastern side of the wall was the only place in the fort that anyone could be in any degree of safety. Into this place we used to gather the splinters broken off the palisades by the enemy's shot and make a little fire, just enough to keep from suffering. We would watch an opportunity to escape from the vigilance of Colonel Fleury and run into this place for a minute or two's respite from fatigue and cold. When the engineer found that the workmen began to grow scarce, he would come to the entrance and call us out. He had always his cane in his hand, and woe betided him he could get a stroke at. At his approach I always jumped over the ditch and ran down on the other side, so that he could not reach me; but he often noticed me and as often threatened me, but threatening was all; he could never get a stroke at me, and I cared but little for his threats.

It was utterly impossible to lie down to get any rest or sleep on account of the mud, if the enemy's shot would have suffered us to do so. Sometimes some of the men, when overcome with fatigue and want of sleep, would slip away into the barracks to catch a nap of sleep, but it seldom happened that they all came out again alive. I was in this place a fortnight and can say in sincerity that I never lay down to sleep a minute in all that time.

---

[21] François Louis Teissèdre de Fleury was a French nobleman who sailed for America in 1777 in hopes of gaining fame and fortune by serving in the Continental army. Unlike many such foreign adventurers, Fleury was a valuable officer. He used his engineering talents to help construct the Delaware defenses, and the Continental Congress later recognized him by having a medal cast in his honor, a rare distinction, for his vital part in the retaking of Stony Point (July 16, 1779). A dispute lingers as to whether he was among the aristocrats who died by the guillotine in Paris during the French Revolution.

The British knew the situation of the place as well as we did. And as their point-blank shot would not reach us behind the wall, they would throw elevated grapeshot from their mortar, and when the sentries had cried, "a shot," and the soldiers, seeing no shot arrive, had become careless, the grapeshot would come down like a shower of hail about our ears.

I will here just mention one thing which will show the apathy of our people at this time. We had, as I mentioned before, a 32-pound cannon in the fort, but had not a single shot for it. The British also had one in their battery upon the Hospital Point, which, as I said before, raked the fort, or rather it was so fixed as to rake the parade in front of the barracks, the only place we could pass up and down the fort. The artillery officers offered a gill of rum for each shot fired from that piece, which the soldiers would procure. I have seen from 20 to 50 men standing on the parade waiting with impatience the coming of the shot, which would often be seized before its motion had fully ceased and conveyed off to our gun to be sent back again to its former owners. When the lucky fellow who had caught it had swallowed his rum, he would return to wait for another, exulting that he had been more lucky or more dexterous than his fellows….

We continued here, suffering cold, hunger, and other miseries till the 14th day of November. On that day at the dawn we discovered 6 ships of the line, all 64s, a frigate of 36 guns, and a galley in a line just below the *chevaux-de-frise*; a 24-gun ship (being an old ship cut down), her guns said to be all brass 24-pounders, and a sloop of 6 guns in company with her, both within pistol shot of the fort on the western side. We immediately opened our batteries upon them, but they appeared to take very little notice of us; we heated some shot, but by mistake 24-pound shot were heated instead of 18, which was the caliber of the guns in that part of the fort. The enemy soon began their firing upon us, and there was music indeed. The soldiers were all ordered to take their posts at the palisades, which they were ordered to defend to the last extremity, as it was expected the British would land under the fire of their cannon and attempt to storm the fort. The cannonade was severe, as well it might be, six 64-gun ships, a 36-gun frigate, a 24-gun ship, a galley, and a sloop of 6 guns, together with 6 batteries of 6 guns each and a bomb battery of 3 mortars, all playing at once upon our poor little fort, if fort it might be called.

Some of our officers endeavored to ascertain how many guns were fired in a minute by the enemy, but it was impossible; the fire was incessant. In the height of the cannonade it was desirable to hoist a signal flag for some of our galleys that were lying above us to come down to our assistance. The officers inquired who would undertake it; as none appeared willing for some time, I was about to offer my services; I considered it no more exposure of my life than it was to remain where I was. The flagstaff was of easy ascent, being an old ship's mast, having shrouds to the ground and the round top still remaining. While I was still hesitating, a sergeant of the artillery offered himself; he accordingly ascended to the round top, pulled down the flag to affix the signal flag to the halyard, upon which the enemy, thinking we had struck, ceased firing in every direction and cheered. "Up with the flag!" was the cry of our officers in every part of the fort. The flags were accordingly hoisted, and the firing was immediately renewed.

The sergeant then came down and had not gone half a rod from the foot of the staff when he was cut in two by a cannon shot. This caused me some serious reflections at the time. He was killed! Had I been at the same business I might have been killed, but it might have been otherwise ordered by Divine Providence; we might have both lived. I am not predestinarian enough to determine it. The enemy's shot cut us up; I saw five artillerists belonging to one gun cut down by a single shot, and I saw men who were stooping to be protected by the works, but not stooping low enough, split like fish to be broiled.

About the middle of the day some of our galleys and floating batteries, with a frigate, fell down and engaged the British with their long guns, which in some measure took off the enemy's fire from the fort. The cannonade continued without interruption on the side of the British throughout the day. Nearly every gun in the fort was silenced by mid-day. Our men were cut up like cornstalks; I do not know the exact number of the killed and wounded but can say it was not small, considering the numbers in the fort, which were only the able part of the Fourth and Eighth Connecticut regiments with a company or two of artillery, perhaps less than 500 in all.

The cannonade continued, directed mostly at the fort, till the dusk of the evening. As soon as it was dark we began to make preparations for evacuating the fort and endeavoring to escape to the Jersey shore. When the firing had in some measure subsided and I could look about me, I found the fort exhibited a picture of desolation; the whole area of the fort was as completely ploughed as a field, the buildings of every kind hanging in broken fragments and the guns all dismounted, and how many of the garrison sent to the world of spirits I knew not.[22] If ever destruction was complete, it was here. The surviving part of the garrison were now drawn off and such of the stores as could conveniently be taken away were carried to the Jersey shore.

I happened to be left with a party of 70 or 80 men to destroy and burn all that was left in the place. I was in the northwest battery just after dark when the enemy were hauling their shipping on that side higher up to a more commanding position. They were so nigh that I could hear distinctly what they said on board the sloop. One expression of theirs I well remember—"We will give it to the d——d rebels in the morning." The thought that then occupied my mind I as well remember, 'The d——d rebels will show you a trick which the devil never will; they will go off and leave you.' After the troops had left the fort and were embarking at the wharf, I went to the waterside to find one of my messmates to whom I had lent my canteen in the morning, as there were three or four hogsheads of rum in the fort, the heads of which we were about to knock in, and I was desirous to save a trifle of their contents; there being nothing to eat, I thought I might have something to drink. I found him, indeed, but lying in a long line of dead men who had been brought out of the fort to be conveyed to the main, to have the last honors conferred upon them which it was in our power to give. Poor young man! He was the most intimate associate I had in the army, but he was gone with many more as deserving of regard as himself.

I returned directly back into the fort to my party and proceeded to set fire to everything that would burn, and then repaired immediately to the wharf where three bateaux were waiting to convey us across the river. And now came on another trial. Before we could embark the buildings in the fort were completely in flames, and they threw such a light upon the water that we were as plainly seen by the British as though it had been broad day. Almost their whole fire was directed at us; sometimes our boat seemed to be almost thrown out of the water, and at length a shot took the sternpost out of the rear boat. We had then to stop and take the men from the

---

[22] Modern estimates indicate that the patriots suffered 60 casualties (20 killed and 40 wounded) during the final defense of Fort Mifflin. Martin's comments suggest a higher casualty rate. The rebel defenders finally abandoned Fort Mifflin late at night on November 15–16. Five evenings later they vacated Fort Mercer, thereby conceding control of the Delaware River to the British.

crippled boat into the other two; and now the shot and water flew merrily, but by the assistance of a kind Providence we escaped without any further injury and landed a little after midnight on the Jersey shore.

We marched a little back into some pitch-pine woods, where we found the rest of the troops that had arrived before us. They had made up some comfortable fires and were enjoying the warmth, and that was all the comfort they had to partake of (except rest), for victuals was out of the question. I wrapped myself up in my blanket and lay down upon the leaves and soon fell asleep, and continued so till past noon, when I awoke from the first sound sleep I had had for a fortnight. Indeed, I had not laid down in all that time. The little sleep I had obtained was in cat naps, sitting up and leaning against the wall; and I thought myself fortunate if I could do that much. When I awoke I was as crazy as a goose shot through the head.

We left our flag flying when we left the island, and the enemy did not take possession of the fort till late in the morning after we left it. We left one man in the fort who had taken too large a dose of "the good creature." He was a deserter from the German forces in the British service. The British took him to Philadelphia, where (not being known by them) he engaged again in their service—received two or three guineas bounty, drew a British uniform, and came back to us again at the Valley Forge. So they did not make themselves independent fortunes by the capture of him.

Here ends the account of as hard and fatiguing a job, for the time it lasted, as occurred during the Revolutionary War. Thomas Paine, in one of his political essays, speaking of the siege and defense of this post, says, "They had nothing but their bravery and good conduct to cover them." He spoke the truth. I was at the siege and capture of Lord Cornwallis, and the hardships of that were no more to be compared with this than the sting of a bee is to the bite of a rattlesnake. But there has been but little notice taken of it; the reason of which is there was no Washington, Putnam, or Wayne there. Had there been, the affair would have been extolled to the skies. No, it was only a few officers and soldiers who accomplished it in a remote quarter of the army. Such circumstances and such troops generally get but little notice taken of them, do what they will. Great men get great praise, little men nothing. But it always was so and always will be. Said the officers in King David's army, when going out against rebel Absalom, "Thou shalt not go out with us, for if half of us die they will not care for us. But now thou art worth 10,000 of us." And this has been the burden of the song ever since, and I presume ever will be.[23]

We now prepared to leave Red Bank. I was ordered on a baggage guard; it was not disagreeable to me as I had a chance to ride in a wagon a considerable part of the night. We went in advance of the troops, which made it much easier getting along. We had been encouraged during the whole siege with the promise of relief. "Stand it out a little longer and we shall be relieved," had been the constant cry. The second day of our march we met two regiments advancing to relieve us. When asked where they were going, they said to relieve the garrison in the fort. We informed them that the British had done that already.

Our guard passed through Haddington [Haddonfield] in the night; heard nothing of the goose or murdered cat. We arrived early in the morning at a pretty village called Milltown or Mount Holly. Here we waited for the troops to come up. I was as near starved with hunger as ever I wish to be. I strolled into a large yard where was several sawmills and a gristmill. I went into the latter, thinking it probable that the dust made there was more palatable than that made in the former, but I found nothing there to satisfy my hunger. But there was a barrel standing behind the door with some salt in it. Salt was as valuable as gold with the soldiers. I filled my pocket with it and went out. In the yard and about it was a plenty of geese, turkeys, ducks, and barn-door fowls; I obtained a piece of an ear of Indian corn, and seating myself on a pile of boards, began throwing the corn to the fowls, which soon drew a fine battalion of them about me. I might have taken as many as I pleased, but I took up one only, wrung off its head, dressed and washed it in the stream, seasoned it with some of my salt, and stalked into the first house that fell in my way, invited myself into the kitchen, took down the gridiron, and put my fowl to cooking upon the coals. The women of the house were all the time going and coming to and from the room; they looked at me but said nothing—"They asked me no questions, and I told them no lies." When my game was sufficiently

[23] II Samuel 19:1–6. As King David grieved for his fallen rebel son Absalom, his field commander Joab upbraided him for not mourning the loss of those valiant soldiers who had died for the sake of preserving David's kingdom. Thus Martin was asking why the deeds of ordinary persons always seem to have less meaning than those of reputedly great persons, even in the case of a willful rebel son who would have destroyed his father's kingdom.

broiled, I took it by the *hind* leg and made my exit from the house with as little ceremony as I had made my entrance. When I got into the street, I devoured it after a *very* short grace and felt as refreshed as the old Indian did when he had eaten his crow roasted in the ashes with the feathers and entrails.

We marched from hence and crossed the Delaware again between Burlington and Bristol.... We marched a little distance and stopped "to refresh ourselves." We kindled some fires in the road, and some broiled their meat; as for myself, I ate mine raw. We quickly started on and marched till evening, when we went into a wood for the night. We did not pitch our tents; and about midnight it began to rain very hard, which soon put out all our fires, and we had to lie "and weather it out."

The troops marched again before day; I had sadly sprained my ankle the day before, and it was much swelled. My lieutenant told me to stay where I was till day and then come on. Just as I was about to start off, our brigadier general[24] and suite passed by and seeing me there alone, stopped his horse and asked me what I did there. I told him that Lieutenant S— ordered me to remain there till daylight. Says he, "Lieutenant S— deserves to have his throat cut," and then went on....

I hobbled on as well as I could; the rain and traveling of the troops and baggage had converted the road into perfect mortar, and it was extremely difficult for me to make headway. I worried [wearied] on, however, till sometime in the afternoon when I went into a house where I procured a piece of a buckwheat slapjack. With this little refreshment I proceeded on and just before night overtook the troops. We continued our march until sometime after dark, when we arrived in the vicinity of the main army. We again turned into a wood for the night; the leaves and ground were as wet as water could make them; it was then foggy and the water dropping from the trees like a shower. We endeavored to get fire by flashing powder on the leaves, but this and every other expedient that we could employ failing, we were forced by our old master, Necessity, to lay

---

[24] James M. Varnum was a lawyer-turned-soldier from Rhode Island. The Continental Congress named him a brigadier general in February 1777. In November 1777 he was in overall command of forts Mifflin and Mercer, but he did not directly participate in the defense of either fort. More politician than general, Varnum resigned his Continental military commission in 1779 and later served as a delegate to the Continental Congress from Rhode Island.

down and sleep if we could, with three others of our constant companions, Fatigue, Hunger, and Cold.

Next morning we joined the grand army near Philadelphia, and the heavy baggage being sent back to the rear of the army, we were obliged to put us up huts by laying up poles and covering them with leaves, a capital shelter from winter storms. Here we continued to fast; indeed we kept a continual Lent as faithfully as ever any of the most rigorous of the Roman Catholics did. But there was this exception; we had no fish or eggs or any other substitute for our commons. Ours was a real fast and, depend upon it, we were sufficiently mortified.

About this time the whole British army left the city, came out, and encamped, or rather lay, on Chestnut Hill in our immediate neighborhood. We hourly expected an attack from them; we had a commanding position and were very sensible of it. We were kept constantly on the alert, and wished nothing more than to have them engage us, for we were sure of giving them a drubbing, being in excellent fighting trim, as we were starved and as cross and ill-natured as curs. The British, however, thought better of the matter, and, after several days maneuvering on the hill, very civilly walked off into Philadelphia again.

Starvation seemed to be entailed upon the army and every animal connected with it. The oxen, brought from New England for draught, all died, and the southern horses fared no better; even the wild animals that had any concern with us suffered. A poor little squirrel, who had the ill luck to get cut off from the woods and fixing himself on a tree standing alone and surrounded by several of the soldier's huts, sat upon the tree till he starved to death and fell off the tree. He, however, got rid of his misery soon. He did not live to starve by piecemeal six or seven years....

Soon after the British had quit their position on Chestnut Hill, we left this place, and after marching and countermarching back and forward some days, we crossed the Schuylkill on a cold, rainy, and snowy night upon a bridge of wagons set end to end and joined together by boards and planks. And after a few days more maneuvering we at last settled down at a place called "the Gulf"[25] (so named on account of a remarkable chasm in the hills); and here we encamped some time, and here we had liked to have encamped forever—for starvation here *rioted* in its glory....

[25]   On Gulf Creek about three miles west of the Schuylkill River and about five miles east of Valley Forge, today the site of West Conshohocken, Pennsylvania.

While we lay here, there was a Continental thanksgiving ordered by Congress; and as the army had all the cause in the world to be particularly thankful, if not for being well off, at least that it was no worse, we were ordered to participate in it. We had nothing to eat for two or three days previous, except what the trees of the fields and forests afforded us. But we must now have what Congress said—a sumptuous thanksgiving to close the year of high living we had now nearly seen brought to a close. Well, to add something extraordinary to our present stock of provisions, our country, ever mindful of its suffering army, opened her sympathizing heart so wide upon this occasion as to give us something to make the world stare. And what do you think it was, reader? Guess. You cannot guess, be you as much of a Yankee as you will. I will tell you: It gave each and every man *half* a *gill* of rice and a *tablespoonful* of vinegar!!

After we had made sure of this extraordinary superabundant donation, we were ordered out to attend a meeting and hear a sermon delivered upon the happy occasion. We accordingly went, for we could not help it.... I remember the text, like an attentive lad at church. I can *still* remember that it was this, "And the soldiers said unto him, And what shall we do? And he said unto them, Do violence to no man, nor accuse anyone falsely." The preacher ought to have added the remainder of the sentence to have made it complete: "And be content with your wages."[26] But that would not do, it would be too apropos; however, he heard it as soon as the service was over, it was shouted from a hundred tongues....

The army was now not only starved but naked. The greatest part were not only shirtless and barefoot but destitute of all other clothing, especially blankets. I procured a small piece of raw cowhide and made myself a pair of moccasins, which kept my feet (while they lasted) from the frozen ground, although as I well remember the hard edges so galled my ankles while on a march that it was with much difficulty and pain that I could wear them afterwards; but the only alternative I had was to endure this inconvenience or to go barefoot, as hundreds of my companions had to, till they might be tracked by their blood upon the rough frozen ground. But hunger, nakedness, and sore shins were not the only difficulties we had at that time to encounter; we had hard duty to perform and little or no strength to perform it with.

---

[26] Luke 3:14. The person responding to the soldiers' query was John the Baptist.

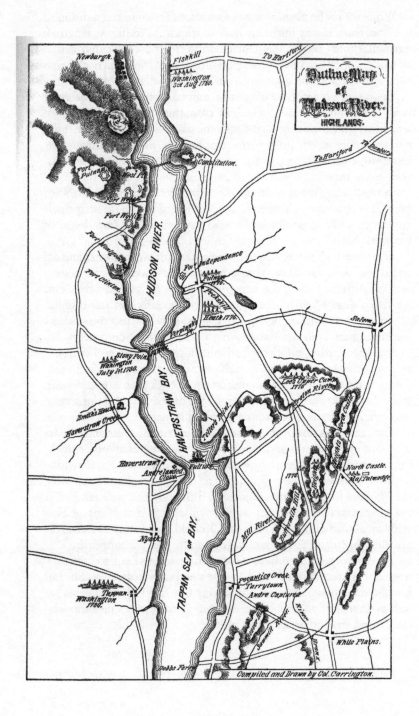

not direct me to the place as it was very dark. I tried to beg a draught of water from them, but they were as rigid as Arabs. At length I persuaded them to sell me a drink for three pence, Pennsylvania currency, which was every cent of property I could then call my own, so great was the necessity I was then reduced to.

I lay here two nights and one day and had not a morsel of anything to eat all the time, save half of a small pumpkin, which I cooked by placing it upon a rock, the skin side uppermost, and making a fire upon it. By the time it was heat[ed] through I devoured it with as keen an appetite as I should a pie made of it at some other time.

The second evening after our arrival here I was warned to be ready for a two days command. I never heard a summons to duty with so much disgust before or since as I did that; how I could endure two days more fatigue without nourishment of some sort I could not tell.... However, in the morning ... I went to the parade where I found a considerable number ordered upon the same business, whatever it was. We were ordered to go to the quartermaster general and receive from him our final orders. We accordingly repaired to his quarters, which was about three miles from camp; here we understood that our destiny was to go into the country on a foraging expedition, which was nothing more nor less than to procure provisions from the inhabitants for the men in the army and forage for the poor perishing cattle belonging to it, at the point of the bayonet. We stayed at the quartermaster general's quarters till sometime in the afternoon, during which time a beef creature was butchered for us. I well remember what fine stuff it was; it was quite transparent. I thought at that time what an excellent lantern it would make. I was, notwithstanding, very glad to get some of it, bad as it looked. We got, I think, two days allowance of it and some sort of bread kind, I suppose....

We were then divided into several parties and sent off upon our expedition. Our party consisted of a lieutenant, a sergeant, a corporal, and 18 privates. We marched till night when we halted, and ... this day we arrived at Milltown, or Downingstown, a small village halfway between Philadelphia and Lancaster, which was to be our quarters for the winter. It was dark when we had finished our day's march. There was a commissary and a wagonmaster general stationed here, the commissary to take into custody the provisions and forage that we collected, and the wagonmaster general to regulate the conduct of the wagoners and direct their motions. The next day after our arrival at this place we were put into a small house in which was only one room, in the center of the village. We were immediately furnished with rations of good and wholesome beef and flour, built us up some berths to sleep in, and filled them with straw, and felt as happy as any other pigs that were no better off than ourselves. And now having got into winter quarters and ready to commence our foraging business, I shall here end my account of my second campaign.

Chapter IV

Campaign of 1778

JPM forages for food and supplies to help sustain his suffering comrades enduring the Valley Forge winter. Participates in combat against retreating British forces at the Battle of Monmouth and performs light infantry duty north of the main British base in New York City.

> A serene and cloudless atmosphere
> Betokens that a storm is near;
> So when Dame Fortune proves most kind,—
> Be sure, Miss-Fortune's close behind.

As there was no cessation of duty in the army, I must commence another campaign as soon as the succeeding one is ended. There was no going home and spending the winter season among friends and procuring a new recruit [rest] of strength and spirits. No—it was one constant drill, summer and winter; like an old horse in a mill, it was a continual routine.[1]

The first expedition I undertook in my new vocation was a foraging cruise. I was ordered off into the country in a party consisting

---

[1] On the other hand, Martin was on detached service during the Valley Forge winter. He lived and ate heartily and well, unlike his suffering comrades in the Continental army campsite. More than one-fourth of the roughly 11,000 patriot soldiers who entered Valley Forge did not survive the winter. The numbers of deaths would have been greater, had not Continentals like Martin kept scouring the countryside on foraging duty with orders to commandeer everything from blankets and clothing to soap and medicines.

of a corporal and six men. What our success was I do not now
remember; but I well remember the transactions of the party in the
latter part of the journey. We were returning to our quarters on
Christmas afternoon, when we met three ladies, one a young married woman with an infant in her arms; the other two were maid-
ens, for aught I knew then or since, they passed for such. They were
all comely, particularly one of them; she was handsome. They
immediately fell into familiar discourse with us, were very inquisi-
tive like the rest of the sex, asked us a thousand questions respecting our business, where we had been and where going, &c. After we
had satisfied their curiosity, or at least had endeavored to do so,
they told us that they (that is, the two youngest) lived a little way
on our road in a house which they described, desired us to call in
and rest ourselves a few minutes, and said they would return as
soon as they had seen their sister and babe safe home.

As for myself, I was very unwell, occasioned by a violent cold I
had recently taken, and I was very glad to stop a short time to rest
my bones. Accordingly, we stopped at the house described by the
young ladies, and in a few minutes they returned as full of chat as
they were when we met them in the road. After a little more information respecting our business, they proposed to us to visit one of
their neighbors, against whom it seemed they had a grudge, and
upon whom they wished to wreak their vengeance through our
agency. To oblige the ladies we undertook to obey their injunctions.
They very readily agreed to be our guides as the way lay across
fields and pastures full of bushes. The distance was about half a
mile and directly out of our way to our quarters. The girls went
with us until we came in sight of the house. We concluded we could
do no less than fulfill our engagements with them; so we went into
the house, the people of which appeared to be genuine Pennsylvania
farmers and very fine folks.

We all now began to relent, and after telling them our business,
we concluded that if they would give us a canteen (which held about
a quart) full of whiskey and some bread and cheese, we would
depart without any further exactions. To get rid of us, doubtless,
the man of the house gave us our canteen of whiskey, and the good
woman gave us a fine loaf of wheaten flour bread and the whole of
a small cheese, and we raised the siege and departed. I was several
times afterwards at this house and was always well treated. I believe
the people did not recollect me, and I was glad they did not, for
when I saw them I had always a twinge or two of conscience for thus
dissembling with them at the instigation of persons who certainly

were no better than they should be, or they would not have employed strangers to glut their vengeance upon innocent people, innocent at least as it respected us. But after all, it turned much in their favor. It was in our power to take cattle or horses, hay, or any other produce from them; but we felt that we had done wrong in listening to the tattle of malicious neighbors, and for that cause we refrained from meddling with any property of theirs ever after. So that good came to them out of intended evil....

We had now five miles to travel to reach our quarters, and I was sick indeed, but we got to our home sometime in the evening, and I soon went to sleep; in the morning I was better.

When I was inoculated with the smallpox I took that delectable disease, the itch; it was given us, we supposed, in the infection. We had no opportunity, or, at least we had nothing to cure ourselves with during the whole season; all who had the smallpox at Peekskill had it.[2] We often applied to our officers for assistance to clear ourselves from it, but all we could get was, "Bear it as patiently as you can, when we get into winter quarters you will have leisure and means to rid yourselves of it." I had it to such a degree that by the time I got into winter quarters I could scarcely lift my hands to my head. Some of our foraging party had acquaintances in the artillery, and by their means we procured sulphur enough to cure all that belonged to our detachment.

Accordingly, we made preparations for a general attack upon it. The first night one half of the party commenced the action by mixing a sufficient quantity of brimstone and tallow, which was the only grease we could get, at the same time not forgetting to mix a plenty of hot whiskey toddy, making up a hot blazing fire and laying down an oxhide upon the hearth. Thus prepared with arms and ammunition, we began the operation by plying each other's outsides with brimstone and tallow and the inside with hot whiskey sling. Had the animalcule of the itch been endowed with reason they would have quit their entrenchments and taken care of themselves when we had made such a formidable attack upon them; but

---

[2] The "itch" had little to do with smallpox, rather with infestations of lice, a common malady for soldiers because they rarely washed or bathed themselves or had freshly laundered clothing. Lice represent a variety of small, parasitic insects that can infest human hair and skin, biting and sucking blood from their host. Lice serve as bearers of the rickettsia of typhus, a potential killer disease characterized by unusually high fevers and red spots on the skin. Typhus claimed the lives of many Valley Forge soldiers.

as it was we had to engage arms in hand, and we obtained a complete victory, though it had like to have cost some of us our lives. Two of the assailants were so overcome, not by the enemy but by their too great exertions in the action, that they lay all night naked upon the field; the rest of us got to our berths somehow, as well as we could; but we killed the itch, and we were satisfied, for it had almost killed us. This was a decisive victory, the only one we had achieved lately. The next night the other half of our men took their turn, but taking warning by our mishaps they conducted their part of the battle with comparatively little trouble or danger to what we had experienced on our part.

I shall not relate all the minute transactions which passed while I was on this foraging party, as it would swell my narrative to too large a size. I will, however, give the reader a brief account of some of my movements.... We fared much better than I had ever done in the army before, or ever did afterwards. We had very good provisions all winter and generally enough of them. Some of us were constantly in the country with the wagons; we went out by turns and had no one to control us.... When we were in the country we were pretty sure to fare well, for the inhabitants were remarkably kind to us. We had no guards to keep; our only duty was to help load the wagons with hay, corn, meal, or whatever they were to take off, and when they were thus loaded, to keep them company till they arrived at the commissary's at Milltown; from thence the articles, whatever they were, were carried to camp in other vehicles under other guards.

I do not remember that during the time I was employed in this business, which was from Christmas to the latter part of April, ever to have met with the least resistance from the inhabitants, take what we would from their barns, mills, corncribs, or stalls; but when we came to their stables, then look out for the women. Take what horse you would, it was one or the other's "pony," and they had no other to ride to church; and when we had got possession of a horse we were sure to have half a dozen or more women pressing upon us, until by some means or other, if possible, they would slip the bridle from the horse's head, and then we might catch him again if we could. They would take no more notice of a charged bayonet than a blind horse would of a cocked pistol. It would answer no purpose to threaten to kill them with the bayonet or musket; they knew as well as we did that we would not put our threats in execution, and when they had thus liberated a horse (which happened but seldom) they would laugh at us and ask us why we did not do as we threatened, kill them, and then they would generally ask us into their houses and treat us with as much kindness as though nothing had happened.

The women of Pennsylvania, taken in general, are certainly very worthy characters. It is but justice, as far as I am concerned, for me to say that I was always well treated both by them and the men, especially the Friends or Quakers, in every part of the state through which I passed, and that was the greater part of what was then inhabited. But the southern ladies had a queer idea of the Yankees (as they always called the New Englanders); they seemed to think that they were a people quite different from themselves, as indeed they were in many respects; I could mention things and ways in which they differed, but it is of no consequence; they were clever and that is sufficient. I will, however, mention one little incident just to show what their conceptions were of us.

I happened once to be with some wagons, one of which was detached from the party. I went with this team as its guard; we stopped at a house, the mistress of which and the wagoner were acquainted. (These foraging teams all belonged in the neighborhood of our quarters.) She had a pretty female child about four years old. The teamster was praising the child, extolling its gentleness and quietness, when the mother observed that it had been quite cross and crying all day. "I have been threatening," said she, "to give her to the Yankees." "Take care," said the wagoner, "how you speak of the Yankees, I have one of them here with me." "La!" said the woman. "Is he a Yankee? I thought he was a Pennsylvanian; I don't see any difference between him and other people."

I have before said that I should not narrate all the little affairs which transpired while I was on this foraging party. But if I pass them all over in silence the reader may perhaps think that I had nothing to do all winter, or at least, that I *did* nothing, when in truth it was quite the reverse. Our duty was hard, but generally not altogether unpleasant; I had to travel far and near, in cold and in storms, by day and by night, and at all times to run the *risk* of abuse, if not of injury, from the inhabitants when *plundering* them of their property (for I could not, while in the very act of taking their cattle, hay, corn, and grain from them against their wills, consider it a whit better than plundering—sheer privateering). But I will give them the credit of never receiving the least abuse or injury from an individual during the whole time I was employed in this business. I doubt whether the people of New England would have borne it as patiently, their "steady habits" to the contrary notwithstanding.

Being once in a party among the Welch mountains,[3] there came on a tedious rainstorm which continued three or four days. I happened to be at a farmer's house with one or two of the wagon masters. The man of the house was from home and the old lady rather crabbed; she knew our business and was therefore inclined to be *rather* unsociable. The first day she would not give us anything to eat but some scraps of cold victuals, the second day she grew a little more condescending, and on the third day she boiled a potful of good beef, pork, and sauerkraut for us. "Never mind," said one of the wagon masters to me, "mother comes on, she will give us roasted turkeys directly." ...

While the storm continued, to pass our time several of our party went to a tavern in the neighborhood. We here gambled a little for some liquor by throwing a small dart or stick, armed at one end with a pin, at a mark on the ceiling of the room; while I was at this amusement I found that the landlord and I bore the same name, and upon further discourse I found that he had a son about my age, whose given name was the same as mine. This son was taken prisoner at Fort Lee on the Hudson River in the year 1776, and died on his way home. These good people were almost willing to persuade themselves that I was their son. There were two very pretty girls, sisters to the deceased young man, who seemed wonderfully taken up with me, called me "brother," and I fared none the worse for my name. I used often, afterwards, in my cruises to that part of the state to call in as I passed, and was always well treated by the whole family. The landlord used to fill my canteen with whiskey, or peach or cider brandy to enable me, as he said, to climb the Welch mountains. I always went there with pleasure and left with regret. I often wished afterwards that I could find more namesakes.

I was sent one day with another man of our party to drive some cattle to the quartermaster general's quarters. It was dark when we arrived there. After we had delivered the cattle, an officer belonging to the quartermaster general's department asked me if I had a canteen. I answered in the negative (I had left mine at my quarters). "A soldier," said he, "should always have a canteen," and I was sorry that I was just then deficient of that article, for he gave us a half-pint tumblerful of genuine old Jamaica spirits, which was ... "as smooth as oil." It was too late to return to our quarters that night, so we concluded to go to camp about three miles distant and see

---

[3] Located in Lancaster and Chester counties, Pennsylvania.

our old messmates. Our stomachs being empty, the spirits began to take hold of both belly and brains. I soon became very faint, but as good luck would have it my companion happened to have a part of a dried neat's[4] tongue, which he had plundered somewhere in his travels. We fell to work upon that and soon demolished it, which refreshed us much and enabled us to reach camp without suffering shipwreck. There was nothing to be had at camp but a little rest and that was all we asked.

In the morning it was necessary to have a pass from the commander of the regiment to enable us to pass the guards on our return to our quarters in the country. My captain gave me one, and then it must be countersigned by the colonel. When I entered the colonel's hut, "Where have you been" (calling me by name) "this winter?" said he. "Why, you are as fat as a pig." I told him I had been foraging in the country. "I think," said he, "you have taken care of yourself; I believe we must keep you here and send another man in your stead, that he may recruit [rest] himself a little." I told him that I was sent to camp on *particular* business and with strict orders to return, and that no one else could do so well. Finally he signed my pass, and I soon hunted up the other man when we left the camp in as great a hurry as though the plague had been there.

But the time at length came when we were obliged to go to camp for good and all, whether we chose it or not. An order from headquarters required all stationed parties and guards to be relieved, that all who had not had the smallpox might have an opportunity to have it before the warm weather came on. Accordingly, about the last of April we were relieved by a party of southern troops. The commissary,[5] who was a native of Connecticut, although at the commencement of the war he resided in Philadelphia, told us that he was sorry we were going away, for said he, "I do not much like these men with one eye (alluding to their practice of gouging).[6] I am acquainted with you, and if any men are wanted here I should prefer those from my own section of the country to entire strangers."

---

[4] An animal of the bovine family, most likely then an ox's tongue.

[5] Jeremiah Wadsworth, a wealthy merchant from Connecticut who served as the army's commissary general from April 1778 until December 1779. His tireless labors kept Washington's Continentals fairly well-supplied with food. In the months preceding his appointment, the supply system for the army had collapsed, representing a major reason for so much privation at Valley Forge.

[6] Referring to the practice, apparently more common among southerners, of gouging out opponents' eyes when engaging in fisticuffs.

Although we would have very willingly obliged him with our company, yet it could not be so, we must go to camp at all events. We accordingly marched off and arrived at camp the next day, much to the *seeming* satisfaction of our old messmates, and as much to the real dissatisfaction of ourselves; at least it was so with me.

Thus far, since the year commenced, "Dame Fortune had been kind," but now "Miss-Fortune" was coming in for *her* set in the reel.... During the past winter I had had enough to eat and been under no restraint; I had picked up a few articles of comfortable summer clothing among the inhabitants; our lieutenant had never concerned himself about us; we had scarcely seen him during the whole time. When we were off duty we went when and where we pleased "and had none to make us afraid"; but now the scene was changed. We must go and come at bidding and suffer hunger besides.

After I had joined my regiment I was kept constantly, when off other duty, engaged in learning the Baron de Steuben's new Prussian exercise; it was a continual drill.[7]

About this time I was sent off from camp in a detachment consisting of about 3,000 men, with 4 fieldpieces, under the command of the young General Lafayette.[8] We marched to Barren Hill, about 12 miles from Philadelphia; there are crossroads upon this hill, a branch of which leads to the city. We halted here, placed our guards,

[7] Friedrich Wilhelm Augustus, Baron von Steuben, was a pretended Prussian noblemen. He arrived in America late in 1777 and offered his services as an unpaid volunteer who could train the army's troops. Washington gladly welcomed him to Valley Forge, and Steuben soon had the Continentals training according to a uniform set of regulations, a modified version of the highly successful Prussian system. His vigorous yet humorous manner eased the soldiers' despair, even as they mastered standardized methods for drilling, marching, and firing their weapons. The "Baron's" efforts quickly transformed the army into a more effective fighting force. In early May 1778 the Continental Congress, on Washington's recommendation, acknowledged Steuben's contributions by naming him the army's Inspector General with a major general's rank and pay.

[8] Marie Joseph Paul Yves Roch Gilbert du Motier, the Marquis de Lafayette, was a romantic young French aristocrat not yet 20 years old when he came to America in 1777 and volunteered his services. Out of courtesy the Continental Congress awarded him a major general's commission without pay or command (July 31, 1777). Because of his bravery at the Battle of Brandywine, Lafayette gained the lasting respect of Washington, who treated him like a son. On May 18, Washington selected Lafayette, who was pressing him for a command assignment, to lead a force of 2,200 Continental and militia troops, among them Martin, toward Philadelphia to reconnoiter British troop dispositions and movements.

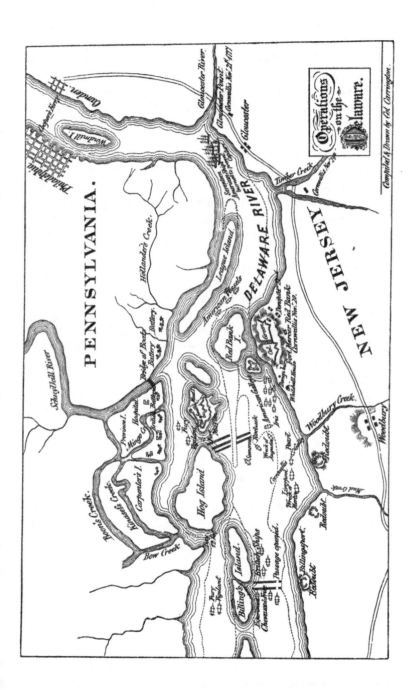

Operations on the Delaware.

Compiled & Drawn by Col. Carrington.

PENNSYLVANIA.

NEW JERSEY.

DELAWARE RIVER.

Schuylkill River.

Philadelphia.

Camden.

Morgan's Bay.

Windmill I.

Gloucester River.

Carpenter Point.
Cornwallis Nov. 24. 1777.

Gloucester.

Timber Creek.
Cornwallis Nov. 20.

Hollander's Creek.

League Island.

American Vessels.

Red Bank I.

Thompson.
Red Bank.
Cornwallis Nov. 20.

Woodbury Creek.

Woodbury.

Redoubt.

Mud Creek.

Redoubt.

Hog Island.

Bow Creek.

Boon's Creek.

Kinnack's Creek.

Carpenter's I.

Mingo.

Province I.

Billing's Island.

Fort Mifflin.

Port Royal.

Billingsport.
Redoubt.

more of them that time, for before we had reached the river the alarm guns were fired in our camp and the whole army was immediately in motion. The British, fearing that they should be outnumbered in their turn, directly set their faces for Philadelphia and set off in as much or more haste than we had left Barren Hill. They had during the night left the city with such silence and secrecy, and by taking what was called the New York road, that they escaped detection by all our parties, and the first knowledge they obtained of the enemy's movements was that he was upon their backs, between them and us on the hill. The Indians, with all their alertness, had like to have "bought the rabbit"; they kept coming in all the afternoon in parties of four or five, whooping and hallooing like wild beasts. After they had got collected they vanished; I never saw any more of them. Our scouting parties all came in safe, but I was afterwards informed by a British deserter that several of the enemy perished by the heat and their exertions to get away from a retreating enemy.

The place that our detachment was now at was the Gulf, mentioned in the preceding chapter, where we kept the rice and vinegar thanksgiving of starving memory. We stayed here till nearly night, when no one coming to visit us we marched off and took up our lodgings for the night in a wood. The next day we crossed the Schuylkill again and went on to Barren Hill once more; we stayed there a day or two and then returned to camp with keen appetites and empty purses. If anyone asks why we did not stay on Barren Hill till the British came up, and have taken and given a few bloody noses?—all I have to say in answer is that the general well knew what he was about; he was not deficient in either courage or conduct, and that was well known to all the Revolutionary army.

Soon after this affair we left our winter cantonments, crossed the Schuylkill, and encamped on the left bank of that river, just opposite to our winter quarters. We had lain here but a few days when we heard that the British army had left Philadelphia and were proceeding to New York through the Jerseys. We marched immediately in pursuit; we crossed the Delaware at Carroll's [Coryell's] Ferry above Trenton,[11] and encamped a day or two between that town and Princeton. Here I was again detached with a party of 1,000 men,

---

[11] Running between New Hope, Pennsylvania, and Lambertville, New Jersey, about 15 miles north of Trenton.

as light troops, to get into the enemy's route and follow him close to favor desertion and pick up stragglers.[12]

... Our detachment marched in the afternoon and toward night we passed through Princeton; some of the patriotic inhabitants of the town had brought out to the end of the street we passed through some casks of ready-made toddy. It was dealt out to the men as they passed by, which caused the detachment to move slowly at this place. The young ladies of the town, and perhaps of the vicinity, had collected and were sitting in the stoops and at the windows to see the noble exhibition of a thousand half-starved and three-quarters naked soldiers pass in review before them. I chanced to be on the wing of a platoon next to the houses, as they were chiefly on one side of the street, and had a good chance to notice the ladies, and I declare that I never before nor since saw more beauty, considering the numbers, than I saw at that time; they were *all* beautiful ....

We passed through Princeton and encamped on the open fields for the night, the canopy of heaven for our tent. Early next morning we marched again and came up with the rear of the British army. We followed them several days, arriving upon their camping ground within an hour after their departure from it. We had ample opportunity to see the devastation they made in their route; cattle killed and lying about the fields and pastures, some just in the position they were in when shot down, others with a small spot of skin taken off their hind quarters and a mess of steak taken out; household furniture hacked and broken to pieces; wells filled up and mechanics'

---

[12]   In the spring of 1778 the king's ministers had to consider the possible global implications of France's decision to enter the war on behalf of the Americans. They justifiably fretted about French land and naval forces trying to conquer highly valued British sugar islands in the West Indies or perhaps even England itself.

Meanwhile, General Howe, comfortably ensconced in Philadelphia during the winter of 1777–78, had asked to be relieved of his command. In May 1778, General Henry Clinton superseded Howe, and he did so with secret orders to reconcentrate British forces in the vicinity of New York City. These massed troops would then be available, if the need arose, for rapid dispersal to more threatened British holdings in other parts of the globe.

On June 18, Clinton completed the evacuation of Philadelphia and commenced his retreat across New Jersey with 10,000 troops. Washington followed, moving his army eastward from Coryell's Ferry at an angle that would permit his force to intercept Clinton's. He also sent out advance columns, such as the one Martin joined, to annoy the enemy's flanks, even as his general officers hotly debated whether to bring on a general engagement.

and farmers' tools destroyed. It was in the height of the season of cherries; the innocent industrious creatures could not climb the trees for the fruit, but universally cut them down. Such conduct did not give the Americans any more agreeable feelings toward them than they entertained before.

It was extremely hot weather, and the sandy plains of that part of New Jersey did not cool the air to any great degree, but we still kept close to the rear of the British army; deserters were almost hourly coming over to us, but of stragglers we took only a few.... We this night turned into a new ploughed field, and I laid down between two furrows and slept as sweet as though I had laid upon a bed of down.

The next morning, as soon as the enemy began their march, we were again in motion and came to their last night's encamping ground just after sunrise. Here we halted an hour or two, as we often had to do, to give the enemy time to advance, our orders being not to attack them unless in self-defense. We were marching on as usual, when about 10 or 11 o'clock we were ordered to halt and then to face to the right about. As this order was given by the officers in rather a different way than usual, we began to think something was out of joint somewhere, but what or where our united wisdom could not explain; the general opinion of the sol- diers was that some part of the enemy had by some means got into our rear. We, however, retraced our steps till we came to our last night's encamping ground, when we left the route of the enemy and went off a few miles to a place called Englishtown.[13] It was uncom- monly hot weather, and we put up booths to protect us from the heat of the sun, which was almost insupportable. Whether we lay here one or two nights, I do not remember; it matters not which. We were early in the morning mustered out and ordered to leave all our baggage under the care of a guard (our baggage was trifling), taking only our blankets and provisions (our provisions were less), and prepare for immediate march and action.

The officer who commanded the platoon that I belonged to was a captain, belonging to the Rhode Island troops, and a fine brave

[13] Englishtown is roughly five miles west of Monmouth Court House (modern-day Freehold), where the retreating British army, exhausted by oppressive summer heat, had arrived during the afternoon of June 26 and encamped in a strong defensive position. Washington had ordered the retrograde movement because his advance troops were too far ahead of the main Continental force and thus lay exposed to a possible enemy attack with no prospect of reinforcing support.

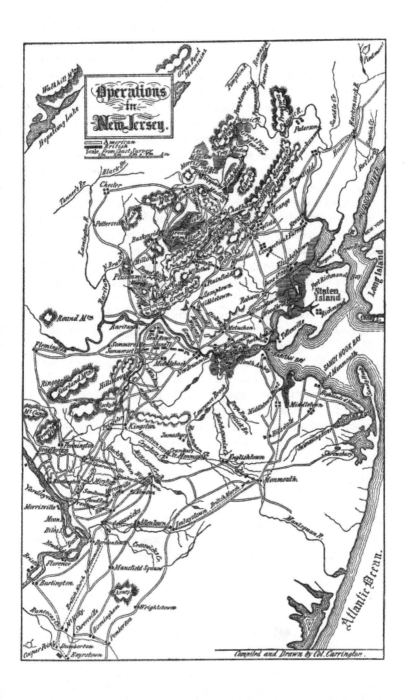

man he was; he feared nobody nor nothing. When we were paraded, "Now," said he to us, "you have been wishing for some days past to come up with the British, you have been wanting to fight. Now you shall have fighting enough before night." The men did not need much haranguing to raise their courage, for when the officers came to order the sick and lame to stay behind as guards, they were forced to exercise their authority to the full extent before they could make even the invalids stay behind, and when some of their arms were about to be exchanged with those who were going into the field, they would not part with them. "If their arms went," they said, "*they* would go with them at all events."[14]

After all things were put in order, we marched but halted a few minutes in the village, where we were joined by a few other troops, and then proceeded on. We now heard a few reports of cannon ahead; we went in a road running through a deep narrow valley, which was for a considerable way covered with thick wood; we were some time in passing this defile. While in the wood we heard a volley or two of musketry, and upon inquiry we found it to be a party of our troops who had fired upon a party of British horse; but there was no fear of horse in the place in which we then were.

It was 10 or 11 o'clock before we got through these woods and came into the open fields. The first cleared land we came to was an Indian cornfield, surrounded on the east, west, and north sides by thick tall trees; the sun shining full upon the field, the soil of which was sandy, the mouth of a heated oven seemed to me to be but a trifle hotter than this ploughed field; it was almost impossible to breathe. We had to fall back again as soon as we could into the woods; by the time we had got under the shade of the trees and had taken breath, of which we had been almost deprived, we received orders to retreat, as all the left wing of the army, (that part being under the command of General Lee) were retreating. Grating as this order was to our feelings, we were obliged to comply.

We had not retreated far before we came to a defile, a muddy, sloughy brook. While the artillery were passing this place, we sat

[14] At this juncture, as the Battle of Monmouth was about to unfold, Martin was under the brigade command of General James M. Varnum, but his actual commander was Colonel John Durkee of the 4th Connecticut regiment, since Varnum was elsewhere. On June 27, Washington had brought the strength of the flanking detachment at Englishtown up to 5,000. He had decided on a major strike against the rear flank of Clinton's retreating army; however, he had also placed General Charles Lee, his second in command who had persistently argued against any form of an engagement, in charge of this force. As Lee advanced toward Monmouth Court House on the morning of the 28th, he did so with no developed plan of battle.

down by the roadside. In a few minutes the Commander in Chief and suite crossed the road just where we were sitting. I heard him ask our officers "by whose order the troops were retreating," and being answered, "by General Lee's," he said something, but as he was moving forward all the time this was passing, he was too far off for me to hear it distinctly; those that were nearer to him said that his words were—"d—n him." Whether he did thus express himself or not I do not know. It was certainly very unlike him, but he seemed at the instant to be in a great passion; his looks if not his words seemed to indicate as much.[15]

After passing us he rode on to the plain field and took an observation of the advancing enemy. He remained there some time upon his old English charger, while the shot from the British artillery were rending up the earth all around him. After he had taken a view of the enemy he returned and ordered the two Connecticut brigades to make a stand at a fence, in order to keep the enemy in check while the artillery and other troops crossed the before-mentioned defile…. When we had secured our retreat, the artillery formed a line of pieces upon a long piece of elevated ground. Our detachment formed directly in front of the artillery as a covering party, so far below on the declivity of the hill that the pieces could play over our heads. And here we waited the approach of the enemy, should he see fit to attack us.

[15] Lee's detachment made contact with the British rear guard, numbering 1,500 to 2,000, around 10 a. m. Clinton, who was a good tactician, sensed that a force much larger than a flanking party was mounting a strike, so he ordered additional troops from his retreating column to wheel about and return for the fight. Under inexplicable circumstances but mostly because of Lee's lack of leadership, the Americans began a confused retreat back toward Englishtown with British units in pursuit. The hour was somewhat past noontime, and the temperature was approaching an unseasonable 100 degrees when Washington rode up trying to stop the retreat. When he found Lee, there was a sharp exchange. Washington ordered Lee to leave the field. Then he reformed the Americans and personally directed an impressive stand that gained the patriots at least a pyrrhic victory that day.

Regarding the enigmatic Charles Lee, he was a former British officer who had resettled in America before the war, accepted a Continental major general's commission in June 1775, and expressed disdain for Washington's command abilities before his own capture by the British in late 1776. Exchanged in April 1778, Lee rejoined the army at Valley Forge, apparently with the idea that American troops would always fail when fighting against massed British regulars. Immediately after Monmouth, Lee demanded a court martial to clear his name. The military panel ruled against him on various charges, especially in failing to execute orders and showing disrespect for his superior officer. His recommended penalty was suspension from the service for a year, which the Continental Congress sustained. Lee in turn wrote an insolent letter to Congress, and the delegates dropped him permanently from the roll of general officers.

By this time the British had come in contact with the New England forces at the fence, when a sharp conflict ensued. These troops maintained their ground, till the whole force of the enemy that could be brought to bear had charged upon them through the fence; and after being overpowered by numbers and the platoon officers had given orders for their several platoons to leave the fence, they had to force them to retreat, so eager were they to be revenged on the invaders of their country and rights.

As soon as the troops had left this ground the British planted their cannon upon the place and began a violent attack upon the artillery and our detachment, but neither could be routed. The cannonade continued for some time without intermission, when the British pieces being mostly disabled, they reluctantly crawled back from the height which they had occupied and hid themselves from our sight.

Before the cannonade had commenced, a part of the right wing of the British army had advanced across a low meadow and brook and occupied an orchard on our left. The weather was almost too hot to live in, and the British troops in the orchard were forced by the heat to shelter themselves from it under the trees. We had a four-pounder on the left of our pieces which kept a constant fire upon the enemy during the whole contest. After the British artillery had fallen back and the cannonade had mostly ceased in this quarter, and our detachment had an opportunity to look about us, Colonel Cilley[16] of the New Hampshire line, who was attached to our detachment, passed along in front of our line, inquiring for General Varnum's men (who were the Connecticut and Rhode Island men belonging to our command). We answered, "Here we are." He did not hear us in his hurry, but passed on: In a few minutes he returned, making the same inquiry. We again answered, "Here we are." "Ah!" said he, "you are the boys I want to assist in driving those rascals from yon orchard."

We were immediately ordered from our old detachment and joined another, the whole composing a corps of about 500 men. We instantly marched toward the enemy's right wing, which was in the orchard, and kept concealed from them as long as possible by keeping behind the bushes. When we could no longer keep ourselves concealed, we marched into the open fields and formed our line. The British immediately formed and began to retreat to the main body of their army.

[16]   Joseph Cilley was commander of the 1st New Hampshire regiment from April 1777 until his retirement in January 1781.

Colonel Cilley, finding that we were not likely to overtake the enemy before they reached the main body of the army on account of fences and other obstructions, ordered three or four platoons from the right of our corps to pursue and attack them, and thus keep them in play till the rest of the detachment could come up.

I was in this party. We pursued without order; as I passed through the orchard I saw a number of the enemy lying under the trees, killed by our fieldpiece, mentioned before. We overtook the enemy just as they were entering upon the meadow, which was rather bushy. When within about five rods of the rear of the retreating foe, I could distinguish everything about them. They were retreating in line, though in some disorder; I singled out a man and took my aim directly between his shoulders (they were divested of their packs). He was a good mark, being a broad-shouldered fellow. What became of him I know not; the fire and smoke hid him from my sight. One thing I know, that is, I took as deliberate aim at him as ever I did at any game in my life. But after all I hope I did not kill him, although I intended to at the time.

By this time our whole party had arrived, and the British had obtained a position that suited them, as I suppose, for they returned our fire in good earnest, and we played the second part of the same tune. They occupied a much higher piece of ground than we did and had a small piece of artillery, which the soldiers called a grasshopper. We had no artillery with us. The first shot they gave us from this piece cut off the thigh bone of a captain, just above the knee, and the whole heel of a private in the rear of him. We gave it to poor Sawney[17] (for they were Scotch troops) so hot that he was forced to fall back and leave the ground they occupied. When our commander saw them retreating and nearly joined with their main body, he shouted, "Come, my boys, reload your pieces, and we will give them a set-off." We did so, and gave them the parting salute, and the firing on both sides ceased. We then laid ourselves down under the fences and bushes to take breath, for we had need of it; I presume everyone has heard of the heat of that day, but none can realize it that did not feel it. Fighting is hot work in cool weather, how much more so in such weather as it was on the 28th of June, 1778.

After the action in our part of the army had ceased, I went to a well a few rods off to get some water. Here I found the wounded captain,

---

[17] A common nickname for a Scotsperson, derived from the word sandy. Certainly not a term of endearment in the situation of combat.

mentioned before, lying on the ground and begging his sergeant, who pretended to have the care of him, to help him off the field or he should bleed to death; the sergeant and a man or two he had with him were taken up in hunting after plunder. It grieved me to see the poor man in such distress, and I asked the sergeant why he did not carry his officer to the surgeons; he said he would directly. "Directly!" said I, "why he will die directly." I then offered to assist them in carrying him to a meetinghouse[18] a short distance off where the rest of the wounded men and the surgeons were. At length he condescended to be persuaded to carry him off. I helped him to the place and tarried a few minutes to see the wounded and two or three limbs amputated, and then returned to my party again, where we remained the rest of the day and the following night, expecting to have another hack at them in the morning, but they gave us the slip.

As soon as our party had ceased firing, it began in the center and then upon the right, but as I was not in that part of the army, I had no "adventure" in it; but the firing was continued in one part or the other of the field the whole afternoon. Our troops remained on the field all night with the Commander in Chief. A regiment of Connecticut forces were sent to lie as near the enemy as possible and to watch their motions, but they disappointed us all. If my readers wish to know how they escaped so slyly without our knowledge, after such precautions being used to prevent it, I must tell them I know nothing about it....[19]

---

[18] Most likely the Old Tennent church, standing between Englishtown and Freehold.

[19] The Battle of Monmouth added little to the luster of British arms. Clinton lost 251 troops killed and 170 wounded, some of whom died from sunstroke. In addition, an estimated 600 Hessians deserted during the land passage from Philadelphia to New York, meaning that the British force lost at least one-tenth of its total strength before making good its escape by reaching the peninsula of Sandy Hook (June 30) on the southern side of New York Bay. There waiting British transports carried Clinton's army to safety in New York City.

The patriots at Monmouth suffered 267 casualties, 37 of whom died from sunstroke. Another 95 were missing. Still, Washington's army controlled the battlefield at the end of the day and could claim victory by that measure alone. Even more important, although the British still held firmly to their main base of operations in New York City, they had gained little else after two years of hard campaigning. Even worse, France was now America's ally, and the war would soon expand into a global contest. As if mesmerized by so many undesirable turn of events, Henry Clinton made no further attempts to campaign actively in either New England or the middle states. Monmouth thus proved to be the last major battle in the northern theater of the Revolutionary War.

One little incident happened during the heat of the cannonade, which I was eyewitness to, and which I think would be unpardonable not to mention. A woman whose husband belonged to the artillery and who was then attached to a piece in the engagement, attended with her husband at the piece the whole time. While in the act of reaching a cartridge and having one of her feet as far before the other as she could step, a cannon shot from the enemy passed directly between her legs without doing any other damage than carrying away all the lower part of her petticoat. Looking at it with apparent unconcern, she observed that it was lucky it did not pass a little higher, for in that case it might have carried away something else, and continued her occupation.[20]

The next day after the action each man received a gill of rum, but nothing to eat. We then joined our regiments in the line and marched for Hudson's River. We marched by what was called "easy marches," that is we struck our tents at 3 o'clock in the morning, marched 10 miles and then encamped, which would be about 1 or 2 o'clock in the afternoon. Every third day we rested all day. In this way we went to King's Ferry, where we crossed the Hudson.

Each brigade furnished its own ferrymen to carry the troops across. I was one of the men from our brigade; we were still suffering for provisions. Nearly the last trip the bateau that I was in made, while crossing the river empty, a large sturgeon (a fish in which this river abounds) seven or eight feet in length, in his gambolings[21] sprang directly into the boat without doing any other damage than breaking down one of the seats of the boat. We crossed and took in our freight and recrossed, landed the men and our prize, gave orders to our several messmates as to the disposal of it, and proceeded on our business till the whole of the brigade had crossed the river,

---

[20] The woman was Mary Ludwig Hays McCauly of Carlisle, Pennsylvania, later sanitized as the legendary "Molly Pitcher" to suit nineteenth-century sensibilities about proper spheres of activity for women. McCauly most likely was a domestic servant before the war who actually served in the ranks of the Continental army. The British army permitted 1 woman in the ranks for every 10 men; the Continental ratio was 1 in 15. Women performed various duties, everything from nursing and cooking to scavenging the fields of slaughter for vital equipment after battles and burying the dead. As in McCauly's case, they also occasionally engaged in combat. These women should not be confused with "camp followers" who traveled along with husbands and children or, in many instances, were prostitutes. Mary McCauly lived until 1832 making a meager living as a charwoman. She did receive a small pension for her services late in her life.

[21] Leaping or jumping out of the water.

which was not long, we working with new energy in expectation of having something to eat when we had done our job. We then repaired to our messes to partake of the bounty of Providence, which we had so unexpectedly received. I found my share, which was about the seventh part of it, cooked, that is, it was boiled in salt and water, and I fell to it and ate, perhaps a pound and a half, for I well remember that I was as hungry as a vulture and as empty as a blown bladder. Many of the poor fellows *thought* us happy in being thus supplied; for my part I *felt* happy.

From King's Ferry the army proceeded to Tarrytown,[22] and from thence to the White Plains. Here we drew some small supplies of summer clothing of which we stood in great need. While we lay here, I, with some of my comrades who were in the battle of White Plains in the year '76, one day took a ramble on the ground where we were then engaged with the British and took a survey of the place. We saw a number of the graves of those who fell in that battle; some of the bodies had been so slightly buried that the dogs or hogs, or both, had dug them out of the ground. The skulls and other bones and hair were scattered about the place. Here were Hessian skulls as thick as a bombshell. Poor fellows! They were left unburied in a foreign land; they had, perhaps, as near and dear friends to lament their sad destiny as the Americans who lay buried near them. But they should have kept at home; we should then never have gone after them to kill them in their own country. But, the reader will say, they were forced to come and be killed here; forced by their rulers who have absolute power of life and death over their subjects. Well then, reader, bless a kind Providence that has made such a distinction between *your* condition and *theirs*. And be careful too that you do not allow yourself ever to be brought to such an abject, servile, and debased condition.

We lay at the White Plains some time. While here I was transferred to the Light Infantry,[23] when I was immediately marched

---

[22] Tarrytown, located on the east bank of the Hudson River, is about 10 miles below King's Ferry and would have represented the approximate halfway point on a southeastward march to White Plains.

[23] A term for specially designated companies of soldiers who carried little equipment so that they could travel "lightly" and quickly, normally as skirmishers or rangers making contact with enemy forces in advance of their own armies. Washington had formed his first light infantry "Corps of Rangers" in August 1777 under the famous Virginia rifleman, Daniel Morgan. Besides being young and robust, those chosen for light infantry duty were normally adept marksmen who had also proven their capacity to remain calm under the stress of battle. Martin was not yet 18 years old when he was

down to the lines. I had hard duty to perform during the remainder of the campaign. I shall not go into every particular, but only mention a few incidents and accidents which transpired.

There were three regiments of Light Infantry, composed of men from the whole main army. It was a motley group—Yankees, Irishmen, Buckskins, and what not. The regiment that I belonged to was made up of about one half New Englanders, and the remainder were chiefly Pennsylvanians—two sets of people as opposite in manners and customs as light and darkness. Consequently there was not much cordiality subsisting between us; for to tell the sober truth, I had in those days as lief [gladly] have been incorporated with a tribe of western Indians as with any of the southern troops, especially of those which consisted mostly (as the Pennsylvanians did) of foreigners. But I *was* among them and in the same regiment too, and under their officers (but the officers, in general, were gentlemen), and had to do duty with them. To make a bad matter worse, I was often when on duty the only Yankee that happened to be on the same tour for several days together. "The bloody Yankee," or "the d—d Yankee," was the mildest epithets that they would bestow upon me at such times. It often made me think of home, or at *least* of my regiment of fellow Yankees.

Our regiment was commanded by a Colonel Butler,[24] a Pennsylvanian.... He was a brave officer, but a fiery austere hothead. Whenever he had a dispute with a brother officer, and that was pretty often, he would never resort to pistols and swords, but always to his fists. I have more than once or twice seen him with a "black eye," and have seen other officers that he had honored with the same badge.

As I have said before, I shall not be *very* minute in relating my "adventures" during my continuance in this service. The duty of the

---

selected to serve in the light infantry detachments formed at White Plains under the overall command of Colonel David Henley. Their orders were to monitor, harass, and disrupt British movements and activities north of Manhattan Island in the wake of Clinton's reconcentration of forces in and around New York City.

[24] Richard Butler was a native of Ireland who had migrated to Pennsylvania and became involved in the Indian trade. Awarded a captain's commission in 1776, he quickly moved up the Continental ranks and became a colonel of the 9th Pennsylvania in June 1777. He also served with Morgan's Corps of Rangers that year. In 1791 the roughhewn Butler died in battle while trying to clear Indians from the Ohio country.

Light Infantry is the hardest, while in the field, of any troops in the army, if there is any *hardest* about it. During the time the army keeps the field they are always on the lines near the enemy, and consequently always on the alert, constantly on the watch. Marching and guard-keeping, with all the other duties of troops in the field, fall plentifully to *their* share....

We had not been long on the lines when our regiment was sent off, lower down toward the enemy upon a scouting expedition. We marched all night. Just at day-dawn we halted in a field and concealed ourselves in some bushes; we placed our sentinels near the road, lying down behind bushes, rocks, and stoneheaps. The officers had got wind of a party of the enemy that was near us. A detachment of cavalry which accompanied us had taken the same precaution to prevent being discovered that the infantry had.

We had not been long in our present situation before we discovered a party of Hessian horsemen advancing up the road, directly to where we were lying in ambush for them. When the front of them had arrived "within hail," our colonel rose up from his lurking place and very civilly ordered them to come to him. The party immediately halted, and as they saw but one man of us, the commander seemed to hesitate and concluded, I suppose, not to be in too much of a hurry in obeying our colonel's command; but that it was the best way for him to retrace his steps. Our colonel then, in a voice like thunder, called out to him, "*Come here, you rascal!*" But he paid very little attention to the colonel's summons and began to endeavor to free himself from what, I suppose, he thought a bad neighborhood. Upon which our colonel ordered the whole regiment to rise from their ambush and fire upon them; the order was quickly obeyed and served to quicken their steps considerably. Our horsemen had, while these transactions were in progress, by going round behind a small wood, got into their rear. We followed the enemy hard up, and when they met our horsemen there was a trifle of clashing. A part forced themselves past our cavalry and escaped; about 30 were taken and a number killed. We had none killed and but two or three of the horsemen slightly wounded. The enemy were armed with short rifles.

There was an Irishman belonging to our infantry, who, after the affray was over, seeing a wounded man belonging to the enemy lying in the road and unable to help himself, took pity on him, as he was in danger of being trodden upon by the horses; and having shouldered him was staggering off with his load in order to get him to a place of more safety. While crossing a small worn-out bridge over a very muddy brook, he happened to jostle the poor fellow more than usual, who cried out, "Good rebel, don't hurt poor Hushman." "Who do you call a rebel, you scoundrel?" said the Irishman and tossed him off his shoulders as unceremoniously as though he had been a log of wood. He fell with his head into the mud, and as I passed I saw him struggling for life, but I had other business on my hands than to stop to assist him. I did sincerely pity the poor mortal, but pity him was all I could then do. What became of him after I saw him in the mud I never knew; most likely he there made his final exit. The infantry marched off with the prisoners and left the horsemen to keep the field till we were out of danger with our prize; consequently I never heard anything more of him. But the Irishman reminded me "that the *tender* mercies of the wicked are cruel."

Soon after this I had another fatiguing job to perform. There was a militia officer, a colonel (his name I have forgotten, though I think it was Jones), who had collected some stores of flour, pork, &c. for the use of the militia in his neighborhood when any small parties of them were required for actual service. A party of the enemy, denominated "Cowboys" (Refugees)[25] had destroyed his stores. He solicited some men from the Light Infantry to endeavor to capture some of the gang whom he was personally acquainted with, who belonged to, or were often at, Westchester, a village near King's Bridge. Accordingly, a captain and 2 subaltern officers and 80 men (of which I was one) was sent from our regiment, then lying in the village called Bedford,[26] to his assistance.

We marched from our camp in the dusk of the evening and continued our march all night. We heard repeatedly during the night the tories firing on our sentries that belonged to the horse guards, who were stationed on the lines near the enemy. This was

[25] A "neutral ground" encompassing much of Westchester County, New York, existed between American and British lines. British outposts ran from the area of King's Bridge just north of Manhattan Island eastward to the Bronx River. Farther north the patriots maintained a line running southeastward from Dobbs Ferry on the Hudson River to Mamaroneck, New York, on Long Island Sound. In between roving bands of partisans engaged in savage campaigns of pillage, rapine, and murder that had little to do with service to either side. Those partisans who claimed loyalty to the Crown were known as Refugees or Cowboys; those supposedly committed to the patriot cause were known as Skinners. In reality, the true allegiance of both was only to serving themselves.

[26] In southeastern New York about 10 miles from Ridgefield, Connecticut.

often practiced by those villains, not only upon our cavalry but the infantry also when they thought they could do it with impunity. We arrived at the colonel's early in the morning and stayed there through the day.

At night the lieutenant of our detachment with a small party of men, guided by two or three militia officers, were sent off in pursuit of some of those shooting gentry whom the colonel suspected. We first went to a house where were a couple of free blacks who were strongly suspected of being of the number. The people of the house denied having any knowledge of such persons, but some of the men inquiring of a small boy belonging to the house, he very innocently told us that there were such men there and that they lay in a loft over the hogsty. We soon found their nest but the birds had flown. Upon further inquiry, however, we found their skulking place and took them both.

We then proceeded to another house, a mile or two distant. Here we could not get any intelligence of the vermin we were in pursuit of. We, however, searched the house but found none. But we (the soldiers) desired the man who attended us with a light to show us into the dairy-house, pretending that the suspected persons might be there, and he accordingly accompanied us there. We found no enemy in this place, but we found ... plenty of good bread, milk, and butter; we were as hungry as Indians and immediately "fell to, and spared not," while the man of the house held the candle and looked at us as we were devouring his eatables. I could not see his heart and of course could not tell what sort of thoughts "harbored there," but I could see his face and that indicated pretty distinctly what passed in his mind; he said *nothing*, but I believe he had as lief [gladly] his bread and butter had been arsenic as what it was. We cared little for his thoughts or his maledictions; they did not do us half so much hurt as his victuals did us good.

We then returned to our party at the colonel's, where we arrived before daybreak. We stayed here through the day ... and prepared for our expedition after the Cowboys. At dark we set off, accompanied by the militia colonel and three or four subaltern militia officers; this was the third night I had been on my feet, the whole time without any sleep, but go we must.... We kept on still through the fields, avoiding the houses as much as possible. I shall never forget how tired and beat out I was. Every grove of trees or piece of woods ... I hoped would prove a resting place, but there was no rest.

About two o'clock we took to the high road when we were between the village of Westchester and King's Bridge. We then came back to the village, where we were separated into small divisions, ... and immediately entered all the suspected houses at once. What we had to do must be done quickly, as the enemy were so near that they might have been informed of us in less than half an hour. There were several men in the house into which I was led, but one only appeared to be obnoxious to the officer who led us. This man was a tory Refugee in green uniform; we immediately secured him.... We directly left the house with our prisoner and joined the other parties and hurried off with all possible speed.

When we had got away and daylight appeared, we found that we had 12 or 14 prisoners, the most or all of whom had been concerned in the destruction of the colonel's stores. We did not suffer the grass to grow long under our feet until we considered ourselves safe from the enemy that we had left behind us; we then slackened our pace and took to the road, where it was easier getting along than in the fields. Oh! I was so tired and hungry when we arrived at the colonel's, which was not till sundown or after.

The most of the fellows we had taken belonged in the neighborhood of this place. As we passed a house just at night, there stood in the door an elderly woman, who seeing among the prisoners some that she knew, she began to open her batteries of blackguardism upon us for disturbing what she termed the king's peaceable subjects. Upon a little closer inspection, who should her ladyship spy among the herd but one of her own sons. Her resentment was then raised to the highest pitch, and we had a drenching shower of imprecations let down upon our heads. "Hell for war!" said she, "why, you have got my son Josey too." Poor old simpleton! She might as well have saved her breath to cool her porridge.

We here procured another day's ration of the good colonel's pork and bread. We stayed through the night and got some sleep and rest. Early next morning we left our prisoners, blacks and all, to the care of the militia, who could take care of them after we had taken them for them, and marched off for our encampment at Bedford, where we arrived at night, sufficiently beat out and in a good condition to add another night's sleep to our stock of rest.

We lay at Bedford till the close of the season. Late in the autumn the main army lay at New Milford, in the northwestern part of Connecticut.[27] While there the Connecticut troops drew some

---

[27] Martin's statement is misleading. Washington's "main army" resided in the vicinity of White Plains during the autumn of 1778 before crossing the Hudson River and establishing winter quarters in the vicinity of Middlebrook, New Jersey. The Connecticut regiments marched first to New Milford in late October and then to the Redding-Danbury area for their winter encampment.

winter clothing. The men belonging to that state, who were in the Light Infantry, had none sent them; they, therefore, thought themselves hardly dealt by. Many of them, fearing they should lose their share of the clothing (of which they stood in great need), absconded from the camp at Bedford and went to New Milford. This caused our officers to keep patrolling parties around the camp during the night to prevent their going off....

I had often heard of some of the low bred Europeans, especially Irishmen, boxing with each other in good fellowship, as they termed it; but I could not believe it till I was convinced by actual demonstration. While we tarried here, I was one day at a sutler's[28] tent, or hut, where were a number of what we Yankees call "Old Countrymen." Soon after entering the hut, I observed one who was to appearance "pretty well over the bay." Directly there came in another who, it appeared, was an old acquaintance of the former's; they seemed exceeding glad to see each other, and so must take a drop of "the cratur" together; they then entered into conversation about former times. The first-mentioned was a stout athletic fellow; the other was a much smaller man. All of a sudden the first says, "Faith, Jammy, will you take a box?" "Aye, and thank ye too," replied the other. No sooner said than done, out they went, and all followed to see the sport, as they thought it, I suppose.

It was a cold, frosty day in the month of December. The ground all around the place was ploughed and frozen as hard as a pavement. They immediately stripped to the buff, and a broad ring was directly formed for the combatants (and they needed a broad one), when they prepared for the battle. The first pass they made at each other, their arms drawing their bodies forward, they passed without even touching either; the first that picked them up was the frozen ground, which made the claret, as they called the blood, flow plentifully. They, however, with considerable difficulty put themselves into a position for a second bout, when they made the same pass-by as at the first. The little fellow, after getting upon his feet again, as well as he could, cried out, "I am too drunk to fight," and crawled off as fast as he was able to the sutler's hut again; the other followed, both as bloody as butchers, to drink friends again where no friendship had been lost. And there I left them and went to my tent, thankful that Yankees, with all their follies, lacked such a *refined* folly as this.

---

[28] Sutlers were civilian peddlers, normally licensed, who followed after the troops to sell them provisions, especially alcohol.

The main army about this time quitted the eastern side of the Hudson River and passed into New Jersey to winter quarters. The Connecticut and New Hampshire troops went to Reading [Redding] and Danbury in the western part of Connecticut.[29] The Light Infantry, likewise, broke up their encampment at Bedford and separated to join their respective regiments in the line. On our march to join our regiment, some of our *gentlemen officers*, happening to stop at a tavern, or rather a sort of grogshop, took such a seasoning that two or three of them became "quite frisky," as the old Indian said of his young squaw. They kept running and chasing each other backward and forward by the troops as they walked along the road, acting ridiculously. They soon, however, broke up the sport, for two of them at last, got by the ears, to the no small diversion of the soldiers (for nothing could please them better than to see the officers quarrel among themselves). One of the officers used his sword in the scabbard, the other a cane.... Some of the other officers who had not dipped their bills quite so deep parted them, at the same time representing to them the ridiculous situation they stood in, fighting like blackguards in sight of the soldiers. At length shame, so far as they had reason to let it operate beginning to take hold of them, the other officers persuaded them to shake hands in token of future friendship, but they carried wonderful long faces all the rest of the day.

We arrived at Reading [Redding] about Christmas or a little before, and prepared to build huts for our winter quarters. And now came on the time again between grass and hay, that is the winter campaign of starving. We had not long been under the command of General Putnam[30] before the old gentleman heard, or

---

[29] Redding is some 15 miles inland from Long Island Sound and just south of Danbury in western Connecticut, close to the eastern border of New York. In late April 1777 a British force had raided and sacked the village of Danbury, which then served as a Continental army supply depot.

[30] Israel Putnam, a farmer and tavern keeper from Connecticut, was nearing 60 years of age when the Revolutionary War broke out. He had earlier gained a dazzling reputation for his fighting prowess in the French and Indian War. The Continental Congress named him a major general in June 1775, and at the Battle of Bunker Hill (June 17, 1775) he supposedly uttered the immortal words, "Don't fire until you see the whites of their eyes." During the New York campaign of 1776, it became self-evident that Putnam was either beyond his prime or lacked the capacity for effective field leadership. As such, Washington kept giving Putnam non-critical assignments, such as commanding the Continentals wintering in the Danbury-Redding area. A paralytic stroke in late 1779 resulted in Putnam's retirement.

fancied he heard, that a party of the enemy were out somewhere "down below." We were alarmed about midnight, and as cold a night as need be, and marched off to find the enemy (if he could be found). We marched all the remaining part of the night and all the forenoon of the next day, and when we came where they were, they were not there at all at all, as the Irishman said.

We now had nothing more to do but to return as we came, which we immediately set about. We marched back to Bedford, near the encamping ground I had just left. We were conducted into our bedroom, a large wood, by our landlords, the officers, and left to our repose, while the officers stowed themselves away snugly in the houses of the village, about half a mile distant. We struck us up fires and lay down to rest our weary bones, all but our jawbones; they had nothing to weary them. About midnight it began to rain, which soon put out all our fires, and by three or four o'clock it came down in torrents. There *we* were, but where our careful officers were, or what had become of them we knew not, nor did we much care. The men began to squib off their pieces in derision of the officers, supposing they were somewhere among us and careless of our condition; but none of them appearing, the men began firing louder and louder, till they had brought it to almost a running fire. At the dawn, the officers, having I suppose heard the firing, came running from their warm, dry beds, almost out of breath exclaiming, "Poor fellows! Are you not almost dead?" We might have been for aught they knew or cared. However, they marched us off to the village, wet as drowned rats, put us into the houses, where we remained till the afternoon and dried ourselves.

It cleared off toward night, and about sundown we marched again for camp, which was about 20 miles distant. We marched till sometime in the evening when we were ordered to get into the houses, under the care of the non-commissioned officers, the commissioned officers having again taken care of themselves at an early hour of the night. Myself and 10 or 15 others of our company, being under the charge of our orderly sergeant, could not get any quarters, as the people at every house made some excuse, which he thought all true. We kept pushing on till we had got three or four miles in advance of the troops; we then concluded to try for lodgings no longer, but to make the best of our way to camp, which we did, and arrived there in the latter part of the night. I had nothing to do but to endeavor to get a little rest, for I had no cooking, although I should have been very glad to have had it to do.

The rest of the troops arrived in the course of the day, and at night I think we got a little something to eat, but if we did not, I know what I got by the jaunt, for I got a pleurisy which laid me up for some time. When I got so well as to work I assisted in building our winter huts. We got them in such a state of readiness that we moved into them about New Year's Day. The reader may take my word, if he pleases, when I tell him we had nothing extraordinary, either of eatables or drinkables, to keep a new year or housewarming. And as I have got into winter quarters again, I will here bring my third campaign to a close.

Chapter V

Campaign of 1779

JPM and his comrades endure horrible shortages and harsh winter conditions, almost to the breaking point of open mutiny, then engage in defending Connecticut and New York's Hudson Highlands region from various British attacks during the summer campaign season.

> You may think what you please, sir, I too can think—
> I think I can't live without victuals and drink;
> Your oxen can't plough, nor your horses can't draw,
> Unless they have something more hearty than straw;—
> If that is their food, sir, their spirits must fall—
> How can *I* labor with—nothing at all?

We got settled in our winter quarters at the commencement of the new year and went on in our old Continental line of starving and freezing. We now and then got a little bad bread and salt beef (I believe chiefly horse-beef, for it was generally thought to be such at the time). The month of January was very stormy, a good deal of snow fell, and in such weather it was a mere chance if we got anything at all to eat. Our condition at length became insupportable. We concluded that we *could* not or *would* not bear it any longer; we were now in our own state and were determined that if our officers would not see some of our grievances redressed, the state should. Accordingly, one evening after roll calling, the men generally turned out (but without their arms) and paraded in front of their huts. We had no need of informing the officers; we well knew that they would hear of our muster without our troubling ourselves to inform them.

We had hardly got paraded before all our officers, with the colonel at their head, came in front of the regiment, expressing a deal of sorrow for the hardships we were compelled to undergo, but much more for what they were pleased to call our mutinous conduct.[1] This latter expression of their sorrow only served to exasperate the men, which the officers observing, changed their tone and endeavored to soothe the Yankee temper they had excited, and with an abundance of fair promises persuaded us to return to our quarters again.

But hunger was not to be so easily pacified and would not suffer many of us to sleep. We were therefore determined that none others should sleep. Martial law was very strict against firing muskets in camp. Nothing could, therefore, raise the officers' "lofty ideas" sooner, or more, than to fire in camp; but it was beyond the power or vigilance of all the officers to prevent the men from "making void the law" on that night. Finding they were watched by the officers, they got an old gun barrel which they placed in a hut that was unfinished; this they loaded a third part full, and putting a slow match to it would then escape to their own huts, when the old barrel would speak for itself with a voice that would be heard. The officers would then muster out, and some running and scolding would ensue; but none knew who made the noise, or where it came from. This farce was carried on the greater part of the night; but at length the officers getting tired of running so often to catch Mr. Nobody without finding him, that they soon gave up the chase,

---

[1]   The colonel now in charge of Martin's 8th Connecticut was Giles Russell, since John Chandler had left the service in March 1778, apparently because of ill health. The Connecticut soldiers who settled into winter quarters in the Redding-Danbury area were in the brigades of generals Jedediah Huntington and Samuel Holden Parsons, the latter including Martin's regiment. These Continental veterans were very much in an indignant frame of mind, their anger focusing on their deplorable living conditions, lack of decent food and clothing, and absence of pay. Encamped as they were on Connecticut soil, they started whispering among themselves about marching to Hartford, the state capital, where they intended to confront the General Assembly and resign en masse unless they gained satisfaction in redressing their grievances. Martin does not mention that General Putnam, who was in overall command, arrested the soldiers suspected of fomenting the turmoil. This near mutiny soon fizzled out, but such collective protest, as demonstrated again by these same Connecticut long-termers in May 1780, continued to occur as various Continental brigades rose up in exasperation over the privation they were enduring.

and the men seeing they could no longer gull the officers, gave up the business likewise.

We fared a little better for a few days after this memento to the officers; but it soon became an old story, and the old system commenced again as regular as fair weather to foul. We endeavored to bear it with our usual fortitude, until it again became intolerable, and the soldiers determined to try once more to raise some provisions, if not at least to raise another dust.

Accordingly, one evening after dark we all turned out again with our arms, appointed a commander and were determined that time, if we could not be better accommodated, to march into the center of the state and disperse to our homes, in presence of as many of our fellow citizens as chose to be spectators. After we had organized ourselves and regulated the plan for our future operations, it was the design of our regiment to have marched to our field officers' quarters, and through them to demand of our country better usage; but before we had got all our little matters of etiquette settled, our adjutant came up (he having been over at the village on some errand best known to himself), and seeing us in arms upon the parade at that time of night, mistrusted [suspected] something was in the wind. He passed us without saying a word and went directly and informed the other officers, all of whom were soon upon the parade.

Our major was the first that arrived. He was a ... bold-looking man, and made a fine appearance. He came on to the right of the regiment, and soon after the colonel and other officers came in front. The commanding sergeant ordered the men to shoulder arms and then to present (which is a token of respect), and then to order them again. The major then addressed the sergeant thus: "Well, Sergeant ——, you have got a larger regiment than we had this evening at roll call, but I should think it would be more agreeable for the men to be asleep in their huts this cold night, than to be standing on the parade, for I remember that they were very impatient at roll call on account of the cold."

"Yes, sir," said the sergeant, "Solomon says that 'the abundance of the rich will not suffer *him* to sleep',[2] and we find that the

---

[2] Ecclesiastes 5:12. The theme of Ecclesiastes is to be content with one's circumstances, since life is so fleeting. The sergeant was emphasizing that the soldiers, no matter how patient and dutiful, had reached the point where they could no longer endure their abominable living conditions in the Continental army.

abundance of poverty will not suffer us to sleep." By this time the colonel had come to where the major and sergeant were arguing the case, and the old mode of flattery and promising was resorted to and produced the usual effect; we all once more returned to our huts and fires, and there spent the remainder of the night muttering over our forlorn condition.

It was now the beginning of February. Many of the men had obtained furloughs to go home and visit their friends, before I had left the Light Infantry, and many since; I now made application and obtained one for 15 days' absence. I prepared for the journey (which was about 30 miles) and started from the camp about 9 o'clock in the morning, intending to go the whole distance that day. I had not a mouthful of anything to eat or to carry with me. I had, it is true, two or three shillings of old Continental money, worth about as much as its weight in rags. I, however, set off for home; the hopes of soon seeing my friends and the expectation of there filling my belly once more buoyed up my spirits until I had got within about five miles of home. When coming to a tavern about sunset, I consulted with myself whether I had not better call and get me a glass of spirits, as I did not possess wherewith to procure me a meal of victuals, concluding that I should soon be where I could get that gratis; I accordingly did call and drank a glass of spirits and water, and immediately pursued my journey.

I soon came to where I was obliged to leave the high road and take to one that struck across the country and a ferry. By the time I had got to this road I had become so faint that I thought I could not reach the nearest house, which was more than a mile distant. I was acquainted with this road, but the main road which led to a large village I was unacquainted with any further than where I then was. I sat down and rested myself a few minutes, and I had need of it. I concluded to keep on the main road, being confident that I should find a house in a less distance than on the other. I went on, often having to rest myself from mere faintness.

I traveled, however, nearly a mile and a half without seeing the least sign of a house. At length after much fatigue, I came to an old house, standing, as the Irishman said, out of doors. I made [walked] up to it and knocked at the door. "Who's there?" cried an old woman from within. "A friend," I replied. "What do you want?" said she. "I want to rest here tonight." "I cannot entertain you," said she, "I am alone and cannot let a stranger in." I told her I could not and would not go any further. After some inquiring on her part and answering on mine, she condescended to admit me. She need not to have feared me, for had she been a virgin and as beautiful as Helen, I should have had no inclination to have soiled her chastity that night; I had something else to employ my thoughts upon.

However loath the old lady was to admit me, she used me extremely well, for she provided me with a good supper and a field bed before the fire, where I slept soundly till the morning, nor would she let me depart in the morning till I had breakfasted. While she was preparing my breakfast, I chopped off a backlog and put it on the fire, which was all the compensation she required, nor even that, it was my own will; we then parted with mutual thanks, and I proceeded on my journey....

When I came to the ferry, it was frozen over and covered with snow a foot deep. I went into the ferryman's house, one of whose daughters was wife to the drum major of our regiment; she made a bitter complaint to me against her husband, said he came home from the army and spent all her earnings, gave the whole family the itch, and then went off to camp, leaving her and her children to shift for themselves as well as they could. I could have told her a little more of his *amiable* conduct than she knew, but I thought she might as well get her information from some other quarter....

I arrived at my good old grandsire's about eight or nine o'clock in the morning, with a keen appetite for my breakfast, although I had ate one that day. I believe the old people were glad to see me. They appeared to be much so, and I am quite sure I was glad to see them and all my other friends, if I had any. I had now an opportunity of seeing the place of my boyhood, visit old acquaintances, and ramble over my old haunts; but my time was short, and I had of course to employ every minute to the best advantage.

I remained at home till my furlough had fully expired. I intended my country should give me a day to return to camp. The day before I intended to set off for the army, my lieutenant arrived at home to spend a week with his family. He called upon me and told me that if I chose I might stay and accompany him to camp, and he would be responsible for me. I did not want much persuasion to comply with his desire, and accordingly remained another week and then went with the lieutenant to camp and had no fault found.

I had not been at camp more than a week before I was sent off with a large detachment to New London to guard the fortifications in and about that town.[3] On our march we passed through the place of my residence when at home; the detachment tarried a night there, so I had an opportunity of being at home another night. We marched in the morning and remained the following night at New Haven. I was quartered for the night in a house in the skirts of the town. There was a young lady belonging to the house, who, as it was Sabbath eve, had gone out to see the "daughters of the land," like Dinah of old.[4] Just as we were about to lie down, I went to the back door of the house, where was a small field of dry cornstalks. I met the young lady with a gallant, just at the door; the moment he saw me he left his sweetheart and went off through the cornstalks, making as much noise as if a whirlwind had passed through them. I thought he was a brave fellow, thus to leave his mistress in the power of those he was afraid of himself, and not stop so long as to ask quarters for her, but upon the first alarm to desert her to save his own four quarters from receiving damage. Many pretended heroes have done the same, perhaps worse.

We went by easy marches, and nothing of consequence occurred until we arrived at New London. Here we were put into houses, and here too we almost starved to death; and I believe should have quite starved had we not found some clams, which kept us from absolutely dying. We had nothing to eat except now and then a little miserable beef or a little fresh fish and a very little bread, baked by a baker belonging to the town, which had some villainous drug incorporated with it that took all the skin off our mouths. I sincerely believe it was done on purpose to prevent our eating. I was not free from a sore mouth the whole time I stayed there....

We stayed here starving until the 1st of May, when we received orders to march to camp and join our regiments.... While on our march we halted in a village; here I went into a house, with several

---

[3] Going back to the Danbury raid of 1777, rumors persisted of British plans for additional strikes against Connecticut towns. These stories built to a new crescendo in the autumn of 1778, which caused Governor Jonathan Trumbull to insist upon the presence of Continental troops in Connecticut during the winter. Washington conceded by placing soldiers in the Redding-Danbury area. When reports circulated of an imminent British sortie against the seaport community of New London, located on the Thames River in eastern Connecticut a few miles inland from the Atlantic Ocean, General Putnam ordered 400 of these Continentals, including Martin, to help provide for that town's defense.

[4] Genesis 34:1–30 tells the story of Dinah, the daughter of Jacob and Leah, and her rape by Shechem, the son of Hamor, with deadly consequences.

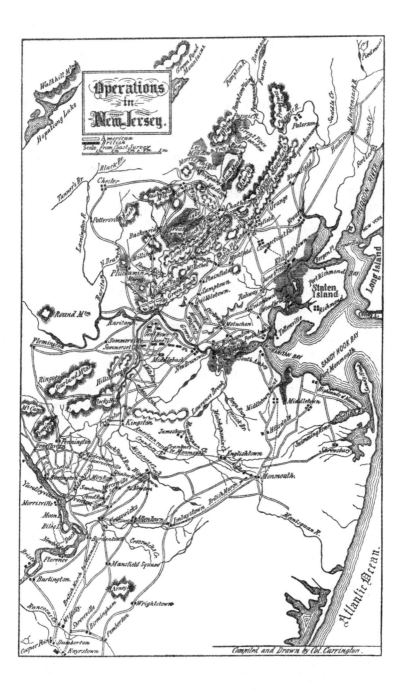

We were immediately ordered to march, which order was quickly put in execution. We went directly to the Fishkill on the Hudson, and from thence down nearly opposite to West Point.[6] We remained here some days; I was the most of that time on a stationed guard, keeping the horses that belonged to the army at pasture. I procured some damaged cartridges, and after converting the balls into shot and getting out of hearing from the camp, diverted myself by killing birds or squirrels, or any such game. This I often practiced, though I ran the risk of a keelhauling if detected. Here I had a good opportunity to exercise myself at the business, being at a considerable distance from camp. Pigeons were plenty, and we fared pretty comfortably with what provisions we were allowed otherwise.

After being relieved from this guard, I was detached with a small party to ... Peekskill in the southern edge of the Highlands. We took up our quarters in some old barracks; there was a number of bombshells and some old damaged wagon wheels lying near the barracks. One day, after diverting ourselves by filling the shells with water, plugging them up, and setting them on the fire, while the water boiling, the steam would force the plug out with a report as loud as that of a pistol.

Tired with exercising ourselves at this diversion, we began to contrive some other mischief, when 4 or 5 of us took one of the old wagon wheels, and after considerable trouble and fatigue we carried the wheel about 30 or 40 forty rods up the mountain, at the back of the barracks and a considerable distance from them, when we gave the wheel the liberty to shift for itself and find its own way back. It went very regular for a few turns, when taking a glancing stroke against something, it took a course directly for the barracks and just in that part, too, where the men were, who we could hear distinctly laughing and talking. Ah me! What would I not have given had I never meddled with the ugly thing, but it was then too late to repent; the evil one had come. I confess I felt myself in a forlorn case. The barracks were only a single board thick, and those rotten and old, and the wheel might have gone through them and the men, too, that stood in its route, without scarcely retarding its progress. We all stood breathless waiting the result, when as it happened (and well for us there was such a thing as chance) the wheel, when within about 15 feet of the barracks, and with the motion

---

[6] Fishkill lies in New York on the east bank of the Hudson River across from Newburgh, which is about 10 miles north of West Point.

almost of a cannon ball struck something that gave it an elevation of 20 or 30 feet into the air, and passed over the barracks and several rods beyond them before it struck the ground again. The reader may rest satisfied that this last circumstance did not cause many tears of grief to fall.

The Americans had a fortification upon Verplanck's Point, on the eastern side of the Hudson opposite Stony Point garrisoned by a captain and about 100 men. The British took this place and made the garrison prisoners, after a close siege of about a week, and fortified the point.[7] They appeared by their conduct to have a strong inclination to possess West Point. To make a diversion in their own favor and draw off some of our forces from the vicinity of that fortress, they sent the infamous Governor Tryon into Connecticut with his banditti, who took possession first of New Haven and plundered it, and then embarked and went and plundered and burnt Fairfield and Norwalk. The two Connecticut brigades were then sent in pursuit of them. We marched nearly down to the seacoast when, the enemy getting scent of us, they took to their shipping and made the best of their way back to New York. We returned as soon as possible.[8]

[7] Martin's recollection is somewhat confused. The British captured Fort Lafayette at Verplanck's (normally rendered Verplancks) Point along with its defenders, who were North Carolina troops, on June 1, the same day that they seized Stony Point. There was no prolonged siege.

[8] Martin seems to have read Clinton's strategy in reverse order. The suspected British push up the Hudson River in May had the effect of drawing Continental troops away from Connecticut to protect New York's threatened Highlands region, including West Point. Then in early July, Clinton, supposedly in retaliation for privateering strikes against British shipping, launched a series of vicious raids against coastal towns in western Connecticut. Having marched for the Highlands, the Connecticut brigades of Huntington and Parsons did not get back to their home state in time to challenge the British raiders. Meanwhile, local militia resistance proved ineffective as troops under William Tryon plundered New Haven on July 5 before sacking and burning Fairfield (July 8), Green's Farm (July 9), and Norwalk (July 11). The raids, rumored for so long, all but obliterated the latter three communities. Ironically, the Continentals who had spent the winter in Connecticut were not in position to provide the very defense that had caused their placement there in the first place. Clinton, as such, had outmaneuvered his patriot adversaries.

William Tryon had trained as a soldier during his youth in England, had married into a wealthy, well-connected family, and had served as governor of North Carolina and New York before the collapse of royal authority in America. He remained in New York during the Revolutionary War, holding the local rank of major general. Using his earlier military experience in a variety of ways, he was active in training loyalist regiments, and he led the strike against Danbury as well as the raids of 1779 against the Connecticut coastal towns. Ill health caused Tryon to retire to England in 1780.

Being on our march the 15th day of July and destitute of all kinds of eatables, just at night I observed a cheese in a press before a farmer's door, and we being about to halt for the night, I determined to return after dark and lay siege to it; but we went further than I expected before we halted, and a smart shower of rain with thunder happening at the time, the cheese escaped. It cleared off with a brisk wind at northwest and cold; we were all wet to the skin and had no tents with us, lying on the western side of a cleared hill. I never came nearer perishing with the cold in the middle of summer in all my life, either before or since.

In the night we heard the cannon at Stony Point, and early next morning had information of the taking of that place by the Light Infantry of our army under the command of General Wayne.[9] Our officers were all on tiptoe to show their abilities in executing some extraordinary exploit. Verplanck's Point was the word. "Shall the Light Infantry get all the honor, and we do nothing!" said they. Accordingly, we set off full tilt to take Verplanck's Point; we marched directly for the Peekskill and arrived near there early in the day. We there received information that the British at Verplanck's Point were reinforced and advancing to attack *us*. We were quite knocked on the head by this news. However, we put ourselves in as good a condition as our circumstances would admit and waited their approach; they were afraid of us, or we of them, or both, for

---

[9]   In late June, even before Clinton's raids on the Connecticut towns, Washington had called upon General "Mad" Anthony Wayne of Pennsylvania to consider possible plans for retaking Stony Point. Once the raids on the Connecticut towns were under way, Washington knew for sure how dispersed Clinton's forces were, and he ordered Wayne to proceed. Late at night on July 15–16, Wayne led his Light Infantry corps, about 1,200 troops, up the slopes of Stony Point in a bayonet assault. In the action that ensued the Americans overwhelmed and captured the British defenders, about 600 in number.

Stony Point was a brilliant triumph but had no lasting effect, other than to raise patriot morale. Washington lacked sufficient troop strength to assign a garrison force to Stony Point, and the British reestablished their hold there on July 19, a day after Wayne withdrew his corps.

Anthony Wayne was among Washington's most talented general officers. He became colonel of the 4th Pennsylvania regiment early in 1776 and campaigned that year in Canada. Thereafter his assignments were with the main Continental army. He served with distinction at Brandywine, Germantown, and Monmouth before his notable triumph at Stony Point. In 1794 Wayne's crushing victory over Native Americans at Fallen Timbers in the Ohio country was decisive in opening that region to white settlers.

we did not come in contact that time. And thus ended the taking of Verplanck's Point and our honorable expectations....[10]

Sometime late in the fall, the British evacuated all their works and retired to New York. A large detachment, of which I was one, was sent to Verplanck's Point to level the British works. We were occupied in this business nearly two weeks, working and starving by day, and at night having to lie in the woods without tents. Some of our men got some peas which had been left there by the British, but one might as well have boiled gravel stones soft.... After we finished leveling the works we returned to camp.[11]

While lying at or near the Peekskill, a man belonging to the cavalry was executed for desertion to the enemy, and as none of the corps to which he belonged were there, no troops were paraded, as was customary on such occasions, except a small guard.[12] The ground on which the gallows was erected was literally covered with pebble stones. A brigade major attended the execution, his duty on these occasions being the same as the high sheriff's in civil matters.

---

[10] Washington considered but did not attempt a coordinated attack on British-controlled Fort Lafayette at Verplancks Point. A major problem was that patriot troop strength east of the Hudson River was too dispersed to mount an effective strike at the same time that Wayne's corps assaulted Stony Point. The Connecticut brigades were not available because they were just then on the road back to Peekskill after having marched to Connecticut in response to Clinton's raids on the coastal towns.
[11] Rumors began circulating in late summer that a powerful French naval fleet under the command of Charles Hector Théodat, the Comte d'Estaing, then cruising in the West Indies, was sailing north to join Washington's army in combined land-naval operations against New York City. First Clinton began to strengthen his local defenses. Then in late October he ordered the abandonment of Rhode Island, which the British had controlled since late 1776, and the withdrawal of his garrison forces from Stony and Verplancks points, all to assure a maximum concentration of troops to defend New York City and environs. Even before Clinton made these decisions, however, d'Estaing had suffered a defeat in early October while engaging in joint operations with American troops to expel a British force from Savannah, Georgia, at which point he gave up any notion of sailing farther north that year.
[12] As the war lengthened, desertion rates declined among long-term Continental veterans, mainly because of the deep bonds of friendship formed among comrades who had endured so much together. Desertions still occurred, however, and those getting caught while attempting to go over to the enemy could expect to be executed. Rank-and-file soldiers, who could empathize with anyone wanting to escape the service, detested having to witness such object lessons in regard to what might happen to them, should they try to desert. In this instance, Martin and his comrades also expressed their resentment about the blatant greed of the hangman, a civilian who had most likely given nothing of himself to the cause of liberty. They gathered on November 12 to watch the execution of Josiah Edwards, who had served in the 2nd Continental Light Dragoons of Colonel Elisha Sheldon.

He had somewhere procured a ragamuffin fellow for an executioner, to preserve his own immaculate reputation from defilement. After the culprit had hung the time prescribed by law, or custom, the hangman began stripping the corpse, the clothes being his perquisite. He began by trying to pull off his boots, but for want of a bootjack he could not readily accomplish his aim; he kept pulling and hauling at them, like a dog at a root, until the spectators, who were very numerous (the guard having gone off), growing disgusted, began to make use of the stones by tossing several at his pretty carcass. The brigade major interfering on behalf of his aide-de-camp, shared the same usage; they were both quickly obliged "to quit the field." As they retreated the stones flew merrily. They were obliged to keep at a proper distance until the soldiers took their own time to disperse, when they returned and completed their honorable business.

We remained at and near Peekskill till sometime in the month of December. The cold weather having commenced earlier than usual, we had hard combating with hunger, cold, nakedness, and hard duty, but were obliged to grapple with them all as well as we could. As the old woman said by her husband, when she baked him instead of his clothes, to kill the vermin, "You must grin and bear it."

About the middle of this month (December) we crossed the Hudson at King's Ferry and proceeded into New Jersey for winter quarters. The snow had fallen nearly a foot deep.... Our destination was at a place in New Jersey called Basking Ridge.[13] It was cold and snowy; we had to march all day through the snow and at night take up our lodgings in some wood where, after shoveling away the snow, we used to pitch three or four tents facing each other, and then join in making a fire in the center. Sometimes we could procure an armful of buckwheat straw to lie upon, which was deemed a luxury. Provisions, as usual, took up but a small part of our time, though much of our thoughts.

We arrived on our wintering ground in the latter part of the month of December, and once more, like the wild animals, began to make preparations to build us a "city for habitation." The soldiers,

---

[13]   The winter campsite is known as Jockey Hollow, nestled among sharply rising hills just to the southwest of Morristown and to the northwest of Basking Ridge in New Jersey. Jockey Hollow has been preserved under the care of the Morristown National Historical Park. The housing location assigned to the Connecticut line was to the southeast of the Henry Wick farm and near the historic Mendham-Elizabethtown road.

when immediately going about the building of their winter huts, would always endeavor to provide themselves with such tools as were necessary for the business (it is no concern of the reader's, as I conceive, by what means they procured their tools) ... to expedite the erection and completion of their dwelling places. Do not blame them too much, gentle reader, if you should chance to make a shrewd Yankee guess how they *did* procure them; remember, they were in distress, and you know when a man is in that condition he will not be over scrupulous how he obtains relief, so he does obtain it.

We encamped near our destined place of operation and immediately commenced. It was upon the southerly declivity of a hill; the snow, as I have already observed, was more than a foot deep, and the weather none of the warmest. We had to level the ground to set our huts upon; the soil was a light loam. When digging just below the frost, which was not deep, the snow having fallen early in the season, we dug out a number of toads, that would hop off when brought to the light of day as lively as in summertime. We found by this where toads take up their winter quarters, if we can never find where swallows take up theirs.

As this will be the last time that I shall have occasion to mention my having to build huts for our winter habitations, I will, by the reader's leave, just give a short description of the fashion and manner of erecting one of those log towns.

After the ground was marked out by the quartermasters, much after the same manner as for pitching tents in the field, we built the huts in the following manner: Four huts, 2 in front and 2 in the rear, then a space of 6 or 8 feet, when 4 more huts were placed in the same order, and so on to the end of the regiment, with a parade in front and a street through the whole, between the front and rear, the whole length 12 or 15 feet wide. Next in order in the rear of these huts the officers of the companies built theirs with their waiters in the rear of them. Next the field officers in the same order; every two huts, that is one in front and one in the rear, had just their width in front indefinitely, and no more, to procure the materials for building; the officers had all in the rear. No one was allowed to transgress these bounds on any account whatever, either for building or firewood.

The next thing is the erecting of the huts. They were generally about 12 by 15 or 16 feet square (all uniformly of the same dimensions).... A chimney was ... built at the center of the backside, composed of stone as high as the eaves and finished with sticks and clay, if clay was to be had, if not, with mud. The last thing was to hew stuff and build us up cabins or berths to sleep in, and then the buildings were fitted for the reception of *gentleman soldiers*, with all their *rich* and *gay* furniture.

Such were the habitations we had to construct at this time. We got into them about the beginning of the year, when the weather became intensely cold. Cold weather and snow were plenty, but beef and bread were extremely scarce in the army. Let it be recollected that this was what has been termed the "hard winter," and hard it was to the poor soldiers.... So here I will close the narrative of my campaign of 1779. And happy should I then have thought myself if that had ended the war, but I had to see a little more trouble before that period arrived.

Chapter VI

Campaign of 1780

JPM survives the most brutal winter during the war, engages in a line mutiny in protest of food and supply shortages, joins the Corps of Sappers and Miners, and comments on the traitorous activities of Benedict Arnold.

> The soldier defending his country's rights,
> Is griev'd when that country his services slights;
> But when he remonstrates and finds no relief,
> No wonder his anger takes place of his grief.

The winter of 1779 and '80 was very severe; it has been denominated "the hard winter," and hard it was to the army in particular, in more respects than one. The period of the Revolution has repeatedly been styled "the times that tried men's souls." I often found that those times not only tried men's souls, but their bodies too; I know they did mine, and that effectually.

Sometime in the month of January there happened a spell of remarkably cold weather. In the height of the cold, a large detachment from the army was sent off on an expedition against some fortifications held by the British on Staten Island. The detachment was commanded by Major General John Sullivan.[1] It was supposed

---

[1] Martin's recollection was faulty. The commander was Major General William Alexander, Lord Stirling. Sullivan, claiming bad health, had recently retired from the service after leading a punitive expedition against the Six Nations of Iroquois in New York.

by our officers that the bay before New York was frozen sufficiently to prevent any succors being sent to the garrisons in their
works. It was therefore determined to endeavor to surprise them
and get possession of their fortifications before they could obtain
help. Accordingly, our troops were all conveyed in sleighs and
other carriages; but the enemy got intelligence of our approach
(doubtless by some tory) before our arrival on the island. When we
arrived we found Johnny Bull[2] prepared for our reception. He was
always complaisant, especially when his own honor or credit was
concerned. We accordingly found them all waiting for us, so that
we could not surprise them, and to take their works by storm
looked too hazardous; to besiege them in regular form was out of
the question, as the bay was not frozen so much as we expected.
There was an armed brig lying in the ice not far from the shore; she
received a few shots from our fieldpieces for a morning's salutation.
We then fell back a little distance and took up our abode for the
night upon a bare bleak hill, in full rake of the northwest wind with
no other covering or shelter than the canopy of the heavens, and no
fuel but some old rotten rails which we dug up through the snow,
which was two or three feet deep; the weather was cold enough to
cut a man in two.

We lay on this accommodating spot till morning when we began
our retreat from the island. The British were quickly in pursuit; they
attacked our rear guard and made several of them prisoners, among
whom was one of my particular associates. Poor young fellow!
I have never seen or heard anything from him since. We arrived at
camp after a tedious and cold march of many hours, some with
frozen toes, some with frozen fingers and ears, and half-starved into
the bargain. Thus ended our Staten Island expedition.[3]

Soon after this there came on several severe snowstorms. At one
time it snowed the greater part of four days successively, and there
fell nearly as many feet deep of snow, and here was the keystone of
the arch of starvation. We were absolutely, literally starved; I do

[2]   A common nickname for English subjects, used here somewhat sarcastically in
referencing British troops.
[3]   Washington hoped to drive the British from their defenses on Staten Island, some
20 miles southeast of Morristown. Involving about 3,000 American troops, the raid
occurred on January 14–15, 1780. The British force, having gained intelligence of an
imminent strike, was on full alert, despite the severe, subzero weather. Casualties
were slight, although an estimated 500 ill-clad patriot soldiers suffered severe cases
of frostbite.

solemnly declare that I did not put a single morsel of victuals into my mouth for four days and as many nights, except a little black birch bark which I gnawed off a stick of wood, if that can be called victuals. I saw several of the men roast their old shoes and eat them, and I was afterwards informed by one of the officers' waiters that some of the officers killed and ate a favorite little dog that belonged to one of them. If this was not "suffering," I request to be informed what can pass under that name. If "suffering" like this did not "try men's souls," I confess that I do not know what could....[4]

We continued here, starving and freezing, until I think sometime in the month of February, when the two Connecticut brigades were ordered to the lines near Staten Island. The small parties from the army which had been sent to the lines were often surprised and taken by the enemy or cut to pieces by them. These circumstances, it seems, determined the Commander in Chief to have a sufficient number of troops there to withstand the enemy, even should they come in considerable force. And now a long continuance of our hardships appeared unavoidable. The First Brigade took up its quarters in a village called Westfield, and the Second in another called Springfield; we were put into the houses with the inhabitants. A fine addition we were, doubtless, to their families, but as we were so plentifully furnished with necessaries, especially in the article of food, we could not be burdensome to them, as will soon appear.

I think it necessary before I proceed further, to prevent much repetition, to give some information of the nature and kind of duty we had to perform while here, that the reader may form a clearer idea of the hardships we had to encounter in the discharge of it.... We were stationed about six miles from Elizabethtown, which is situated near the waters which separate Staten Island from the main. We had to send a detachment to this place which continued on duty there several days; it consisted of about 200 men and had to form several guards while there. We had another guard, which

---

[4] "The hard winter" of 1779–80, as described by Martin, was probably the most severe of the century, far worse in terms of frigid temperatures and heavy snowfalls than the Valley Forge winter of 1777–78. Food shortages for the some 10,000 Continentals housed in more than 1,000 rudely-built log huts in the Jockey Hollow region represented a major problem, and the specter of starvation was ever present. Killer diseases were not as devastating as at Valley Forge, however, largely because so many of these veteran soldiers had already endured and gained immunity from the maladies that had taken so many lives in earlier years.

consisted of about 100 men, at a place called Woodbridge; this guard stayed there 2 days before they were relieved, and was 10 miles from our quarters. Woodbridge also lay by the same waters....[5]

Our duty all the winter and spring was thus. Suppose I went upon the Woodbridge guard, I must march from the parade at 8 o'clock in the morning, go a distance of 10 miles and relieve the guard already there, which would commonly bring it to about 12 o'clock; stay there 2 days and 2 nights, then be relieved and take up the afternoon of that day to reach our quarters at Westfield, where as soon as I could get into my quarters, and generally before I could lay by my arms, warned for Elizabethtown the next day. Thus it was the whole time we lay here, which was from the middle of February to the latter part of May following. It was Woodbridge and Elizabethtown, Elizabethtown and Woodbridge, alternately, till I was absolutely sick of hearing the names mentioned....

The guard kept at Woodbridge, being so small, and so far from the troops, and so near the enemy that they were obliged to be constantly on the alert. We had three different houses that we occupied alternately during the night: The first was an empty house, the second the parson's house, and the third a farmer's house. We had to remove from one to the other of these houses three times every night, from fear of being surprised by the enemy.

There was no trusting the inhabitants, for many of them were friendly to the British, and we did not know who were or who were not, and consequently were distrustful of them all, unless it were one or two. The parson was a staunch whig, as the friends to the country were called in those times, and the farmer mentioned before was another, and perhaps more that we were not acquainted with; be that as it would, we were shy of trusting them. Here, especially in the night, we were obliged to keep about one half of the guard upon sentry, and besides these, small patrolling parties on all the roads leading toward the enemy; but with all the vigilance we

---

[5] Springfield, where the Second Brigade resided, is to the northwest of today's Elizabeth, New Jersey. Not quite halfway on a line running southeast from Springfield to Woodbridge is Westfield, where Martin and other First Brigade troops took up quarters. Elizabethtown and Woodbridge, the latter about 10 miles south of the former, served as advance rebel posts in most immediate contact with the northern and southern portions of Staten Island. The British did not consider launching any major troop movements westward from Staten Island that winter.

could exercise, we could hardly escape being surprised and cut off by the enemy. They exerted themselves more than common to take some of our guards, because we had challenged them to do it and had bid them defiance....

At another time I was upon the Elizabethtown station. Being one night on my post as sentinel, I observed a stir among the troops composing the detachment; I inquired the cause of a passing officer, who told me the British were upon Holstead's Point, which was a point of land about two miles from the main body of the detachment, where we had a guard consisting of a sergeant, a corporal, and 10 privates. The circumstances were as follows: The guard informed the man of the house where the guard was kept (a Mr. Holstead, the owner of the land that formed the point) that they had heard boats pass and repass at some distance below during the night. He said they were the British, and that they had landed some of the Refugees,[6] as that neighborhood abounded with such sort of cattle, but that it would be next to impossible to detect them, as they had so many friends in that quarter, and many of the enemy belonging to those parts, they knew every lurking place in all the neighboring country; the only way for the guard was to be vigilant and prevent a surprise. When the guard was relieved in the morning, the new one was informed of these circumstances and cautioned to be on the lookout.

Accordingly at night, they consulted with Mr. Holstead, who advised them to place a sentinel at a certain spot that had been neglected, for said he, "They know your situation better than you do yourselves; and if they come, they will enter your precincts by the way I have pointed out to you, and," continued he, "they will come about the time of the setting of the moon."

Agreeable to his advice, the sergeant stationed a sentinel at that place and prepared for them. Just as had been predicted, about the time the moon was setting, which was about 10 o'clock, they came, and at the same point. The first sentinel that occupied that post had not stood out his trick before he saw them coming; he immediately hailed them by the usual question, "Who comes there?" They answered him, that if he would not discharge his piece they would not hurt him, but if he did they would kill him. The sentinel, being true to his trust, paid no regard to their threats, but fired his piece and ran for the house to alarm the guard. In his way he had to cross

[6]   In this instance loyalist soldiers serving under British arms.

a hedge fence, in passing which he got entangled in the bushes, as it was supposed, and the enemy coming up thrust a bayonet through him. They then inflicted 12 more wounds upon him with bayonets and rushed on for the house to massacre the remainder of the guard, but they had taken the alarm and left the house. The Refugees (for such they were) entered the house, but found none of the men to murder. Mr. Holstead had two young daughters in the house, one of which secreted herself in a closet and remained throughout the whole transaction undiscovered. The other they caught and compelled to light a candle and attend them about the house in search of the Rebels, but without finding any, or offering any other abuse to the young lady (which was indeed a wonder).

When they could find none to wreak their vengeance upon, they cut open the knapsacks of the guard and strewed the Indian meal about the floor, laughing at the poverty of the Yankee soldiery, who had nothing but hog's fodder, as they termed it, to eat. After they had done all the mischief they could in the house, they proceeded to the barn and drove off five or six head of Mr. Holstead's young cattle, took them down upon the point and killed them, and went off in their boats that had come across from the island for that purpose, to their den among the British.

There was another young man belonging to the guard on his post at the extremity of the point. When the Refugees came down to embark, they cut off this man's retreat, there being a sunken marsh on each side of the point covered with dry flags and reeds. When he challenged them, they answered him the same as they did the other sentinel. But he paid as little attention to their threats as the other had done, although apparently in a much worse situation, but fired his musket and sprang into the marsh among the reeds, where he sunk to his middle in the mud, and there remained unperceived till they went off, and thus preserved his life.

Such maneuvers the British continued to exhibit the whole time we were stationed here, but could never do any other damage to us than killing poor Twist (the name of the young man). Unfortunate young man! I could not restrain my tears when I saw him next day, with his breast like a sieve caused by the wounds. He lost his own life by endeavoring to save the lives of others; massacred by his own countrymen, who ought to have been fighting in the common cause of the country instead of murdering him.

I have been more particular in relating this circumstance, that the reader may be informed what people there were in the times of the Revolution. Mr. Holstead told me that almost the whole of his neighborhood had joined the enemy and that his next-door neighbor was in this very party. There was a large number in this place and its vicinity by the name of Hetfield, who were notorious rascals. A certain captain of militia, resident in these parts, who upon some occasion had business to transact within the reach of these miscreants, they caught and hanged him up without ceremony, judge, or jury. General Washington demanded the perpetrators of this infernal deed of the British authorities in New York, but they declined complying with his demand. He, therefore, selected a British captain, a prisoner, a son—and I believe an only son—of an opulent English lady, and put him in close confinement, threatening to execute him unless the murderer were given up to justice. But his distressed mother by her strong maternal intercession with the king and court of France, prevailed on them; and their remonstrances to General Washington, joined with his own benevolent feelings, so far wrought upon him that he set the captain at liberty, and thus these murderous villains escaped the punishment due to their infernal deeds.[7]

We remained on this tedious duty ... till the middle of May, when we were relieved, but we remained at our quarters 8 or 10 days after that. Our duty was not quite so hard now as it had been, but that faithful companion, hunger, stuck as close to us as ever; he was a faithful associate, I will not say friend, for indeed poverty is no friend, nor has *he* many admirers, though he has an extensive

---

[7] Holstead no doubt told Martin about the relatives and friends of the ruthless eastern New Jersey loyalist, John Smith Hetfield. Holstead could not have been the original source of the story that followed, since these events played themselves out in 1782. The patriot militia captain was Joshua Huddy, who was captured in March 1782 at Toms River, New Jersey, and summarily hanged three weeks later on the bogus charge of having killed a loyalist refugee named Philip White. Appalled by such barbaric handling of a helpless prisoner of war, Washington insisted that General Clinton turn over the person responsible to stand trial for murder. Clinton refused, at which point Washington had a lottery held among British prisoners whose rank was similar to Huddy's. The unfortunate winner was Captain Charles Asgill, about 20 years old and the scion of a powerful English noble family. Washington, with backing from his general officers, intended to hang him in retaliation for Huddy's death. Fortunately for Asgill, he had the protection of a written agreement that stipulated how he was to be treated as a prisoner. To have executed him would have represented a major breach of rules governing the conduct of civilized warfare. So Washington hesitated, even as Lady Asgill appealed far and wide for her innocent son's release. Asgill's protected status in combination with his mother's entreaties finally resulted in his release.

acquaintance. The soldiers were well acquainted with him during the whole period of the Revolutionary War....

We left Westfield about the 25th of May and went to Basking Ridge to our old winter cantonments. We did not reoccupy the huts which we built, but some others that the troops had left, upon what account I have forgotten. Here the monster Hunger still attended us. He was not to be shaken off by any efforts we could use, for here was the old story of starving, as rife as ever. We had entertained some hopes that when we had left the lines and joined the main army, we should fare a little better, but we found that there was no betterment in the case. For several days after we rejoined the army, we got a little musty bread and a little beef about every other day, but this lasted only a short time and then we got nothing at all. The men were now exasperated beyond endurance; they could not stand it any longer; they saw no other alternative but to starve to death, or break up the army, give all up, and go home. This was a hard matter for the soldiers to think upon. They were truly patriotic; they loved their country, and they had already suffered everything short of death in its cause; and now, after such extreme hardships to give up all was too much, but to starve to death was too much also. What was to be done? Here was the army starved and naked, and there their country sitting still and expecting the army to do notable things while fainting from sheer starvation. All things considered, the army was not to be blamed. Reader, suffer what we did and you will say so too.

We had borne as long as human nature could endure, and to bear longer we considered folly. Accordingly, one pleasant day the men spent the most of their time upon the parade growling like sore-headed dogs. At evening roll call they began to show their dissatisfaction by snapping at the officers and acting contrary to their orders. After their dismissal from the parade, the officers went as usual to their quarters, except the adjutant, who happened to remain, giving details for next day's duty to the orderly sergeants, or some other business, when the men (none of whom had left the parade) began to make him sensible that they had something in train. He said something that did not altogether accord with the soldiers' ideas of propriety, one of the men retorted; the adjutant called him a mutinous rascal, or some such epithet, and then left the parade. This man, then stamping the butt of his musket upon the ground, as much as to say, I am in a passion, called out, "Who will parade with me?" The whole regiment immediately fell in and formed.[8]

We had made no plans for our future operations, but while we were consulting how to proceed, the 4th Regiment, which lay on our left, formed and came and paraded with us. We now concluded to go in a body to the other two regiments that belonged to our brigade and induce them to join with us.[9] These regiments lay 40 or 50 rods in front of us, with a brook and bushes between. We did not wish to have anyone in particular to command, lest he might be singled out for a court martial to exercise its demency upon; we therefore gave directions to the drummers to give certain signals on the drums; at the first signal we shouldered our arms, at the second we faced, at the third we began our march to join with the other two regiments, and went off with music playing.

By this time our officers had obtained knowledge of our military maneuvering, and some of them had run across the brook by a nearer way than we had taken (it being now quite dark) and informed the officers of those regiments of our approach and supposed intentions. The officers ordered their men to parade as quick as possible *without* arms. When that was done, they stationed a camp guard, that happened to be near at hand, between the men and their huts, which prevented them from entering and taking their arms, which they were very anxious to do. Colonel Meigs[10] of the 6th Regiment exerted himself to prevent his men from obtaining their arms until he received a severe wound in his side by a

[8]   What follows is an invaluable account of the Connecticut line mutiny of May 25, 1780. The primary spark was a winter's worth of inadequate provisions, especially food, a reflection of yet another breakdown in the Continental army's supply system reminiscent of the Valley Forge days. Even more serious mutinies were yet to come, particularly the uprisings of the Pennsylvania and New Jersey lines in January 1781.

[9]   Colonel John Durkee commanded the 4th regiment. The two other regiments were the 3rd and the 6th under colonels Samuel Wyllys and Return Jonathan Meigs respectively.

[10]   Connecticut patriot Return Jonathan Meigs assumed command of the 6th regiment in September 1777. He was in charge of Connecticut soldiers assigned to General Anthony Wayne's Corps of Light Infantry in 1779 and gained honor for himself as well as his troops in the patriot victory at Stony Point. His accidental wounding during the mutiny at Jockey Hollow may have blunted the agitation, or so Washington believed. Retiring from the service in early 1781, Meigs later was active in the development of the Ohio country and in working for harmonious relations between Indians and white settlers.

bayonet in the scuffle, which cooled his courage at the time. He said he had always considered himself the soldier's friend and thought the soldiers regarded him as such, but had reason now to conclude he might be mistaken. Colonel Meigs was truly an excellent man and a brave officer. The man, whoever he was that wounded him, doubtless had no particular grudge against him; it was dark and the wound was given, it is probable, altogether unintentionally....

When we found the officers had been too crafty for us, we returned with grumbling instead of music, the officers following in the rear growling in concert. One of the men in the rear calling out, "Halt in front," the officers seized upon him like wolves on a sheep and dragged him out of the ranks, intending to make an example of him for being a "mutinous rascal"; but the bayonets of the men pointing at their breasts, as thick as hatchel[11] teeth, compelled them quickly to relinquish their hold of him. We marched back to our own parade and then formed again. The officers now began to coax us to disperse to our quarters, but that had no more effect upon us than their threats. One of them slipped away into the bushes, and after a short time returned, counterfeiting to have come directly from headquarters. Said he, "There is good news for you, boys, there has just arrived a large drove of cattle for the army." But this piece of finesse would not avail. All the answer he received for his labor was, "Go and butcher them," or some such slight expression.

The lieutenant colonel of the 4th Regiment now came on to the parade. He could persuade *his* men, he said, to go peaceably to their quarters. After a good deal of palaver he ordered them to shoulder their arms, but the men taking no notice of him or his order he fell into a violent passion, threatening them with the bitterest punishment if they did not immediately obey his orders. After spending a whole quiver of the arrows of his rhetoric, he again ordered them to shoulder their arms, but he met with the same success that he did at the first trial. He therefore gave up the contest as hopeless and left us and walked off to his quarters, chewing the cud of resentment all the way, and how much longer I neither knew nor cared. The rest of the officers, after they found that they were likely to meet with no better success than the colonel, walked off likewise to their huts.

While we were under arms, the Pennsylvania troops, who lay not far from us, were ordered under arms and marched off their parades

---

[11] A tool with long, sharp iron teeth used to separate the coarse from the fibrous strands of flax and hemp.

upon, as they were told, a secret expedition. They had surrounded us, unknown to either us or themselves (except the officers). At length ... they inquired of some of the stragglers, what was going on among the Yankees? Being informed that they had mutinied on account of the scarcity of provisions, "Let us join them," said they, "let us join the Yankees; they are good fellows, and have no notion of lying here like fools and starving." Their officers needed no further hinting; the troops were quickly ordered back to their quarters from fear that they would join in the same song with the Yankees. We knew nothing of all this for some time afterwards.

After our officers had left us to our own option, we dispersed to our huts and laid by our arms of our own accord, but the worm of hunger gnawing so keen kept us from being entirely quiet. We therefore still kept upon the parade in groups, venting our spleen at our country and government, then at our officers, and then at ourselves for our imbecility in staying there and starving in detail for an ungrateful people who did not care what became of us, so they could enjoy themselves while we were keeping a cruel enemy from them.

While we were thus venting our gall against we knew not who, Colonel Stewart[12] of the Pennsylvania line, with two or three other officers of that line, came to us and questioned us respecting our unsoldierlike conduct (as he termed it). We told him he needed not to be informed of the cause of our present conduct, but that we had borne till we considered further forbearance pusillanimity [cowardice]; that the times, instead of mending, were growing worse; and finally that we were determined not to bear or forbear much longer. We were unwilling to desert the cause of our country, when in distress; that we knew her cause involved our own; but what signified our perishing in the act of saving her, when that very act would inevitably destroy us, and she must finally perish with us.

[12] Walter Stewart, like Meigs, was an officer admired by rank-and-file troops. Only about 24 years old at the time of the Connecticut mutiny, young Stewart had moved quickly through the ranks, especially after serving as an aide-de-camp to General Horatio Gates in 1776. In June 1777 he assumed command of a Pennsylvania state regiment, which fought with distinction at Brandywine, and his reward for performing so ably at Monmouth in late June 1778 was command of a Continental regiment, the 2nd Pennsylvania. Stewart was also known as a convincing speaker, and some contemporaries referred to him as the most handsome man in the Continental army.

"Why do you not go to your officers," said he, "and complain in a regular manner?" We told him we had repeatedly complained to them, but they would not hear us. "Your officers," said he, "are gentlemen; they *will* attend to you. I know them; they cannot refuse to hear you. But," said he, "your officers suffer as much as you do. We all suffer. The officers have no money to purchase supplies with any more than the private men have, and if there is nothing in the public store we must fare as hard as you. I have no other resources than you have to depend upon; I had not a sixpence to purchase a partridge that was offered me the other day. Besides," said he, "you know not how much you injure your own characters by such conduct. You Connecticut troops have won immortal honor to yourselves the winter past by your perseverance, patience, and bravery, and now you are shaking it off at your heels. But I will go and see your officers, and talk with them myself." He went, but what the result was I never knew. This Colonel Stewart was an excellent officer, much beloved and respected by the troops of the line he belonged to. He possessed great personal beauty; the Philadelphia ladies styled him *the Irish Beauty*.

Our stir did us some good in the end, for we had provisions directly after, so we had no great cause for complaint for some time.

About this time there were about 3,000 men ordered out for a particular field day, for the Prussian General Baron de Steuben to exercise his maneuvering functions upon. We marched off our regimental parades at dawn of day and went three or four miles to Morristown, to a fine plain where we performed a variety of military evolutions. We were furnished with a plenty of blank cartridges, had 8 or 10 fieldpieces, and made a great noise, if nothing more. About one or two o'clock we ceased and were supplied with a gill of rum each. Having had nothing to eat since the night before, the liquor took violent hold, and there were diverse queer tricks exhibited both by officers and men.... This day was nearly equal to the whiskey scrape at the Schuylkill in 1777.[13]

---

[13]   The date of this event was April 24, a month before the Connecticut mutiny. Washington had called for a formal review to honor Chevalier Anne-César de la Luzerne, who had arrived in America late in 1779 as the new French minister to the United States. Luzerne may not have witnessed the drunken deportment of officers and soldiers after the review.

In the month of June 5,000 British and Hessian troops advanced into New Jersey, burnt several houses in Elizabethtown and the Presbyterian meetinghouse and most of the village of Springfield. They also barbarously murdered, by shooting, Mrs. Caldwell, the wife of the minister of that place. What their further intentions were could not be ascertained by our commanders. Sometimes it was conjectured that they were aiming at a quantity of public stores deposited in Morristown; sometimes that it was for a diversion in favor of their main army, by endeavoring to amuse us till their forces could push up the North [Hudson] River and attack West Point. Our army was accordingly kept in a situation to relieve either in case of an attack.[14] While we remained in this situation our army was infested by spies from the British; I saw three of those vermin one day hanging on one gallows. The enemy soon after recoiled into their shell again at New York....

Another affair happened soon after this which did not set very well on my stomach at the time. I had been on a detached party for four or five days and had had nothing to eat for at least eight and forty hours of the latter part of the time. When I came to camp there was nothing there; I strolled off to where some butchers were killing cattle, as I supposed for the general officers (for they must

[14] Late in 1779 General Clinton set sail for South Carolina with an expeditionary force numbering nearly 9,000 soldiers. His objective was to reduce the principal port city of Charleston, which he intended to use as a base of operations in reestablishing royal authority in the South. Before embarking, Clinton placed General Wilhelm, Baron von Knyphausen, in temporary command of British operations back in New York.

Late in May when Knyphausen received intelligence about the Continental army's mutinous disposition as well as reports of growing loyalist sentiment among the New Jersey populace, he decided upon a demonstration of force to see whether the presence of the king's troops might provoke a renunciation of the rebellion by Jersey's civilians and Washington's soldiers alike.

Knyphausen moved into New Jersey on June 7, 1780. That day his force looted and burned the town of Connecticut Farms (modern-day Union), just west of Elizabethtown. One of his soldiers, while passing through the town, shot dead the wife of the Reverend James Caldwell. These actions infuriated New Jersey's patriots, who reacted by persistently harassing Knyphausen's troops. On June 23 the Hessian general led an attack on Springfield, another two and a half miles from Connecticut Farms. A rebel force under General Nathanael Greene offered stout resistance, and Knyphausen finally withdrew to Staten Island, but not before his troops had pillaged and burned nearly every home in Springfield. Knyphausen's expedition thus failed completely in obtaining its objectives and also represented the last major British thrust into New Jersey during the war.

have victuals, let the poor men fare as they would), and by some means procured an old ox's liver. I then went home and soon had a quantity of it in my kettle. The more I seethed it the harder it grew, but I soon filled my empty stomach with it, and, it being night, I turned in; I had not slept long before I awoke, feeling ... "dreadfully."

I worried it out till morning, when, as soon as I thought I could call upon the doctors without too much disturbing their honors, I applied to one for relief. He gave me a large dose of tartar emetic, the usual remedy in the army for all disorders, even sore eyes, though he could not have given me a better one for my then present malady. He gave me ample directions how to proceed, a part of which was to take one half or two thirds of the potion and wait a given time, and if it did not operate then to swallow the remainder. It did not work till I had the whole in my crop, nor then neither. I waited some time for it, but growing impatient, I wandered off into the fields and bushes to see what effect exercise would have; I then sat down upon a log, or stone, or something else and discharged the hard junks of liver like grapeshot from a fieldpiece. I had no water or any other thing to ease my retchings. O, I thought I *must* die in good earnest. The liver still kept coming, and I looked at every heave for my own liver to come next, but that happened to be too well fastened to part from its moorings. Perhaps the reader will think this a trifling matter, happening in the ordinary course of things, but I think it a "suffering," and not a small one neither "of a Revolutionary soldier."

After the British had retreated to New York, our army marched for West Point. We passed through the Highlands by the Clove, a remarkable chasm in the mountains, and came out on the bank of the Hudson River at a place called Buttermilk Falls, where a small stream falls into the river over a high craggy bank, forming a pretty cascade....[15] The Connecticut forces crossed the river to the eastern side and encamped opposite to West Point.... It was now very hot weather, being the latter part of June....

Soon after we were encamped here I was sent off with a working party to work upon some fortifications on Constitution

---

[15]   The Clove extended northeastward into New York from New Jersey's Ramapo Mountains. The rugged valley, which represented a natural pathway in moving toward West Point, was also a notorious hangout for parties of rebels and loyalists who were mostly bandits that preyed on travelers and straggling soldiers. Buttermilk Falls may be found just south of West Point.

Island,[16] a mile or two higher up the river. We ... were to remain there a week. Our duty was chiefly wheeling dirt upon a stone building intended for a magazine. We had to wheel to the top of the wall, which was about 20 feet high upon a way 2 planks wide, and in the passage we had to cross a chasm in the rocks 30 or 40 feet wide and perhaps as many deep. None of us happened to take a dive into it, but it often made my head swim when crossing it at such a rate, and I thought it would not be strange if some of us should feel the bottom before we left there. From the planks, which we wheeled upon, to the bottom of the hole could not be less than 60 feet; if anyone had fallen into it he would have received his discharge from the army without further trouble....

After we had been two or three days at this invigorating business, the troops were inspected by General Steuben. When he found out our situation, he ordered us off immediately. "You may as well knock those men on the head," said he, "as keep them there; they will die if kept there much longer, and they can do no more if you knock their brains out." He had more sense than our officers, but they did not feel the hardships which we had to undergo, and of course cared but little if anything at all about us. We were called off, and I never was so glad to get clear of any duty as I was to get clear of that. A state prison would be preferable to it, for there one might chance to get something to eat, or at least to drink.

And now there was to be a material change in my circumstances, which in the long run was much in my favor. There was a small corps to be raised by enlistments, and in case of the failure of that, by drafts from the line. These men were called "Sappers and Miners," to be attached to the engineer's department.[17] I had known

---

[16]   Located on the east side of the Hudson River across from West Point, the fortifications on the island formed an integral part of an elaborate defensive network designed to block any attempted movement of British warships or troops up the river and beyond the Highlands. In April 1778 the patriots stretched a chain of about 130 tons, which included the weight of its anchors, some five hundred yards across the Hudson to Constitution Island in further strengthening the West Point defenses.

[17]   Washington approved the concept of a Corps of Sappers and Miners in July 1780. The purpose was to train a select body of soldiers in such basic engineering matters as the construction of field fortifications and the maintenance and repair of roads. These troops could then direct fatigue parties in various tasks, everything from the preparation of fieldworks to the digging of tunnels and entrenchments—the latter were known as "saps"—should siege operations become necessary. That Martin was chosen for service with the Sappers and Miners demonstrates the regard his officers had for his native intelligence as well as their positive perception of him as a soldier who could be trusted with significant responsibility.

of this for some time before, but never had a thought of belonging
to it, although I had heard our major (to whose company I belonged)
tell some of our officers ... that if there was a draft from our regiment, he intended I should go; although, he added, he did not wish
to part with me. I, however, thought no more about it till a captain
of that corps applied for a draft of one man from each regiment
throughout the whole army present. The captain was personally
acquainted with our major and told him he would like to have him
furnish him with a man from the regiment that he knew was qualified for a non-commissioned officer;[18] the major then pitched upon
me. How far he was to be justified in his choice the reader may,
perhaps, be enabled to judge by the construction of this present
work; I give him my free consent to exercise his judgment upon it.

I was accordingly transferred to this corps and bid a farewell
forever to my old comrades, as it respected any further associating
with them, or sharing in their sufferings or pleasures. I immediately
went off with this (now my) captain[19] and the other men drafted
from our brigade, and joined the corps in an old meetinghouse at
the Peekskill. It was after dark when we arrived there. I had now
got among a new set, who were to a man entire strangers to me.
I had of course to form new acquaintances, but I was not long in
doing that; I had a pretty free use of my tongue and was sometimes
apt to use it when there was no occasion for it. However, I soon
found myself at home with them. We were all young men and therefore easy to get acquainted.

I found nothing more here for belly timber than I had in the line,
and got nothing to eat till the second day after I had joined the
corps.... We then drew, if I remember right, two days rations of our
good old diet, salt shad; and as we had not as yet associated ourselves into regular messes, as is usual in the army, each man had his

---

[18] Soldiers holding rank above privates, such as corporals and sergeants, and below
company-grade commissioned officers, such as lieutenants and captains. Non-
commissioned officers have the authority to command privates in the execution of
specific assignments.

[19] Martin's new captain was David Bushnell, who grew up in Connecticut and
attended Yale College. Known today as the inventor of the submarine, Bushnell
designed and built a heavy wooden vessel, the *American Turtle*, that could maneuver
under water. During 1776 and 1777 he demonstrated his craft on various occasions
but failed to do any damage to targeted British war vessels. Even though some persons considered him a crackpot, Bushnell possessed solid engineering skills that
made him a worthy choice to head the Corps of Sappers and Miners.

fish divided out by himself. We were on the green before the meet-inghouse, and there were several cows feeding about the place. I went into the house to get something to put my fish into, or some other business, and stayed longer than I intended, or rather ought to have done, for when I came out again, one of the cows was just finishing her meal on my shad; the last I saw of it was the tail of a fish sticking out of the side of her mouth. I was vexed enough to have eaten the weight of it off her carcass, but she took care of that, and I had another opportunity (if well improved) of mortify-ing my body by fasting two days longer; but I got something among the men, as poorly as they were off, to sustain nature till I could get more by some means or other. Such shifts were nothing strange to us.

This Corps of Miners was reckoned an honorable one; it con-sisted of three companies. All the officers were required to be acquainted with the sciences, and it was desirable to have as intel-ligent young men as could be procured to compose it, although some of us fell considerably short of perfection. Agreeable to the arrangement between my former commander and my new captain, I was appointed a sergeant in this corps,[20] which was as high an office as I ever obtained in the army; and I had some doubts in my own mind at the time whether I was altogether qualified for that. However, I was a sergeant, and I think I *did* use my best abilities to perform the duties of the office according to my best knowledge and judgment. Indeed, I can say at this late hour of my life, that my conscience never did, and I trust never will, accuse me of any failure in my duty to my country, but, on the contrary, I always fulfilled my engagements to her, however she failed in fulfilling hers with me. The case was much like that of a loyal and faithful husband and a light-heeled wanton of a wife. But I forgive her and hope she will do better in [the] future.

Soon after I had joined this corps, the army moved down on the west side of the Hudson to Orangetown, commonly called by the inhabitants of those parts, Tappan (pronounced *Tap-pawn*).[21] Just before arriving at our encamping ground, we halted in the road an hour or two. Some four or five of our men, knowing that the regi-ments to which they formerly belonged were near, slipped off for a

[20] Surviving Revolutionary War records indicate that Martin's highest rank was that of a corporal. Such records are notoriously inaccurate or incomplete.
[21] On the west side of the Hudson River contiguous with the border running between New York and New Jersey.

few minutes to see their old messmates. When we came to march again, they not having returned, I was ordered to remain with their arms and knapsacks till they came and then bring them on and join the corps again. I accordingly waited an hour or two before they all returned. As soon as I had got them all together we set off; but the troops arriving and passing in almost every direction, I knew not where to go to find our corps.

After much trouble and vexation (being constantly interrogated by the passing officers, who we were, and how we came to be behind our troops), I concluded, that as most or all the troops had passed us, to stay where I then was and wait the coming up of the baggage of our troops, thinking that the guard or drivers might have directions where to find them. Our baggage happening to be quite in the rear, while we were waiting we had an opportunity to see the baggage of the army pass. When that of the middle states passed us, it was truly amusing to see the number and habiliments of those attending it; of all specimens of human beings, this group capped the whole. A caravan of wild beasts could bear no comparison with it. There was "Tag, Rag and Bobtail"; "some in rags and some in jags," but none "in velvet gowns." Some with two eyes, some with one, and some I believe with none at all. They "beggared all description"; their dialect too was as confused as their bodily appearance was odd and disgusting. There was the Irish and Scotch brogue, murdered English, flat insipid Dutch, and some lingoes which would puzzle a philosopher to tell whether they belonged to this world or some "undiscovered country." I was glad to see the tail end of the train and waited with impatience for the arrival of our baggage, which soon after made its appearance; but the men with the wagons knew no better than myself where to go. We, however, proceeded and soon after met one of the sergeants coming to meet and conduct us to where our people were, which was at Dobbs Ferry,[22] and about three miles from any part of the rest of the army. Most of the artillery belonging to the army was at the same place....

Soon after our arrival here, a British brig [the *Vulture*] passed up the river, the same that conveyed the unfortunate Major André to his bane. Poor man! He had better have stayed where he was better acquainted.... One night, the British brig came down the river with

---

[22]   To reach Dobbs Ferry, Martin had to cross over to the east bank of the Hudson River.

her precious cargo—Arnold—on board.[23] There were several shots discharged at her as she passed the blockhouse, but she went by without paying us much attention. The next day it was reported that General Arnold had deserted; I should as soon have thought West Point had deserted as he, but I was soon convinced that it was true.

Had I possessed the power of foreknowledge, I might twice have put Arnold asleep without anyone knowing it and saved the life of perhaps a better man, and my country much trouble and disgrace. The first time was at the Peekskill in a barn just before André came to his quarters and while their clandestine negotiation was in progress. I was upon a guard. "There are men," says Shakespeare, "who in their sleep mutter all their conceits." Such a one was Arnold, and therefore afraid to sleep near anyone lest he should "babble his conceits" in his sleep. He ordered me and my guard out of the barn that he might have his bed upon the floor. I was so put

---

[23]   General Benedict Arnold, a native of Connecticut, was as valuable a general officer as Washington had in the Continental army. During 1777 he was instrumental in achieving the major American victory over the army of General John Burgoyne at Saratoga, New York. Arnold, however, too often felt slighted by the lack of recognition accorded him for his many contributions to the cause of liberty. His growing disillusionment and resentment spurred him to begin a treasonous correspondence with the British in May 1779.

In 1778 dashing, young Major John André became an aide-de-camp to General Clinton in charge of the general's spying operations. As such, he served as Arnold's chief correspondent. André made clear how anxious the British were to capture West Point, and in the summer of 1780 Arnold maneuvered himself into overall command of the Highlands defenses. He was now perfectly placed to help the British satisfy their objective, for which Arnold expected to receive a general's commission in the British army and a handsome stipend as compensation for the property holdings that he would have confiscated when patriot authorities discovered his treachery.

On September 20 André, now elevated to the post of adjutant general or chief administrator of Clinton's army, sailed up the Hudson River aboard the sloop-of-war *Vulture* to meet secretly with Arnold and complete all arrangements. Three days later André was taken prisoner near Tarrytown as he tried to make a land passage through patriot lines. On his person he carried documents incriminating to Arnold. Had André been dressed in his uniform, he would have received courteous treatment as a prized prisoner, but he was wearing civilian clothing, which left him open to the charge of spying against the Americans. The penalty for such a crime was death by hanging.

On the morning of September 25 when Arnold learned of André's capture, he fled down the Hudson from his headquarters across the river from West Point. Once he reached the *Vulture*, the captain weighed anchor and easily evaded the rebel gunfire coming from Dobbs Ferry in sailing back downriver to New York City.

out of my bias at the time that had I known what plans he had in his head, I should have needed but little persuasion to have had a reckoning with him.

The other time was but three or four days before his desertion. I met him upon the road a little distance from Dobbs Ferry; he was then taking his observations and examining the roads. I thought that he was upon some deviltry. We met at a notch of the roads and I observed he stopped, and sitting upon his horse, seemed minutely to examine each road. I could not help taking notice of him, and thought it strange to see him quite alone in such a lone place. He looked guilty, and well he might, for Satan was in as full possession of him at that instant as ever he was of Judas; it only wanted a musket ball to have driven him out. I had been acquainted with Arnold from my childhood and never had too good an opinion of him....

Our people had a number of spy boats lying a little distance above the ferry. One night one of these boats went down the river and anchored not far from the western shore, which was there very high, placed a sentinel in the boat, and lay down to rest. A British boat getting intelligence of them, rowed up with muffled oars, keeping close under the highland in the shadow of the mountains (the moon being in that quarter), till they had got above them, and then came directly down upon them. The sentinel immediately roused up the men in the boat. One of them, having his musket charged with buckshot (Yankee peas, as the British used to call them), challenged them with, "Who comes there?" They answered, "We will quickly let you know." The man in our boat ... gave them the contents of his musket, which caused a bitter lamentation in the British boat. Our people had now cut their cable and got to their oars. They rowed a small distance and lay to for the enemy's boat to come up, when they all fired into her and again sprang to their oars. Our boat could row much faster than the other, which still followed her. They kept up a constant fire upon each other till they got nearly up to the ferry, where there were a few troops encamped, who running down upon the bank of the river prepared to give the English boat a seasoning; but the enemy, seeing them, gave over the chase and went back down the river. What execution our people did among them was not known, but one of our men received a musket ball directly in the middle of his forehead, which passed out behind his head. This was done about 11 o'clock at night, and I saw him at 9 the next morning, alive, and breathing just like a man in a sound sleep; he died in about an hour after.

About this time Major André was brought from the Highlands to headquarters where he was examined, condemned, and executed. I saw him before his execution, but was on duty on that day and could not attend; otherwise I should. He was an interesting character. There has been a great deal said about him, but he was but a man, and no better, nor had he better qualifications than the brave Captain Hale, whom the British commander caused to be executed as a spy upon Long Island in 1776 without the shadow of a trial, denying him the use of a Bible or the assistance [of] a clergyman in his last moments, and destroying the letters he had written to his widowed mother and other relations. André had every indulgence allowed him that could be granted with propriety. See the contrast—let all who pity André so much look at it and be silent.[24]

We were frequently alarmed while lying at Dobbs Ferry. Being so few and at a distance from the main army, we had constantly to be on the lookout, but never happened to come in contact with the enemy, although they very frequently made us believe we should....

We lay at Dobbs Ferry till the latter part of the month of October, when we marched to West Point for winter quarters. I left this place with regret, more so than any other during my continuance in the army. It was upon an account which I need not mention. Many young men have doubtless felt the same upon similar occasions. If they have, they know my feelings at the time I speak of. But that time has long since gone by and my affections with it, both "gone with the years beyond the flood," never more to return.

We marched for West Point. At the Peekskill we procured bateaux to convey ourselves and baggage up the river to the Point, where we arrived in safety and went into the old barracks until new ones could be built for us, which we immediately commenced. We had to go six miles down the river, and there hew the timber, then carry it on our shoulders to the river, and then raft it to West Point. We, however, soon completed this part of the business ourselves when

---

[24] General Nathanael Greene served as president of the military hearing board that met at Tappan, New York, and condemned André to death after a day-long trial. He was hanged on October 2. By comparison, the patriot martyr Nathan Hale, who went to Long Island in civilian clothing to gather information on British troop arrangements, was peremptorily hanged on direct orders from General Howe. Hale's memorable last words were: "I only regret that I have but one life to lose for my country."

the carpenters took it in hand, and by New Year's Day they were ready to receive us; till then, we had been living in the old barracks, where there were rats enough, had they been men, to garrison 20 West Points.

Our barracks being completed and we safely stowed away in them, I shall here conclude the campaign of 1780.

Chapter VII

Campaign of 1781

JPM and his comrades continue to challenge British and loyalist forces in the region north of New York City, then travel south to participate in the decisive Yorktown campaign in Virginia, resulting in the capture of the army of General Charles, Lord Cornwallis.

> I saw the plundering British bands,
> Invade the fair Virginian lands.
> I saw great WASHINGTON advance
> With Americans and troops of France;
> I saw the haughty Britons yield
> And stack their muskets on the field.

Nothing material occurred to me till the month of February, nor anything then *very* material. About the 20th of that month I took it into my head to apply to my captain for a recommendation to our colonel for a furlough, that I might once more visit my friends, for I saw no likelihood that the war would ever end. The captain told me that the colonel was about sending a non-commissioned officer into Connecticut after two men belonging to our corps who had been furloughed but had stayed beyond the time allowed them, and that he would endeavor to have me sent on this business, and that after I had sent the delinquents to camp, I might tarry a space at home. Accordingly, I soon after received a passport, signed by the colonel, in these terms, "Permit the bearer,—— ——, to pass into the country after some deserters, and to come back." The time, "to come back," not being fixed, I set off, thinking I would regulate that as would best suit my own convenience.

When I arrived at home I found that my good old grandmother was gone to her long home, and my grandsire gone 40 miles back into the country to his son's, and I never saw him afterwards. My sister was keeping the house, and I was glad to see her, as I had not seen her for several years. There was likewise a neighbor's daughter there, who kept as much as she possibly could with my sister and generally slept with her, whom I had seen more than once in the course of my life. Their company and conversation made up for the absence of my grandparents, it being a little more congenial to my age and feelings.

I stayed at home two or three days to recruit [rest] after my journey, when a man belonging to our company (going home on furlough) called and informed me that one of the men I was after had arrived at camp, and as he should pass through the town where the other resided, he agreed to do my errand for me. With this arrangement I was much pleased, as it would save me about 60 miles travel in all, going and coming, and I gave him a dollar to help him along, which was all the money I had. He then went on and did as he agreed. I had nothing now to do but to recreate myself, for as the time of my return to the army was indefinitely set, I did not trouble myself about it.

I spent my time as agreeable as possible among the young people of my acquaintance, for I thought I was old enough to choose my own method of employing my time, being now nearly 21 years of age. I did, indeed, enjoy myself about 10 days as agreeably as ever I did in the same space of time in my life; but as I had no set time to return to camp, I was loath to trespass upon my good colonel's indulgence, and therefore began to think about my return. And as there was two men, one an old associate and the other a private citizen who were going to camp, I thought for company's sake I would go with them, and accordingly did; but I confess that I never left my home with so much regret before....

When I arrived within sight and hearing of the army, or rather the garrison of West Point, it again harrowed up my melancholy feelings that had in a manner subsided on my journey. But upon reaching the barracks where I had left my companions, ... I found our barracks entirely unoccupied, our men all gone, and not a soul could tell me where. What to do I knew not; I had a great mind to set off for home again, but at length concluded that I would try a little longer to find which way the men had gone.

I therefore went to the issuing commissary of the garrison, who was my quondam [former] schoolmate, and he soon informed me that they had gone to Virginia with General Lafayette;[1] I was thunderstruck at this intelligence and blamed myself tenfold for leaving home so soon. The commissary, observing my chagrin, told me that my captain and 8 or 10 of our people were in the country about 20 miles off, where they were undergoing the operation of the smallpox. The next day I went out to them and remained with them two or three days, but that would not do for me. I told the captain that I would go after the men. He said I might act my pleasure as it respected that, but that he should advise me to stay with him till he had got through with the smallpox and the other men that were with him had recovered, and then they should all go together. But that would not content me; I was as uneasy as a fish out of the water. The captain then told me that if I was determined to follow the corps that my arms were with him, and I might take them and go. I took them and went back to West Point to the commissary, where I procured three or four rations of provisions and an order for five or six more, in case I could find any commissary on the way. The commissary filled my canteen with liquor, and thus equipped I set off on my journey alone, not expecting to find the men within less than 400 miles.

I encountered nothing very material on my journey, except it were fatigue and some want, until I arrived at Annapolis in Maryland.[2] There I found what I had so long sought after, the Sappers and Miners; they were returning to West Point. They were on board vessels and were blocked in at Annapolis by some British ships at the mouth of the river. Shortly after I joined them an opportunity offered, and we escaped with our little fleet by sweeping out in a dark night, and went up the bay.

We went directly on to West Point and took possession of our new barracks again and remained there till sometime in the month of May, when we (with the rest of the army in the Highlands) moved

[1] In late December 1780, General Clinton sent a detachment of 1,600 raiders to Virginia under the command of his new brigadier general, Benedict Arnold. Their mission was to destroy military supplies and related goods that Virginians could otherwise dispatch to North and South Carolina to support General Nathanael Greene's patriot troops, who were there dueling with British forces under General Charles, Lord Cornwallis. Once apprized of the damage being wrought by Arnold's raiders, Washington called upon Lafayette to assemble a special detachment of 1,200 light troops and proceed south to help relieve Virginia. Martin's comrades were initially part of this force.

[2] The capital of Maryland located on the west side of Chesapeake Bay at the mouth of the Severn River.

down and encamped at the Peekskill.[3] We remained here awhile
and then moved down near King's Bridge, 15 miles from New York.
A part of the army under the command of General Lincoln fell
down the river in bateaux and landed near old Fort Independence,
where they were soon attacked by the enemy, when a smart skirmish ensued; our corps, among others, immediately marched to
reinforce General Lincoln, but the action ceased, and the enemy
had retired before we could arrive.[4]

We lay on the ground we then occupied till after midnight, when
we advanced further down toward Morrisania.[5] At the dawn of day
we were in close neighborhood with a British redoubt and saw a
single horseman of the enemy reconnoitering us. We sent a platoon
of men around a hill to cut off his retreat, but mistrusting our
scheme he kept off out of our reach, although he was seen near us

---

[3] During the summer of 1780, General Jean Baptiste Donatien de Vimeur, the
Comte de Rochambeau, arrived in Rhode Island with 5,500 French troops ready
to fight in concert with American forces. To settle upon a plan of joint operations
for the 1781 campaign season, Washington met with Rochambeau at Wethersfield,
Connecticut, on May 22. In the absence of French naval support and with troop
numbers inferior to Clinton's, the two generals could not seriously consider
Washington's preferred objective of an all-out assault on New York City. Instead,
they agreed to conduct harassing operations, intending to push in British outposts
and cause Clinton to draw troops out of the South for the better protection of
his New York base. If he did so, the small patriot forces under generals Greene
and Lafayette would thereby gain much-needed relief. Should the French naval
fleet in the West Indies become available later in the campaign season, as
Rochambeau predicted, then broader-scale operations could be undertaken. Once
back in the Highlands, Washington concentrated his Continentals at Peekskill in
preparation for the joint offensive against Clinton's defenses on the northern
flank of New York City.

[4] Benjamin Lincoln of Massachusetts had performed valuable service during the
Saratoga campaign of 1777 in the defeat and capture of General John Burgoyne's
army. The Continental Congress placed him in charge of the southern theater in late
1778, but when Lincoln tried to ward off General Clinton's massive assault on
Charleston, South Carolina, during the spring of 1780, he suffered the indignity of
having to surrender his force. In late June 1781, Washington selected Lincoln to lead
800 troops in a boldly conceived strike against British defensive posts in the vicinity
of King's Bridge. Lincoln's column left Peekskill on the night of July 2–3 but ran into
unexpected enemy resistance and accomplished nothing. Old Fort Independence was
about four miles north of King's Bridge in the vicinity of Valentine's Hill.

[5] The large country estate of wealthy Lewis Morris, who served in the Continental
Congress, signed the Declaration of Independence, and functioned somewhat inac-
tively as a brigadier general of Westchester County militia. The estate was just north
of the point where the Harlem River branches northwest from the East River.

the greater part of the day "cutting his capers." As soon as it was fairly light we halted, and remained there all day and the night following.

The next morning we were joined by the French army from Rhode Island. Between us and the British redoubt there was a large deep gully. Our officers gave leave to as many as chose of our men to go over the gully and skirmish with the small parties of horsemen and footmen that kept patrolling from the redoubt to the gully, watching that none of us took shelter there to annoy them. Accordingly, a number of us kept disturbing their tranquility all day. Sometimes only 4 or 5 of us, sometimes 10 or 12, sometimes we would drive them into the redoubt, when they would reinforce and sally out and drive us all over the gully.

We kept up this sport till late in the afternoon, when myself and two others of our non-commissioned officers went down near the creek that makes the island upon which New York is situated.[6] The two other men that were with me stopped under an apple tree that stood in a small gully. I saw four or five British horsemen on their horses a considerable distance from me on the island. When they saw me they hallooed to me, calling me "a white-livered son of a b—h." (I was dressed in a white hunting shirt, or was without my coat, the latter, I think, as it was warm, and I wore a white under-dress.) We then became quite sociable; they advised me to come over to their side, and they would give me roast turkeys. I told them that they must wait till we left the coast clear, ere they could get into the country to steal them, as they used to do. They then said they would give me pork and 'lasses; and then inquired what execution some cannon had done, just before fired from the island, if they had not killed and wounded some of our men, and if we did not want help, as our surgeons were a pack of ignoramuses. I told them, in reply, that they had done no other execution with their guns than wounding a dog (which was the case), and as they and their surgeons were of the same species of animals, I supposed the poor wounded dog would account it a particular favor to have some of his own kind to assist him.

While we were carrying on this very polite conversation, I observed at a house on the island, in a different direction from the horsemen, a large number of men; but as they appeared to be a

---

[6] A curious description, but since Martin was in the vicinity of Morrisania he was most likely referring to the Harlem River.

motley group, I did not pay them much attention. Just as I was finishing the last sentence of my conversation with the horsemen, happening to cast my eyes toward the house (and very providentially too) I saw the flash of a gun. I instinctively dropped, as quick as a loon could dive, when the ball passed directly over me and lodged in the tree under which my comrades were standing. They saw the upper part of my gun drop as I fell, and said, "They have killed him." But they were mistaken. The people at the house set up a shouting, thinking they had done the job for one poor Yankee, but they were mistaken too, for I immediately rose up, and slapping my backsides to them, slowly moved off.

I do not know that I ever ran a greater risk for my life while I was in the army; indeed I could not, for I verily believe that if I had not "dove at the flash," the ball would have gone directly through my body, but "a miss is as good as a mile," says the proverb. I kept a bright lookout for them as I walked off. They sent another shot after me, and I again dropped, but that did not come so near me as the other, nor did they huzza again. These shots must have come from a rifle, as the distance was more than a quarter of a mile....

This afternoon I had like to have picked up another of their shots. I was standing with another of our men in a narrow gateway talking. A man from the redoubt had crept down behind an old battery near us and fired at us. The ball passed between our noses which were not more than a foot apart. The fellow walked off, and we sent him something to quicken his pace, but our shots did as little execution as his had done....

We lay all night upon the ground which we had occupied during the day. I was exceedingly tired, not having had a wink of sleep the preceding night, and had been on my feet during the last 24 hours; and this night to add to my comfort, I had to take charge of the quarter guard. I was allowed to get what rest I could consistently with our safety. I fixed my guard, placed two sentinels, and the remainder of us laid down. We were with our corps, who were all by dark snug in the arms of Morpheus;[7] the officers slept under a tree near us. My orders were if there was any stir or alarm during the night, to awaken the officers, and if any strangers attempted to pass, to stop them and bring them to the officers to be examined by them.

---

[7] The mythological god of dreams.

Sometime in the night, the sentry by the guard stopped two or three officers who were going past us. The sentry called me up, and I took the strangers to our officers, where they went through an examination and were then permitted to pass on; I returned to my guard and lay down till called up again to relieve the sentinels. All this time I was as unconscious of what was passing as though nothing of the kind had happened, nor could I remember anything of the matter when told of it the next day, so completely was I worn down by fatigue.

We now fell back a few miles and encamped (both Americans and French) at a place called Philipse Manor.[8] We then went to making preparations to lay siege to New York; we made fascines and gabions, the former bundles of brush, and the latter are made in this manner, viz.—after setting sticks in the ground in a circle about two feet or more in diameter, they are interwoven with small brush in form of a basket; they are then laid by for use, which is in entrenching. Three or more rows of them are set down together (breaking joints); the trench is then dug behind and the dirt thrown into them, which when full, together with the trench, forms a complete breastwork. The word is pronounced *gab-beens*. The fascines (pronounced *fas-heens*) are, as I said, bundles of brush bound snugly together, cut off straight at each end; they are of different lengths, from 5 to 12 feet. Their use is in building batteries and other temporary works.

We now expected soon to lay close siege to New York. Our Sappers and Miners were constantly employed with the engineers in front of the army, making preparations for the siege. One day I was sent down toward the enemy with a corporal and 12 men upon a reconnoitering expedition, the engineers having heard that there was a party of Refugees, or Cowboys, somewhere not far from their premises. My orders were to go to a certain place and if I did not see or hear anything of the enemy to return; or if I *did* find them to return as soon as possible and bring word to the officers, unless I thought we were able to cope with them ourselves.

We set off upon our expedition early in the afternoon and went as far as directed by our officers, but saw no enemy. We stopped here awhile and rested ourselves. When we had refreshed ourselves, we thought it a pity to return with our fingers in our mouths and

[8]   The same location where Martin mustered out of the service at the end of the 1776 campaign.

report that we had seen nothing; we therefore agreed *unanimously* to stretch our orders a trifle and go a little further. We were in the fields; about a mile ahead were three or four houses at which I and some others of our party had been before. Between us and the houses there was a narrow wood, mostly of young growth and quite thick. We concluded to go as far as the houses, and if we could not hear anything of the Cowboys there, to return contented to camp.

Agreeably to our plan we set out and had but just entered the wood when we found ourselves flanked by 30 or 40 Cowboys, who gave us a hearty welcome to their assumed territories, and we returned the compliment; but a kind Providence protected every man of us from injury, although we were within 10 rods of the enemy. They immediately rushed from their covert before we had time to reload our pieces; consequently, we had no other alternative but to get off as well and as fast as we could. They did not fire upon us again, but gave us chase, for what reason I know not.

I was soon in the rear of my party, which had to cross a fence composed of old posts and rails with trees plashed down [intertwined] upon it. When I arrived at the fence, the foremost of the enemy was not more than six or eight rods distant, all running after us helter-skelter without any order. My men had all crossed the fence in safety; I alone was to suffer. I endeavored to get over the fence across two or three of the trees that were plashed down. Somehow or other I blundered and fell over, and caught my right foot in a place where a tree had split partly from the stump. Here I hung as fast as though my foot had been in the stocks, my ham lying across the butt of another tree, while my body hung down perpendicularly; I could barely reach the ground with my hands, and of course could make but little exertion to clear myself from the limbs.

The commander of the enemy came to the fence, and the first compliment I received from him was a stroke with his hanger [short sword] across my leg, just under or below the kneepan, which laid the bone bare. I could see him through the fence and knew him; he was, when we were boys, one of my most familiar playmates, was with me a messmate in the campaign of 1776, had enlisted during the war in 1777, but sometime before this had deserted to the enemy, having been coaxed off by an old harridan [a shrew] to whose daughter he had taken a fancy. The old hag of a mother, living in the vicinity of the British, easily inveigled him away. He was a smart active fellow and soon got command of a gang of Refugee-Cowboy plunderers. When he had had his hack at my shins, I began to think it was "neck or nothing," and making one desperate effort, I cleared my foot by leaving my shoe behind before he could have the second stroke at me. He knew me as well as I did him, for as soon as he saw me clear of the fence and out of the reach of his sword, he called me by name and told me to surrender myself, and he would give me good quarters. Thought I, you will wait till I ask them of you. I sprang up and ran till I came to my party, who were about a hundred rods ahead, waiting to see how I should come off.

The enemy never fired a shot at me all the time I was running from them, although nearly the whole of their party was standing on the other side of the fence when I started from it. Whether his conscience smote him and he prevented them from firing at me, or whether they were unprepared, not having had time to reload their pieces in their pursuit of us, or from what other cause, I know not, but they never interfered with me while I was running across the field, 50 or 60 rods, in open sight of them. Thus I escaped; and this was the only time the enemy drew blood from me during the whole war. This same Refugee was the youngster that was with me at the salt hay poling mentioned in the first chapter of this narrative.

We remained at Philipse Manor till the last of July. I had a lame leg, caused by the wound given me by Mr. Refugee, but I lost only a short time from duty. I was favored with easy duty by my officers on account of my wound.

The first of August, I think it was the 1st day of that month, we all of a sudden marched from this ground and directed our course toward King's Ferry near the Highlands, crossed the Hudson, and lay there a few days till the baggage, artillery, &c. had crossed, and then proceeded into New Jersey. We went down to Chatham, where were ovens built for the accommodation of the French troops. We then expected we were to attack New York in that quarter, but after staying here a day or two we again moved off and arrived at Trenton by rapid marches.[9]

It was about sunset when we arrived here and instead of encamping for the night, as we expected, we were ordered immediately on

---

[9]   Martin's dates are off by a month. On August 14 Washington received news that Admiral François Joseph Paul, the Comte de Grasse, was sailing north from the West Indies with a fleet of 29 warships and 3,000 soldiers. Grasse would only come as far as the Chesapeake Bay region, and he refused to stay beyond October 15. Washington and Rochambeau had two months in which to take advantage of this opportunity for combined operations.

board vessels then lying at the landing place, and a little after sunrise found ourselves at Philadelphia. We, that is the Sappers and Miners, stayed here some days, proving and packing off shells, shot, and other military stores. While we stayed here we drew a few articles of clothing, consisting of a few tow shirts, some overalls, and a few pairs of silk-and-oakum stockings. And here or soon after, we each of us received a MONTH'S PAY in specie, borrowed as I was informed by our French officers from the officers in the French army. This was the first that could be called money, which we had received as wages since the year '76, or that we ever did receive till the close of the war, or indeed ever after as wages.[10]

When we had finished our business at Philadelphia, we (the Miners) left the city. A part of our men with myself went down the Delaware in a schooner which had her hold nearly full of gunpowder. We passed Mud Island, where I had experienced such hardships in Nov. '77. It had quite a different appearance to what it had then, much like a fine, fair, warm, and sunny day succeeding a cold, dark, stormy night. Just after passing Mud Island in the afternoon, we

---

Almost fortuitously, they had an obvious target in Lord Cornwallis's army, numbering about 8,000 troops. During mid-May the aggressive Cornwallis had moved into Virginia, combined his force with other units operating there, and tried to engage Lafayette's rebels in a showdown battle. In mid-June, Clinton advised Cornwallis to establish a defensive base, one from which portions of his troops could be withdrawn by water should they be needed at New York City or other points. In early August, Cornwallis began to dig in at Yorktown on the south bank of the York River near Chesapeake Bay. He was to stay on the defensive in what was a most vulnerable position, should Grasse's fleet seal off the bay and Washington and Rochambeau get their troops in position to control the landside surrounding Yorktown.

Washington launched the southward trek of about 450 miles from King's Ferry on August 20–21. The combined forces reached Philadelphia by early September but not before halting a few days in the area of Chatham, New Jersey, about seven miles southeast of Morristown. The purpose of the delay was to confuse Clinton into thinking that a major attack against Staten Island would eventually be launched. The idea was to keep the British commander focused on the need to defend New York above all else, even though only a token patriot force remained behind to protect the Highlands.

[10] Martin does not mention that many soldiers became insubordinate and refused to proceed beyond Philadelphia unless they obtained this minimal form of financial compensation. Nor would they accept all but worthless Continental paper currency. The wealthy and powerful Philadelphia merchant, Robert Morris, who had become the Superintendent of Finance for the Continental Congress, arranged for the loan, which was drawn from Rochambeau's military chest. Morris guaranteed repayment on his own signature, since Congress lacked any form of a respectable credit rating.

had a smart thundershower; I did not feel very agreeably, I confess, during its continuance, with such a quantity of powder under my feet. I was not quite sure that a stroke of the electric fluid might not compel me to leave the vessel sooner than I wished; but no accident happened, and we proceeded down the river to the mouth of Christiana [Christina] Creek,[11] up which we were bound.

We were compelled to anchor here on account of wind and tide. Here we passed an uneasy night from fear of British cruisers, several of which were in the bay. In the morning we got under weigh [way], the wind serving, and proceeded up the creek 14 miles, the creek passing the most of its course through a marsh as crooked as a snake in motion.... We went on till the vessel grounded for lack of water. We then lightened her by taking out a part of her cargo, and when the tide came in we got up to the wharves and left her at the disposal of the artillerists.

We then crossed over land to the head of the Elk, or the head, or rather bottom, of Chesapeake Bay. Here we found a *large* fleet of *small* vessels waiting to convey us and other troops, stores, &c. down the bay. We soon embarked, that is such of us as went by water, the greater part of the army having gone on by land. I was in a small schooner called the *Birmingham*. There was but a small number of our corps of Sappers and Miners in this vessel, with a few artillerists, 6 or 8 officers, and a commissary who had a small quantity of stores on board, among which was a hogshead containing 20 or 30 gallons of rum. To prevent the men from getting more than their share of the liquor, the officers (who loved a little of the "good creature" as well as the men) had the bulkhead between the hold and the cabin taken down and placed the hogshead in the cabin, carefully nailing up the partition again, when they thought that they had the exclusive disposal of the precious treasure. But the soldiers were as wily as they, for the very first night after the officers had snugly secured it, as they thought, the head of the cask being crowded against the bulkhead, the soldiers contrived to loosen one of the boards at the lower end so as to swing it aside, and broached the hogshead on the other head, so that while the officers in the cabin thought they were the sole possessors of its contents, the soldiers in the hold had possession of at least as good a share as themselves.

[11]   Christina Creek meanders inland in a southwesterly direction from Wilmington in northern Delaware and would have carried Martin about halfway to the northern extremities of Chesapeake Bay.

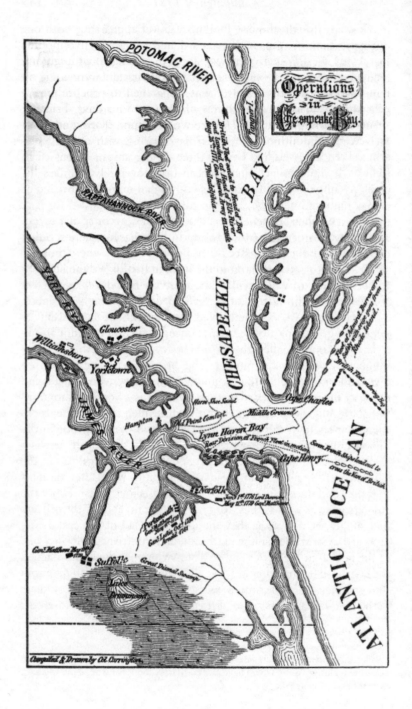

We passed down the bay making a grand appearance with our mosquito fleet to Annapolis (which I had left about five months before for West Point). Here we stopped, fearing to proceed any further at present, not knowing exactly how matters were going on down the bay. A French cutter was dispatched to procure intelligence. She returned in the course of three or four days, bringing word that the passage was clear; we then proceeded and soon arrived at the mouth of [the] James River, where were a number of armed French vessels and two or three 50-gun ships. We passed in sight of the French fleet, then lying in Lynnhaven Bay; they resembled a swamp of dry pine trees. We had passed several of their men-of-war higher up the bay.[12]

We were obliged to stay here a day or two on account of a severe northeast rainstorm.... After the storm had ceased, we proceeded up the [James] river to a place called Burwell's Ferry, where the fleet all anchored.... Soon after landing we marched to Williamsburg,[13] where we joined General Lafayette, and very soon after our whole army arriving, we prepared to move down and pay our old acquaintance, the British at Yorktown, a visit. I doubt not but their wish was not to have so many of us come at once, as their accommodations were rather scanty. They thought, "The fewer the better cheer." We thought, "The more the merrier." We had come a long way to see them and were unwilling to be put off with excuses; we thought the present time quite as convenient (at least for us) as any future time could be, and we accordingly persisted, hoping that, as they pretended to be a very courtly people, they would have the politeness to come out and meet us, which would greatly shorten the time to

[12] Grasse's fleet approached the entrance to Chesapeake Bay in late August and soon anchored in Lynnhaven Bay, about five miles west of Cape Henry along the southern shoreline. A squadron of 14 British vessels had followed the French ships north from the West Indies but had lost contact and proceeded to New York. There joined by five warships, the expanded British fleet under the overall command of Admiral Thomas Graves returned to Chesapeake Bay, only to be defeated in the Battle off the Chesapeake Capes on September 5. Nine days later Graves sailed away with his wounded craft for New York, leaving the French in complete control of the bay and Cornwallis cut off from rescue by sea. With British warships no longer a threat, the flotilla of allied vessels in the northern Chesapeake began sailing southward on September 18. Eight days later Martin and his comrades began debarking at Burwell's Ferry, about six miles south of Williamsburg on the James River.

[13] During the eighteenth century Williamsburg, located on the peninsula between the York and James rivers, served as Virginia's capital. Yorktown is about 12 miles to the southeast.

be spent in the visit, and save themselves and us much labor and trouble; but they were too impolite at this time to do so.

We marched from Williamsburg the last of September. It was a warm day; when we had proceeded about halfway to Yorktown we halted and rested two or three hours. Being about to cook some victuals, I saw a fire which some of the Pennsylvania troops had kindled a short distance off. I went to get some fire while some of my messmates made other preparations.... I had taken off my coat and unbuttoned my waistcoat, it being (as I said before) very warm; my pocketbook containing about five dollars in money and some other articles, in all about seven dollars, was in my waistcoat pocket. When I came among the strangers, they appeared to be uncommonly complaisant, asking many questions, helping me to fire, and chatting very familiarly. I took my fire and returned, but it was not long before I perceived that those kindhearted helpers had helped themselves to my pocketbook and its whole contents. I felt mortally chagrined, but there was no plaster for my sore but patience, and my plaster of that at this time, I am sure, was very small and very thinly spread, for it never covered the wound.

Here, or about this time, we had orders from the Commander in Chief that, in case the enemy should come out to meet us, we should exchange but one round with them and then decide the conflict with the bayonet, as they valued themselves at that instrument. The French forces could play their part at it, and the Americans were never backward at trying its virtue. The British, however, did not think fit at that time to give us an opportunity to soil our bayonets in their carcasses, but why they did not we could never conjecture; we as much expected it as we expected to find them there.

We went on and soon arrived and encamped in their neighborhood without ... molestation. Our Miners lay about a mile and a half from their works in open view of them. Here again we encountered our old associate, hunger. Affairs, as they respected provisions, &c. were not yet regulated. No eatable stores had arrived, nor could we expect they should until we knew what reception the enemy would give us. We were, therefore, compelled to try our hands at foraging again. We, that is, our corps of Miners, were encamped near a large wood. There was a plenty of shoats [young hogs] all about this wood, fat and plump, weighing generally from 50 to 100 pounds apiece. We soon found some of them, and as no owner appeared to be at hand and the hogs not understanding our inquiries (if we made any) sufficiently to inform us to whom they belonged, we made free with some of them to satisfy the calls of nature till we could be better supplied, if better we could be. Our officers countenanced us, and that was all the permission we wanted; and many of us did not want even that.

We now began to make preparations for laying close siege to the enemy. We had holed him, and nothing remained but to dig him out. Accordingly, after taking every precaution to prevent his escape, [we] settled our guards, provided fascines and gabions, made platforms for the batteries to be laid down when needed, brought on our battering pieces, ammunition, &c; on the 5th of October we began to put our plans into execution.[14]

One-third part of all the troops were put in requisition to be employed in opening the trenches. A third part of our Sappers and Miners were ordered out this night to assist the engineers in laying out the works. It was a very dark and rainy night. However, we repaired to the place and began by following the engineers and laying laths [narrow strips] of pine wood end-to-end upon the line marked out by the officers for the trenches. We had not proceeded far in the business before the engineers ordered us to desist and remain where we were, and be sure not to straggle a foot from the spot while they were absent from us. In a few minutes after their departure, there came a man alone to us having on a surtout [long overcoat], as we conjectured (it being exceeding dark), and inquired for the engineers. We now began to be a little jealous for our safety, being alone and without arms, and within 40 rods of the British trenches. The stranger inquired what troops we were, talked familiarly with us a few minutes, when being informed which way the officers had gone, he went off in the same direction, after strictly charging us, in case we should be taken prisoners, not to discover [reveal] to the enemy what troops we were. We were obliged to him for his kind advice, but we considered ourselves as standing in no

[14] By the evening of September 28, the allied troops were within a mile of Cornwallis's entrenchments. Their numbers included 7,800 Frenchmen, 5,700 Continentals, and 3,200 militiamen, which gave the allies a nearly 2 to 1 troop strength advantage over Cornwallis's force of about 8,000. With so favorable a ratio, Washington and Rochambeau could have stormed the Yorktown defenses, but they had no desire to precipitate a human slaughter or commit some tactical blunder that might allow a portion of the weaker enemy force to escape. Thus their decision was to conduct traditional siege operations and squeeze Cornwallis into submission. They would have their troops dig a series of parallel trenches, bring up and mount artillery pieces, and then bombard the British entrenchments until Cornwallis accepted the reality of his army's entrapment and parleyed for surrender terms.

great need of it; for we knew as well as he did that Sappers and Miners were allowed no quarters, at least are entitled to none by the laws of warfare, and of course should take care, if taken and the enemy did not find us out, not to betray our own secret.

In a short time the engineers returned and the afore-mentioned stranger with them. They discoursed together some time when, by the officers often calling him "Your Excellency," we discovered that it was General Washington. Had we dared, we might have cautioned him for exposing himself too carelessly to danger at such a time, and doubtless he would have taken it in good part if we had. But nothing ill happened to either him or ourselves.

It coming on to rain hard, we were ordered back to our tents, and nothing more was done that night. The next night, which was the 6th of October, the same men were ordered to the lines that had been there the night before. We this night completed laying out the works. The troops of the line were there ready with entrenching tools and began to entrench after General Washington had struck a few blows with a pickax, a mere ceremony that it might be said "General Washington with his own hands first broke ground at the siege of Yorktown." The ground was sandy and soft, and the men employed that night ate no "idle bread" (and I question if they ate any other), so that by daylight they had covered themselves from danger from the enemy's shot, who it appeared never mistrusted that we were so near them the whole night, their attention being directed to another quarter. There was upon the right of their works a marsh; our people had sent to the western side of this marsh a detachment to make a number of fires, by which, and our men often passing before the fires, the British were led to imagine that we were about some secret mischief there, and consequently directed their whole fire to that quarter, while we were entrenching literally under their noses.[15]

As soon as it was day they perceived their mistake and began to fire where they ought to have done sooner. They brought out a

[15] Having laid out a line for the first parallel trench on the evening of October 5, a task in which Martin participated, some 1,500 American troops stood ready to dig the next evening. To divert the enemy, the French mounted a feint attack on the British right while the Americans dug away at a distance of about 600 to 700 yards back from the British left. By early the next morning they had completed a trench of about 2,000 feet, which included four redoubts for concentrated cannon placements, running in from the York River on the American right. Artillery pieces were then fitted into assigned positions, and the formal bombardment began in earnest on October 9.

fieldpiece or two without their trenches, and discharged several shots at the men who were at work erecting a bomb battery; but their shot had no effect, and they soon gave it over....

I do not remember exactly the number of days we were employed before we got our batteries in readiness to open upon the enemy, but think it was not more than two or three. The French, who were upon our left, had completed their batteries a few hours before us, but were not allowed to discharge their pieces till the American batteries were ready. Our commanding battery was on the near bank of the [York] river and contained 10 heavy guns; the next was a bomb battery of three large mortars; and so on through the whole line. The whole number, American and French, was 92 cannon, mortars, and howitzers. Our flagstaff was in the 10-gun battery upon the right of the whole. I was in the trenches the day that the batteries were to be opened. All were upon the tiptoe of expectation and impatience to see the signal given to open the whole line of batteries, which was to be the hoisting of the American flag in the 10-gun battery.

About noon the much-wished-for signal went up. I confess I felt a secret pride swell my heart when I saw the "star-spangled banner" waving majestically in the very faces of our implacable adversaries; it appeared like an omen of success to our enterprise, and so it proved in reality. A simultaneous discharge of all the guns in the line followed, the French troops accompanying it with "Huzza for the Americans!" It was said that the first shell sent from our batteries entered an elegant house formerly owned or occupied by the Secretary of State under the British government, and burned directly over a table surrounded by a large party of British officers at dinner, killing and wounding a number of them. This was a warm day to the British.[16]

The siege was carried on warmly for several days, when most of the guns in the enemy's works were silenced. We now began our

---

[16] Martin implies that Thomas Nelson was a loyalist, which was not the case. Nelson was a wealthy Yorktown merchant and the longtime secretary of Virginia, who served in that post from 1743 until his death in 1782. He was residing in his stately home when the allies surrounded Yorktown. A day after allied firing began, "Secretary" Nelson secured permission to leave his battered residence and proceed under a flag of truce to the American lines. He told Washington how effective the initial barrage had been in damaging British entrenchments and gun emplacements. Nelson's nephew, Thomas, Jr., a signer of the Declaration of Independence, was then Virginia's governor and was on the field at Yorktown as a militia general.

second parallel, about halfway between our works and theirs. There were two strong redoubts held by the British on their left. It was necessary for us to possess those redoubts before we could complete our trenches. One afternoon, I, with the rest of our corps that had been on duty in the trenches the night but one before, were ordered to the lines. I mistrusted something extraordinary, serious, or comical was going forward, but what I could not easily conjecture.

We arrived at the trenches a little before sunset. I saw several officers fixing bayonets on long staves. I then concluded we were about to make a general assault upon the enemy's works, but before dark I was informed of the whole plan, which was to storm the redoubts, the one by the Americans and the other by the French.[17] The Sappers and Miners were furnished with axes and were to proceed in front and cut a passage for the troops through the abatis, which are composed of the tops of trees, the small branches cut off with a slanting stroke which renders them as sharp as spikes. These trees are then laid at a small distance from the trench or ditch, pointing outwards, and the butts fastened to the ground in such a manner that they cannot be removed by those on the outside of them; it is almost impossible to get through them. Through these we were to cut a passage before we or the other assailants could enter.

At dark the detachment was formed and advanced beyond the trenches and lay down on the ground to await the signal for advancing to the attack, which was to be three shells from a certain battery near where we were lying. All the batteries in our line were silent, and we lay anxiously waiting for the signal. The two brilliant planets, Jupiter and Venus, were in close contact in the western hemisphere (the same direction that the signal was to be made in). When I happened to cast my eyes to that quarter, which was often, and I caught a glance of them, I was ready to spring on my feet, thinking they were the signal for starting. Our watchword was "Rochambeau," the commander of the French forces' name, a good watchword, for

[17] Martin's assault column, directed at Redoubt No. 10, consisted of 400 troops under the command of Colonel Alexander Hamilton. Colonel William Deux-Ponts led a French force of about the same number against Redoubt No. 9. By virtue of taking these two redoubts, located on the British left near the York River, during the evening of October 14, the allies were able to complete their second parallel trench line at a distance of about 300 yards from the all-but-shattered British entrenchments.

being pronounced *Ro-sham-bow*, it sounded, when pronounced quick, like *rush-on-boys*.

We had not lain here long before the expected signal was given, for us and the French, who were to storm the other redoubt, by the three shells with their fiery trains mounting the air in quick succession. The word up, up, was then reiterated through the detachment. We immediately moved silently on toward the redoubt we were to attack with unloaded muskets. Just as we arrived at the abatis, the enemy discovered us and directly opened a sharp fire upon us. We were now at a place where many of our large shells had burst in the ground, making holes sufficient to bury an ox in; the men having their eyes fixed upon what was transacting before them, were every now and then falling into these holes. I thought the British were killing us off at a great rate. At length one of the holes happening to pick me up, I found out the mystery of the huge slaughter.

As soon as the firing began, our people began to cry, "The fort's our own!" and it was "Rush on boys." The Sappers and Miners soon cleared a passage for the infantry, who entered it rapidly. Our Miners were ordered not to enter the fort, but there was no stopping them. "We will go," said they. "Then go to the d—l," said the commanding officer of our corps, "if you will." I could not pass at the entrance we had made, it was so crowded; I therefore forced a passage at a place where I saw our shot had cut away some of the abatis. Several others entered at the same place.

While passing, a man at my side received a ball in his head and fell under my feet, crying out bitterly. While crossing the trench, the enemy threw hand grenades (small shells) into it; they were so thick that I at first thought them cartridge papers on fire, but was soon undeceived by their cracking. As I mounted the breastwork, I met an old associate hitching himself down into the trench. I knew him by the light of the enemy's musketry, it was so vivid. The fort was taken and all quiet in a very short time. Immediately after the firing ceased, I went out to see what had become of my wounded friend and the other that fell in the passage; they were both dead. In the heat of the action I saw a British soldier jump over the walls of the fort next the river and go down the bank, which was almost perpendicular and 20 or 30 feet high. When he came to the beach he made off for the town, and if he did not make good use of his legs I never saw a man that did.

All that were in the action of storming the redoubt were exempted from further duty that night. We laid down upon the ground and rested the remainder of the night as well as a constant discharge of grape and canister shot would permit us to do, while those who were on duty for the day completed the second parallel by including the captured redoubts within it. We returned to camp early in the morning, all safe and sound, except one of our lieutenants, who had received a slight wound on the top of the shoulder by a musket shot. Seven or eight men belonging to the infantry were killed, and a number wounded....[18]

We were on duty in the trenches 24 hours, and 48 hours in camp. The invalids did the camp duty, and we had nothing else to do but to attend morning and evening roll calls and recreate ourselves as we pleased the rest of the time, till we were called upon to take our turns on duty in the trenches again. The greatest inconvenience we felt was the want of good water, there being none near our camp but nasty frog ponds where all the horses in the neighborhood were watered, and we were forced to wade through the water in the skirts of the ponds, thick with mud and filth, to get at water in any wise fit for use, and that full of frogs. All the springs about the country, although they looked well, tasted like copperas water or like water that had been standing in iron or copper vessels.

I was one day rambling alone in the woods when I came across a small brook of very good water about a mile from our tents. We used this water daily to drink, or we should almost have suffered. But it was "the fortune of war." I was one night in the trenches, erecting a bomb battery; the enemy (it being very dark) were directed in their firing by a large tree. I was ordered by our officers to take two or three men and fell the tree with some old axes as dull as hoes; the tree was very large, and we were two hours in cutting it, although we took Solomon's advice in handling dull tools by "putting to the more strength,"[19] the British all the time urging us to exert ourselves with round and grape shot. They struck the tree a number of times while we were at it, but chanced to do us no harm at all.

In the morning, while the relieves were coming into the trenches, I was sitting on the side of the trench, when some of the New York troops coming in, one of the sergeants stepped up to the breastwork to look about him. The enemy threw a small shell which fell upon

---

[18] Accepted estimates have the American column losing 9 killed and 25 wounded. The French, who faced a larger British force at Redoubt No. 9, suffered 15 killed and 77 wounded.

[19] Ecclesiastes 10:10. Many modern-day biblical scholars would disagree with Martin that these were words given directly by King Solomon.

the outside of the works; the man turned his face to look at it; at that instant a shot from the enemy ... passed just by his face without touching him at all. He fell dead into the trench. I put my hand on his forehead and found his skull was shattered all in pieces and the blood flowing from his nose and mouth, but not a particle of skin was broken. I never saw an instance like this among all the men I saw killed during the whole war.

After we had finished our second line of trenches there was but little firing on either side. After Lord Cornwallis had failed to get off, upon the 17th day of October (a rather unlucky day for the British) he requested a cessation of hostilities for, I think, 24 hours when commissioners from both armies met at a house between the lines to agree upon articles of capitulation.[20] We waited with anxiety the termination of the armistice, and as the time drew nearer our anxiety increased. The time at length arrived; it passed, and all remained quiet. And now we concluded that we had obtained what we had taken so much pains for—for which we had encountered so many dangers and had so anxiously wished. Before night we were informed that the British had surrendered and that the siege was ended.

The next day we were ordered to put ourselves in as good order as our circumstances would admit, to see (what was the completion of our present wishes) the British army march out and stack their arms. The trenches, where they crossed the road leading to the town, were leveled and all things put in order for this grand exhibition. After breakfast on the 19th, we were marched onto the ground and paraded on the right hand side of the road, and the French forces on the left. We waited two or three hours before the British made their appearance; they were not always so dilatory, but they were compelled at last by necessity to appear all armed, with bayonets fixed, drums beating, and faces lengthening.

---

[20] After dark on October 16, Cornwallis tried to execute an escape plan by attempting to move his healthy troops across the York River to Gloucester Point, from where they could push northward into the Virginia countryside away from their Franco-American besiegers. A furious storm drove the advance units back, however, and Cornwallis had to accept entrapment or face annihilation. Early on the morning of the 17th a lone British drummer boy and an officer marched forward with a flag of truce toward the American lines. After much haggling over details on the 18th, representatives from the two sides agreed to terms of surrender, which Cornwallis signed late on the morning of October 19, after which elaborate formal surrender ceremonies took place.

They were led by General O'Hara, with the American General Lincoln on his right, the Americans and French beating a march as they passed out between them.[21] It was a noble sight to us, and the more so, as it seemed to promise a speedy conclusion to the contest. The British did not make so good an appearance as the German forces; but there was certainly some allowance to be made in their favor. The English felt their honor wounded; the Germans did not greatly care whose hands they were in. The British paid the Americans, seemingly, but little attention as they passed them, but they eyed the French with considerable malice depicted in their countenances. They marched to the place appointed and stacked their arms; they then returned to the town in the same manner they had marched out, except being divested of their arms. After the prisoners were marched off into the country our army separated, the French remaining where they then were and the Americans marching for the Hudson.

During the siege we saw in the woods herds of Negroes which Lord Cornwallis (after he had inveigled them from their proprietors), in love and pity to them, had turned adrift with no other recompense for their confidence in his humanity than the smallpox for their bounty and starvation and death for their wages. They might be seen scattered about in every direction, dead and dying with pieces of ears of burnt Indian corn in the hands and mouths, even of those that were dead. After the siege was ended, many of the owners of these deluded creatures came to our camp and engaged some of our men to take them up, generally offering a guinea a head for them. Some of our Sappers and Miners took up several of them that belonged to a Colonel Banister;[22] when he

---

[21]   Cornwallis claimed to be indisposed on the afternoon of October 19 and did not attend the surrender ceremonies. His second in command, General Charles O'Hara, led the defeated British army onto the field. When he offered Washington the symbolic sword of surrender, the American commander pointed toward his own second, Benjamin Lincoln, who graciously accepted the blade, a mark of vindication for the humiliation he had suffered in surrendering his own sword at Charleston May 1780. Then he graciously handed the weapon back to O'Hara, an acknowledgment that the British general had fought like a worthy opponent, regardless of the outcome at Yorktown.

[22]   As British forces marched through the Virginia countryside in the months before Yorktown, they often liberated slaves. Many of these freed persons came down with virulent diseases like smallpox. On occasion the British shepherded them onto patriot plantations to harass and punish rebel resisters by exposing their families and slaves to deadly diseases. After Cornwallis's surrender many planters traveled to Yorktown to reclaim slaves lost to the British army. John Banister, who was from the Petersburg area, was already there, since he was serving as a lieutenant colonel in the Virginia militia. Martin believed that he was performing a humanitarian service in helping to return disease-racked slaves to their masters.

applied for them, they refused to deliver them to him unless he would promise not to punish them. He said he had no intention of punishing them, that he did not blame them at all; the blame lay on Lord Cornwallis. I saw several of those miserable wretches delivered to their master; they came before him under a very powerful fit of the ague. He told them that he gave them the free choice either to go with him or remain where they were, that he would not injure a hair of their heads if they returned with him to their duty. Had the poor souls received a reprieve at the gallows, they could not have been more overjoyed than they appeared to be at what he promised them; their ague fit soon left them.

I had a share in one of them by assisting in taking him up; the fortune I acquired was small, only one dollar. I received what was then called its equivalent in paper money, if money it might be called; it amounted to 1,200 (nominal) dollars, all of which I afterwards paid for one single quart of rum. To such a miserable state had all paper stuff, called money, depreciated.

Our corps of Sappers and Miners were now put on board vessels to be transported up the bay. I was on board a small schooner; the captain of *our* company and 20 others of our men were in the same vessel. There was more than 20 tons of beef on board, salted in bulk in the hold. We were obliged to remain behind to deal out this beef in small quantities to the troops that remained here. I remained part of the time on board and part on shore for 18 days after all the American troops were gone to the northward, and none remaining but the French. It now began to grow cold, and there were two or three cold rainstorms; we suffered exceedingly while we were compelled to stay on shore, having no tents nor any kind of fuel, the houses in the town being all occupied by the French troops.

Our captain at length became tired of this business and determined to go on after the other troops at all events. We accordingly left Yorktown and set our faces toward the Highlands of New York. It was now the month of November and winter approaching; we all wished to be nearer home, or at least to be with the rest of our corps, who were we knew *not* where, nor did they know where we were. They had heard before this that our schooner was cast away and we were drowned. After we left Yorktown we had head winds for several days and made but little progress, getting no farther than [the] Patuxent River[23] in Maryland in that time. We came to anchor

---

[23]   Sailing north from the York River along the western side of Chesapeake Bay, Martin would have first passed the Rappahannock and Potomac rivers in Virginia before reaching the Patuxent River in southern Maryland.

at the mouth of that river about sunset, and as we had been some time on board the vessel, we obtained permission from our captain to go on shore and sleep, as we saw a shelter on shore put up by some of the troops who had gone on before us....

When we had landed and kindled a fire and were most of us sitting down by it, one of our men took up the loaded musket (not knowing it to be so), and placing the butt of the piece on the ground between his legs, asked the owner if his musket was in good order, and cocked and snapped it. I was standing by his side with the muzzle of the piece close by my ear when it proved to be in good order enough to go off, and nearly sent me off with its contents; the fire from it burnt all the hair off the side of my head, and I thought at the instant that my head had gone with it....

We encamped one night ... at Wilmington, a very handsome borough town on the Christiana [Christina] Creek in the state of Delaware. I was quartered for the night at a gentleman's house, who had before the war been a sea captain. He related to me an anecdote that gave me rather a disagreeable feeling, as it may, perhaps, my readers. It was thus: "At the battle of Germantown in the year 1777, a Dutchman (an inhabitant of that town) and his wife fired upon some of the British during the action; whether they killed anyone or not he did not say. But after the battle someone informed against them, and they were both taken and confined in the provost guardhouse in the city, and there kept with scarcely anything to sustain nature and not a spark of fire to warm them. On the morning that the *Augusta* was blown up at Fort Mifflin on Mud Island, the poor old man had got to the prison yard to enjoy the warm sunbeams with a number of other prisoners (my informant among them, he being a prisoner at the time). When they heard the report of the ship's magazine, the poor creature exclaimed, 'Huzza for General Washington! Tomorrow he comes.' The villain Provost Marshal, upon hearing this, put him into the cellar of the prison and kept him there, without allowing him the least article of sustenance till he died. The prisoners cut a small crevice in the floor with a knife through which they poured water and sometimes a little spirits, while he held up his mouth to the place to receive it." Such inhuman treatment was often shown to our people when prisoners by the British during the Revolutionary War. But it needs no comment.

In the morning before we marched, some of us concluded to have a stimulator. I went to a house near by where I was informed they sold liquors. When I entered the house, I saw a young woman in decent morning dishabille [clothing]. I asked her if I could have any liquor there; she told me that her husband had just stepped out and would be in directly, and very politely desired me to be seated. I had sat but a minute or two when there came in from the backyard a great pot-bellied Negro man, rigged off in his superfine broadcloth, ruffled shirt, bowshin, and flat foot.... "My dear," said the lady, "this soldier wishes for a quart of rum." I was thunderstruck; had not the man taken my canteen from me and measured me the liquor, I should certainly have forgotten my errand. I took my canteen and hastened off as fast as possible, being fearful that I might hear or see more of their "dearing," for had I, I am sure it would have given me the ague. However agreeable such "twain's becoming one flesh" was in that part of the Union, I was not acquainted with it in that in which I resided.

We went on to Philadelphia, crossed the river Schuylkill on a pontoon bridge, entered the city, and took up our abode in the barracks.... We stayed here several days. The barracks in this city are, or were then, very commodious; they were two stories high with a gallery their whole length and an ample parade in front; they were capable of sheltering 2,000 or 3,000 men.

After staying in Philadelphia about a fortnight, we left the city and proceeded to the city of Burlington in New Jersey, 20 miles above Philadelphia on the Delaware, which place we understood was to be our winter quarters. We marched about noon, went about 10 miles, and halted for the night. We took up our lodgings in the houses of the inhabitants; the house where I was quartered seemed to belong to a man well off for this world's goods. We were allowed the kitchen and a comfortable fire, and we happened to have, just then, what a soldier of the Revolution valued next to the welfare of his country and his own honor, that is something to eat, and being all in good health and having the prospect of a quiet night's rest; all which comforts happening to us at this time put us in high spirits.

We marched again and crossed a narrow ferry, called Penny Ferry, arrived at Bristol and crossed the Delaware to Burlington, where the artillerists went into barracks, and our corps of Miners were quartered in a large elegant house, which had formerly been the residence of the governor when the state was a British province. The non-commissioned officers, with a few others, had a neat room in one of the wings, and the men occupied the rest of the house, except the rooms in the third story which were taken up by the officers and their attendants. Now we thought ourselves well situated for the winter (as indeed we were, as it respected shelter) after a tedious campaign; but it turned out quite the reverse with several, and myself among the rest, as in the next chapter will appear. Being once more snugly stowed away in winter quarters, it of course ends my sixth campaign.

Chapter VIII

Campaign of 1782

JPM reckons with more disease, hunts for deserters, and enjoys of the company of civilians, now more favorably disposed toward the Continentals with the prospect of peace and independence becoming a real possibility.

> A man with morbid pains oppress'd
> Who feels the nightmare in his breast;
> Rejoices when the pressure's o'er,
> And the distress is felt no more;
> So wars and tumults, when they cease
> Bring comforts in the thoughts of peace.

The arm of British power in America being dislocated by the capture of Lord Cornwallis and his myrmidons, we had not much to disturb us on account of the enemy. I fared rather better than I did when I was here on my journey to Mud Island in 1777. Our duty was not very hard, but I was a soldier yet, and had to submit to soldier's rules and discipline, and soldier's fare.

Either here or just before, our officers had enlisted a recruit. He had lately been discharged from the New Jersey line. After enlisting with us, he obtained a furlough to visit his friends, but receiving no money when he engaged with us (which was, I believe, the sole motive of his entering the service at this time) and obtaining his ends in getting home, he took especial care to keep himself there, at least till he could get another opportunity to try his luck again, which he accordingly did by enlisting in a corps of new levies in his own state—New Jersey. My captain, hearing where he was and how engaged, sent me with two men to find him out and bring him back to his duty.

And now, my dear reader, excuse me for being so minute in detailing this little excursion, for it yet seems to my fancy, among the privations of that war, like one of those little verdant plats of ground [an oasis] amid the burning sands of Arabia so often described by travelers.

One of our captains and another of our men being about going that way on furlough, I and my two men set off with them.... The first night of our expedition we boiled our meat, and I asked the landlady for a little sauce; she told me to go to the garden and take as much cabbage as I pleased, and that boiled with the meat was all we could eat. The next morning we proceeded; it was cool weather and about six inches deep of snow on the ground. After two or three days journeying, we arrived in the neighborhood of the game that we were in pursuit of. It was now sundown, and our furloughed captain and man concluded to stop for the night; here we fell in with some soldiers of the corps that our man belonged to. Our captain inquired if they knew such a man, naming him. They equivocated and asked many questions concerning our business. Our officious captain answered them so much to their satisfaction that Mr. Deserter took so good care of himself that I could not find him, and I cared but little about it. I knew he would get nothing with us, if we caught him, but a striped jacket, and as we concluded the war was nearly ended, we thought it would be but of little service to *him*, nor his company any to *us*.

The captain put me and my two men into the open cold kitchen of a house that they said had sometime or other been a tavern. But as it was in the vicinity of the place where I passed the winter of 1779–80, I was acquainted with several of the inhabitants in the neighborhood, and accordingly sent one of my men to a house hard by, the master of which I knew to be a fine man, and obtained his leave to lodge there. We had a good warm room to sit and lodge in, and as the next day was thanksgiving,[1] we had an excellent supper.

---

[1]   What made these visits a time of thanksgiving good cheer for Martin was not just the abundance of food. The civilian populace, having for so long treated Washington's long-term Continentals with cold indifference if not open disdain, often out of fear of being forced to make contributions to the cause, were now showing newfound generosity toward these same soldiers. With the war effort winding down in 1782, an attitude of peace and harmony was again infusing what for so long had been a viciously divided, war-torn society.

In the morning when we were about to proceed on our journey, the man of the house came into the room and put some bread to the fire to toast. He next produced some cider, as good and rich as wine; then giving each of us a large slice of his toasted bread, he told us to eat it and drink the cider, observing that he had done so for a number of years and found it the best stimulator imaginable. We again prepared to go on, having given up the idea of finding the deserter.

Our landlord then told us that we must not leave his house till we had taken breakfast with him. We thought we were very well dealt by already, but concluded not to refuse a good offer. We therefore stayed and had a genuine New Jersey breakfast, consisting of buckwheat slapjacks, flowing with butter and honey, and a capital dish of chocolate. We then went on, determined not to hurry ourselves so long as the thanksgiving lasted. We found a good dinner at a farmer's house; but I thought that both the good man and his lady looked at us as if they would have been as well pleased with our room as our company....

At night we applied for lodging at a house near the road. There appeared to be none but females in the house, two matronly ladies and two misses. One of the women said she should have no objection to our staying there through the night, were it not that a woman in the house was then lying at the point of death. (I had often heard this excuse made before.) We readily perceived her drift, and, when turning to go away one of the men told her that he did not wish to stay. "For," said he, "if old Corpus should chance to come in the dark for the sick woman, he might in his haste mistake and take me." The woman smiled and we went on.

The next house which looked as if hospitality was an inmate, I applied to and obtained admittance. Here again we found a plenty of thanksgiving fare. The people of this house were acquainted with numbers of the Connecticut soldiers, who had been here during the winter of '79[–80], and made many inquiries respecting them. They seemed to have a particular regard for the Connecticut forces, as that section of the state was originally settled by Connecticut people, and it still retains the name of "the Connecticut Farms."[2]

---

[2] Today the site of Union, New Jersey, and a short distance from Westfield and Springfield, where the two Connecticut brigades lived during the first months of 1780 while performing advanced outpost duty so close to British forces on Staten Island.

The good man of the house would not let us depart in the morning until we had breakfasted. We then bid our kind host farewell and proceeded on.

About noon we called at a house, and while we were warming ourselves in the kitchen and chatting with the young people, the good old housewife came into the room and entered into conversation with us upon the hardships of a soldier's life. She lamented much that we had no mothers nor sisters to take care of us; she said she knew what it was, in a measure, to endure the fatigues and hardships of a camp by the sufferings her sons had undergone in the drafted militia. They had told her how they had suffered hunger and cold, and, to cap all, said she, they came home ragged, dirty, and lousy as beggars. The young men, who were present, did not seem to relish the latter part of her narrative, for they leered like cross colts.

The good woman all the while did not say a word to us about eating, but went off to her room and shut the door; we stayed a few minutes longer and were just going away when the old lady opened her door and said, "Come to your dinners, soldiers," with as much ease and familiarity as though we had belonged to the family. Agreeably to invitation, we went in and found the master of the house sitting in his elbow chair by the fire, who gave us a hearty welcome to the remains of his thanksgiving cheer. We ate a hearty dinner, and an excellent one it was; when after returning them our sincere thanks for their hospitality, we pursued our journey.

This afternoon we passed a place where, on our march to Virginia the past summer, a funny incident occurred, which at the time it happened and at this time excited considerable merriment. Our captain (who we always took pains to discommode) had placed himself on the top of an old rail fence during a momentary halt of the troops. The rail upon which he sat was very slender. Behind him was a meadow and from the fence for about a rod was a bank almost perpendicular. I was sitting on the other end of the rail when our sergeant major, observing the weakness of the fence, came and seated himself by my side, and, giving me a hint, we kept wriggling about till we broke the rail and let the captain take his chance down the bank, among the bushes quite to the bottom, taking good care ourselves not to go with him. When he came back he did not look very well pleased with his Irish hoist. Whether he mistrusted that we had been the cause of his overturn I do not know; he said but little, whatever he might think.

At night we stopped at a large elegant brick house to which the owner bid us welcome. He told me that his house was Lord

Cornwallis' quarters during part of the time he was in the Jerseys in '76 and '77. He said that Cornwallis was a morose, cross man, always quarreling with and beating his servants, that he was glad his pride was humbled, but had much rather have heard that he was killed than taken. Here we again regaled ourselves on thanksgiving viands, which was nearly, or quite, the last; however, we had fared something better than I did at the rice and vinegar thanksgiving in Pennsylvania in the year 1777. We took breakfast here and went on.

We this forenoon passed through a pretty village called Maidenhead (don't stare, dear reader, I did not name it).[3] An hour or two before we came to this place, I saw a pretty young lady standing in the door of a house just by the roadside. I very innocently inquired of her how far it was to Maidenhead. She answered, "Five miles." One of my men who, though young, did not stand in very imminent danger of being hanged for his beauty, observed to the young lady, "that he thought the commodity scarce in the market, since he had to go so far to seek it." "Don't trouble yourself," said she, "about that, there is no danger of its being more scarce on your account." The fellow leered and, I believe, wished he had held his tongue.

The next day we arrived at Trenton, where was a commissary and some public stores.... Accordingly, I made out a return for three men for three days rations. We went to the commissary's, who told us that he had no kind of meat on hand nor any other provisions but flour, that if we chose to take that, he would allow us a pound and a quarter of flour for a pound of beef. We took it and exchanged it at the baker's, pound for pound, and went on; we arrived at our quarters in Burlington sometime in the evening.

Soon after this came on my trouble, and that of several others of the men belonging to our corps. Sometime in the month of January two of our men were taken down with a species of yellow fever; one recovered and the other died. Directly after one belonging to our room was seized with it and removed to the hospital, where he recovered. Next I was attacked with it. This was in February; it took hold of me in good earnest. I bled violently at the nose, and was so reduced in flesh and strength in a few days that I was as helpless as an infant. O! how much I suffered, although I had as good attendance as circumstances would admit. The disorder continued to take

---

[3] Apparently the townsfolk preferred another name as well. They changed Maidenhead to Lawrenceville. The town lies about five miles north of Trenton.

hold of our people till there were more than 20 sick with it. Our officers made a hospital in an upper room in one of the wings of the house, and as soon as the men fell sick they were lodged there.

About the first of March I began to mend, and recovered what little reason I ever possessed, of which I had been entirely deprived from nearly the first attack of the fever. As soon as I could bear it, I was removed from my room to the hospital among those that were recently taken. For what reason I was put with the sick and dying I did not know, nor did I ask; I did not care much what they did with me, but nothing ill resulted from it that I know of. The doctor belonging to the artillery regiment (who attended upon us, we having no doctor in our corps) went home on furlough, and it was a happy circumstance for us, for he was not the best of physicians. Besides, he was badly provided to do with; the apothecary's stores in the Revolutionary army were as ill furnished as any others. The doctor, however, left us under the care of a physician belonging to the city, who was a fine man, and to his efforts under Providence I verily believe I owed my life. He was a skillful, tender-hearted, and diligent man.

Eight men died at this time, the rest recovered, though the most of them very slowly. Some were as crazy as coots for weeks after they had gained strength to walk about. My hair came off my head, and I was as bald as an eagle; but after I *began* to gain strength I soon got about. But it was a grievous sickness to me, the sorest I had ever undergone. Although death is much nearer to *me* now than it was then, yet I never had thought myself so near *death* as I did then.

The spring had now began to open, and warm weather soon came on. We remained here till the month of May, when one of our sergeants and myself obtained permission to go down to Philadelphia for a couple of days to visit some of our acquaintance in that city, but particularly to carry some little clothing to one of our men in the hospital there, who was wounded at the siege of Yorktown and had had his leg amputated above the knee. I carried him among other things a pair of stockings and shoes. His nurse told him that he was more lucky than most other people, for where they got one pair of shoes and stockings he got two. Poor fellow! I never saw nor heard of him afterwards. Thus poor soldiers pass out of notice.

My comrade and I stayed over two days at Philadelphia, intending to return the next day in the packet. That evening one of our noncommissioned officers came down, who informed us that our corps had marched for Hudson's River, and that our arms and clothing were gone on in the baggage wagons and that we must immediately follow. We all, however, stayed there that night, and early next morning we set off by land. We had nothing to burden us, not even provisions or money; consequently, had nothing to hinder us from proving our adroitness at travelling. We walked that day about 40 miles and stopped at night at a small snug house in the state of New Jersey....

We started before sunrise this morning and walked 49 miles, when just before sunset we overtook our corps. I had eaten nothing all day, but drank several draughts of buttermilk which I begged of the farmers' ladies on the road. The next day we arrived at a large house near King's Ferry, usually denominated by the army "the white house," belonging to Smith,[4] the man who conducted Major André on his way toward New York, when he was taken. Our troops stayed here that night and the next day and night, the officers in the house and the men in the barns.

In the evening of the last day we were here, just at dark, one of our officers came and told me that two of the men had deserted and had compelled another man to go with them. As they were all what we called "Old Countrymen," it was conjectured that they had gone to the enemy, and I was accordingly ordered to take nine men, who were then in readiness, and endeavor to overtake them before they could reach New York. I immediately set off, having received my orders, which were to go to what was called the "English Neighborhood,"[5] and if I could not find them or hear of them, to return. The English Neighborhood was from 45 to 50 miles distant from the place we were then at. We traveled so hard that at daylight

[4] Joshua Hett Smith was one of the most enigmatic characters to inhabit the Revolutionary landscape. Apparently an active rebel, Smith became involved in spying activities against the British. In September 1780 he did Benedict Arnold's bidding in relation to meeting with John André, even letting the two conspirators plot in his home, the so-called "white house." Arnold ordered him to guide André back through American lines, but he failed to complete this assignment. Seemingly unaware of André's true identity, Smith nevertheless stood trial for complicity in Arnold's treason. Acquitted in late October 1780, he still went to jail because New York officials thought him a loyalist, but he escaped in May 1781 and gained the safety of British lines. He went on to live in obscurity both in England and the United States.

[5] A heavily wooded area and hangout for loyalists in northeastern New Jersey. Old countrymen were foreigners, such as penniless recent immigrants from Ireland and Scotland, and also included Hessians, who for various reasons had found their way into the Continental service.

I had but three men of the nine left with me, the other six having given out by the way. We were now near our journey's end when the men with me, beginning to grow slack and hearing no tidings of the deserters, we concluded to return.

When we had got 8 or 10 miles on our retrograde movement, we met one of our lieutenants on his way to visit his friends who lived in that quarter. He had with him three men for an escort and had picked up those of my party who had given out by the way. We met him just as he arrived at his father's house, a lucky circumstance for us, as we stopped and got something to eat. He then sent me off alone to a place on the river where some spy boats (as they were called) were stationed, with directions to request the officers commanding them to take up the three deserters, should they see them. I executed this commission and returned to the lieutenant, who then told me to take all the men and return to our corps.

The country all about here was infested by tories, especially a certain district through which I had to pass on my return. The lieutenant charged me not to stop at this place through the night, but to rest short of it or proceed beyond it. I again set out with my 12 men, little heeding the tories. It being some time at night when we arrived at the above-mentioned Tory-land, we pushed on and did not stop till we got quite back to Smith's house. We, particularly myself and the three men who held out all night, were tired enough, having traveled about 90 miles in 24 hours, and I had traveled 5 or 6 miles further than any of them in going to and returning from the spy boats. We were hungry and tired but had nothing to eat. I had six or seven dollars in specie, which one of our corps (an Irishman) had desired me to keep awhile for him to avoid the importunity of his *friends*, but he was not with us. I, however, ventured to make use of one dollar that evening and the next morning in purchasing some bread and cheese and a little something to wet our whistles with. I afterwards paid the man, and he informed me that that dollar did him more good than all the others. I had, the day before this expedition, put on a pair of new shoes which, not having got fitted to my feet, caused blisters upon them as large as cents.[6]

The deserters were, all the time we were in pursuit of them, within three miles of the place where they left us. The man whom

---

[6] That Martin could have covered 90 miles on foot in 24 hours seems almost humanly impossible, especially with new shoes cutting up his feet. He and his comrades were most likely riding horses, since they needed to move faster than the deserters they were trying to capture.

they forced off with them made his escape from them soon after and returned; he told me that they saw us on our return, that they were then in Haverstraw Mountain,[7] not more than a quarter of a mile from us. Thus I had another useless and fatiguing expedition for nothing.

The next morning we set out after our troops, who had gone on for West Point, about 18 or 20 miles. We found them on the eastern side of the river. Here we got some provisions and a day or two after crossed over to West Point, where we encamped and worked some time in repairing the fortifications.

Toward the latter part of the summer we went on to Connecticut Island,[8] opposite to West Point, and were employed awhile in blasting rocks for the repair of the works on that side of the river. It was not so dreary at this time as it was when we were there wheeling dirt upon the magazine in 1780. Our duty was not over hard, but the engineers kept us busy.

In the month of September, while we lay here and our tents were pitched about promiscuously by reason of the ruggedness of the ground, our captain had pitched his marquee in an old gravel pit at some distance from the tents of the men. One day two or three of our young hotheads told me that they and some others of the men, whom they mentioned, were about to have some fun with "the old man," as they generally called the captain. I inquired what their plans were, and they informed me that they had put some powder into a canteen and were going to give him a bit of a hoist. I asked them to let me see their apparatus before they put their project in execution; accordingly, they soon after showed me a wooden canteen with more, as I judged, than three pounds of gunpowder in it, with a stopper of touchwood for a fuse affixed to it, all, they said, in prime order. I told them they were crazy, that the powder they had in the canteen would "hoist" him out of time, but they insisted upon proceeding. It would only frighten him, they said, and that was all they wished to do; it would make him a little more complaisant. I then told them that if they persisted in their determination and would not promise me on the spot to give up their scheme, I would that instant go to the captain and lay the whole affair before him.

At length, after endeavoring without effect to obtain my consent to try a little under his berth, they concluded to give up the affair

---

[7]   An eminence in the Hudson Highlands south of Stony Point.
[8]   A slip of the pen. Martin meant Constitution Island.

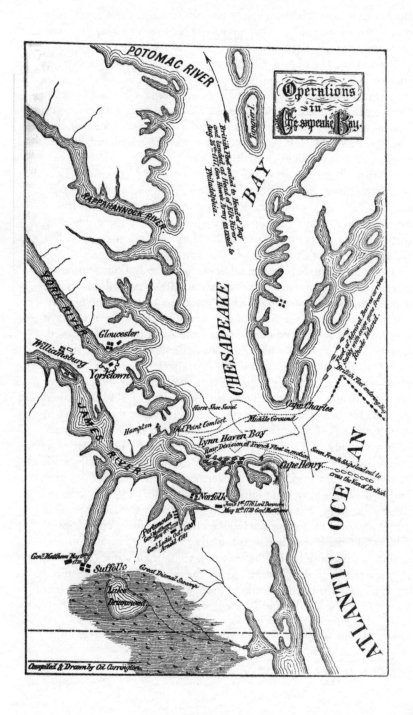

POTOMAC RIVER

Operations in Chesapeake Bay.

British Fleet sailed to Head of Bay and landed, and head of Elk River, and marched by army as route to Philadelphia.

RAPPAHANNOCK RIVER

YORK RIVER

BAY

CHESAPEAKE

Gloucester

Williamsburg

Yorktown

Fleet of Admiral Barras arrives Sandy with army came from Rhode Island.

British Fleet entering Bay.

Horse Shoe Sand

Old Point Comfort

Cape Charles

Middle Ground

Hampton

JAMES RIVER

Lynn Haven Bay

Rear Division of French Fleet in motion

Cape Henry

Seven French Ships lead out to cross the Van of British

Norfolk

Jan'y 1st 1776 Lord Dunmore

May 11th 1779 Gen'l Matthews

ATLANTIC OCEAN

Portsmouth
Gen'l Matthews May 11th 1779
Gen'l Leslie Oct'r 1780
Arnold 1781

Gen'l Matthews May 11th 1779

Suffolk

Great Dismal Swamp

Lake Drummond

Compiled & Drawn by Col. Carrington.

Chapter IX

Campaign of 1783

JPM reflects on the meaning of his experiences as he grew to adulthood as a Continental soldier while also chiding his contemporaries for not appreciating how much he and his long-term comrades had to suffer and sacrifice to bring the new American republic into being.

> When we see th' end of strife and war—
> And gain what we contended for:—
> Remember that our thanks are due
> To HIM whose mercy brings us through.

The winter set in rather early for that part of the country, and not over gentle. We had a quarters guard and a magazine guard to keep; the magazine was situated on one of the highest hills, or rather ledges, on the island. In a cold northeast snowstorm it would make a sentry shake his ears to stand two hours before the magazine. We likewise kept a small guard to protect the slaughterhouse about half the winter; the invalids kept it the other half. All this made the duty of our little corps of less than 70 men rather hard.

I was once upon this slaughterhouse guard when I went to relieve the sentinel there, who was a roommate of mine and a smart, active young man of about 21 years of age. As it was an obscure place, we dispensed with the usual ceremonies in relieving sentries; but this young man standing in the door of the house when I came with the relief, and in his levity endeavoring to cut some odd figure with his musket by throwing it over and catching it again, not considering where or how he stood, he struck the butt of his piece against the upper part of the door, which knocked it out of his hands and, coming down behind him, the bayonet entered the upper part of the calf of his leg and came out a little above the ankle. I had him conveyed to the barracks, where the wound was dressed by an ignoramus boy of a surgeon belonging to the regiment of invalids.

A few days after he complained of a pain in his neck and back. I immediately informed the captain, who had him wrapped up and sent off to the hospital at Newburgh. The men who conveyed him to the hospital returned in the evening and informed us that he was dead, having been seized with the lockjaw, convulsions, or something else caused by the wound. Thus a poor fellow, who had braved the hardships and perils of the war till the very close of it, "died as a fool dieth," causing his own death by his folly. But, perhaps, if another man had been in his stead, he would have acted just as he did....

We passed this winter as contentedly as we could under the hope that the war was nearly over, and that hope buoyed us up under many difficulties which we should hardly have surmounted without its aid. But we were afraid to be *too* sanguine, for fear of being disappointed.

Sometime in the latter part of the month of February, our officers were about to send off some men to Newburgh, 10 or 12 miles up the river, to bring down some clothing. As the ice in the river had not broken up (although it began to be thin and rotten), several of the non-commissioned officers solicited the job for the sake of a frolic. We readily obtained permission, and seven or eight of us set off in the morning on the ice with a large handsled to bring the clothing upon. About a mile and a half above West Point there was a large rent in the ice, quite across the river, in some places not more than a foot or 2 wide, in others 8 or 10. We crossed this place very easily and went on.... When we came to New Windsor,[1] about three or four miles below Newburgh, we conceited we were growing thirsty. We concluded, thereupon, to go on shore and get something to make us breathe freer. We could not get anything but cider, but that was almost as good and as strong as wine. We drank pretty freely of that, and set off again.

It was now nearly sundown, and we had about seven miles to travel. Just before we had arrived at the before-mentioned rent in the ice, we overtook a sleigh drawn by two horses, and owned by a

---

[1] The last cantonment of the Continental army, where an estimated 11,000 Continentals spent the winter of 1782–83.

countryman that I was acquainted with. He had in his sleigh a hogshead of rum belonging to a sutler on West Point. There were 2 or 3 other citizens with him, one of whom was, to appearance, 60 or 70 years of age. When we arrived at the chasm in the ice, the teamster untackled his horses in order to jump them over, and we stopped to see the operation performed. He forced them both over at once; and when they struck the ice on the other side they both went through, breaking the ice for a rod round.

The poor man was in a pitiful taking: He cried like a child. Some of our party told him to choke them out. He had but little faith in the plan; we, however, soon got his leading reins, which happened to be strong new cords, and fixed one round each of the horse's necks with a slip noose. They did not require much pulling before they both sprang out upon the ice together. The owner's tune now turned; he was as joyful as he had been sad before. The next thing was to get the sleigh and rum over. We got it to a narrow spot in the chasm and, all hands taking hold, we ran it over. But when the hinder ends of the sleigh runners came near the edge of the ice, they, with their own weight, broke the ice as bad as the horses had done before. The sleigh arrived safe on the other side, but we were mostly upon the broken, floating ice, but by the aid of Providence we all survived the accident.

The old man that I mentioned happened to be on the same fragment of ice with me; when I had stepped off, I saw him on the edge of the piece, settling down gradually in the water without making the least exertion to help himself. I seized him by the shoulder, and, at one flirt [strong pull], flung him upon the solid ice. He appeared as light as a bag of feathers. He was very thankful and said I had saved his life, and I am not quite sure that I did not.... If the reader says there was no "suffering of a Revolutionary soldier" in this affair, *I say* perhaps there was not; but there was an "adventure."

The great chain that barred the river at West Point had been regularly taken up every autumn and put down every spring ever since it had been in use (that chain which the soldiers used to denominate General Washington's watch chain, every four links of which weighed a ton), but we heard nothing of its being put down this spring, although some idle fellow would report that it was going to be put down immediately. These simple stories would keep the men in agitation, often for days together (for the putting down or the keeping up of the chain was the criterion by which we were to judge of war or peace), when they would get some other piece of information by the ears, which would entirely put the boot on the other leg. The political atmosphere was at this time as full of reports as ever the natural was of smoke, and of about as much consequence.[2]

Time thus passed on to the 19th of April, when we had general orders read which satisfied the most skeptical that the war was over and the prize won for which we had been contending through eight tedious years. But the soldiers said but very little about it; their chief thoughts were more closely fixed upon their situation as it respected the figure they were to exhibit upon their leaving the army and becoming citizens. Starved, ragged, and meager, not a cent to help themselves with, and no means or method in view to remedy or alleviate their condition, this was appalling in the extreme. All that they could do was to make a virtue of necessity and face the threatening evils with the same resolution and fortitude that they had for so long a time faced the enemy in the field.

At length the 11th day of June, 1783, arrived. "The old man," our captain, came into our room with his hands full of papers, and first ordered us to empty all our cartridge boxes upon the floor (this was the last order he ever gave us), and then told us that if we needed them we might take some of them again. They were all immediately gathered up and returned to our boxes. Government had given us our arms, and we considered the ammunition as belonging to them, and he had neither right nor orders to take them from us. He then handed us our discharges, or rather furloughs, for they were in appearance no other than furloughs, permission to return home, but to return to the army again if required. This was policy in government; to discharge us absolutely in our present pitiful, forlorn condition, it was feared, might cause some difficulties, which might be too hard for government to get easily over.[3]

[2]　The chain links, samples of which may be viewed on the grounds of West Point today, actually weighed closer to 180 pounds, rather than Martin's 500-pound estimate. Far more important was Martin's observation about the possible meaning of not placing the chain across the Hudson River that spring.

On April 19, as Martin further notes, soldiers in the Highlands region joyously received news about the Continental Congress's decision four days earlier to approve preliminary articles of peace with Great Britain. American and British commissioners, meeting in Paris, had worked out this draft settlement during the autumn of 1782. On September 3, 1783, the war officially came to an end with formal signing ceremonies in Paris.

[3]　The troops, despite Washington's efforts, did not receive any wages, only certificates of back pay owed to them. Besides muskets, which Congress gave them as presents, and ammunition, which they appropriated for themselves, the soldiers

The powder in our cartridges was soon burnt. Some saluted the officers with large charges; others only squibbed them, just as each one's mind was affected toward them. Our "old man" had a number of these last-mentioned symbols of honor and affection presented him. Some of the men were not half so liberal in the use of powder as they were when they would have given him a canteenful at once.

I confess, after all, that my anticipation of the happiness I should experience upon such a day as this was not realized. I can assure the reader that there was as much sorrow as joy transfused on the occasion. We had lived together as a family of brothers for several years (setting aside some little family squabbles, like most other families); had shared with each other the hardships, dangers, and sufferings incident to a soldier's life; had sympathized with each other in trouble and sickness; had assisted in bearing each other's burdens or strove to make them lighter by council and advice; had endeavored to conceal each other's faults or make them appear in as good a light as they would bear. In short, the soldiery, each in his particular circle of acquaintance, were as strict a band of brotherhood as Masons and, I believe, as faithful to each other. And now we were to be (the greater part of us) parted forever, as unconditionally separated as though the grave lay between us. This I say was the case with the most, I will not say all; there were as many genuine misanthropists [people haters] among the soldiers, according to numbers, as of any other class of people whatever, and some in our corps of Miners; but we were young men and had warm hearts. I question if there was a corps in the army that parted with more

---

received furlough papers, which meant that they could be called back into the service if some unforeseen event reignited the war. The furlough papers would convert into honorable discharges, once the preliminary peace treaty gained formal ratification. Furlough papers could also be used at a later date to claim land warrant certificates, at least for those veterans who had secured enlistment promises of receiving free land, usually in the amount of 100 acres, once the war had reached a successful ending.

Most of the soldiers traded their muskets and pay certificates to get what they needed most, some decent clothing and a pittance of cash to begin reestablishing themselves in civilian life. Most also quickly bartered off their land warrant certificates, if they even obtained them, for whatever necessities they could get. Few of them ever benefited from promises of free land, a matter referenced by Martin in alluding to the so-called "soldiers' lands" in southeastern Ohio. What Washington's long-term Continentals did have, even as numbers of them lived out their lives in poverty, was the personal satisfaction of having made a pivotal contribution to the making of a new republican nation.

regret than ours did, the New Englanders in particular. Ah! it was a serious time.

Some of the soldiers went off for home the same day that their fetters [chains] were knocked off. Others stayed and got their final settlement certificates, which they sold to procure decent clothing and money sufficient to enable them to pass with decency through the country and to appear something like themselves when they arrived among their friends. I was among those; I went up the river to the Wallkill,[4] and stayed some time. When I returned to West Point the certificates were not ready, and it was uncertain when they would be. I had waited so long I was loath to leave there without them.

I had a friend and acquaintance in one of the Massachusetts regiments, who had five or six months to serve in the three years service; there was also in the same regiment a man who had about the same space of time to serve and who wished to hire a man to take his place. My friend persuaded me (although against my inclinations) to take this man's place, telling me that at the expiration of our service, we would go together into the western parts of the state of New York, where there was a plenty of good land to be had as cheap as the Irishman's potatoes ... ; and there we would get us farms and live like heroes. The other man offering me 16 dollars in specie with several other small articles, I consented; and now I had got hobbled again, though but for a short time.

After I had been in this regiment about a month or six weeks, this "friend of mine" told me that he had taken an affront at something, I have forgotten what, and was determined not to stay there any longer, and endeavored to persuade me to go with him. I told him I had so short a time to serve, and, as there was a prospect that I should not have to stay so long as I had engaged to do, I would not go off like a scoundrel, get a bad name, and subject myself to suspicion and danger. I labored to persuade him to relinquish his foolish resolution, and I thought I had; but he a few days after set off with himself, and I have never heard of him since. I hope he did well, for he was a worthy young man.

Soon after this an order was issued that all who had but four months to serve should, after they had cut two cords of wood near

---

[4] What attracted Martin to this area and river about 25 miles northwest of West Point remains unclear. He may have been looking for farmland on which to settle after his discharge from the service.

the garrison for firewood, be discharged. Accordingly, I cut my two cords of wood and obtained an honorable discharge, which the other man might have done if he had not been so hasty in his determination.

I now bid a final farewell to the service. I had obtained my settlement certificates and sold some of them, and purchased some decent clothing, and then set off from West Point. I went into the Highlands where I accidentally came across an old messmate, who had been at work there ever since he had left the army in June last, and, as it appeared, was on a courting expedition. I stopped a few days with him and worked at the farming business; I got acquainted with the people here, who were chiefly Dutch, and as winter was approaching and my friend recommended me to them, I agreed to teach a school among them. A fit person! I knew but little and they less, if possible. 'Like people, like priest.' However, I stayed and had a school of from 20 to 30 pupils, and probably I gave them satisfaction. If I did not, it was all one; I never heard anything to the contrary. Anyhow, they wished me to stay and settle with them.

When the spring opened I bid my Dutch friends adieu and set my face to the eastward, and made no material halt till I arrived in the now state of Maine in the year 1784, where I have remained ever since, and where I expect to remain so long as I remain in existence, and here at last to rest my warworn weary limbs. And here I would make an end of my tedious narrative, but that I deem it necessary to make a few short observations relative to what I have said, or a sort of recapitulation of some of the things which I have mentioned.

When those who engaged to serve during the war enlisted, they were promised a hundred acres of land each, which was to be in their own or the adjoining states. When the country had drained the last drop of service it could screw out of the poor soldiers, they were turned adrift like old worn-out horses, and nothing said about land to pasture them upon. Congress did, indeed, appropriate lands under the denomination of "Soldiers' lands," in Ohio state, or some state, or a future state; but no care was taken that the soldiers should get them. No agents were appointed to see that the poor fellows ever got possession of their lands; no one ever took the least care about it, except a pack of speculators who were driving about the country like so many evil spirits, endeavoring to pluck the last feather from the soldiers. The soldiers were ignorant of the ways and means to obtain their bounty lands, and there was no one appointed to inform them. The truth was, none cared for them; the country was served, and faithfully served, and that was all that was deemed necessary. It was, soldiers, look to yourselves, we want no more of you. I hope I shall one day find land enough to lay my bones in. If I chance to die in a civilized country, none will deny me that. A dead body never begs a grave; thanks for that.

They were likewise promised the following articles of clothing per year. One uniform coat, a woolen and a linen waistcoat, four shirts, four pair of shoes, four pair of stockings, a pair of woolen and a pair of linen overalls, a hat or a leather cap, a stock for the neck, a hunting shirt, a pair of shoe buckles, and a blanket. Ample clothing, says the reader; and ample clothing, say I. But what did we ever realize of all this ample store—why, perhaps a coat (we generally did get that) and one or two shirts, the same of shoes and stockings, and, indeed, the same may be said of every other article of clothing—a few dribbled out in a regiment two or three times in a year, never getting a whole suit at a time, and all of the poorest quality; and blankets of thin baize [woolen material], thin enough to have straws shot through without discommoding the threads. How often have I had to lie whole stormy, cold nights in a wood, on a field, or a bleak hill with such blankets and other clothing like them, with nothing but the canopy of the heavens to cover me. All this too in the heart of winter when a New England farmer, if his cattle had been in my situation, would not have slept a wink from sheer anxiety for them. And if I stepped into a house to warm me when passing, wet to the skin and almost dead with cold, hunger, and fatigue, what scornful looks and hard words have I experienced.

Almost every one has heard of the soldiers of the Revolution being tracked by the blood of their feet on the frozen ground. This is literally true; and the thousandth part of their sufferings has not, nor ever will be told. That the country was young and poor at that time, I am willing to allow; but young people are generally modest, especially females. Now, I think the country (although of the feminine gender, for we say 'she' and 'her' of it) showed but little modesty at the time alluded to, for she appeared to think her soldiers had no private parts; for on our march from the Valley Forge, through the Jerseys, and at the boasted Battle of Monmouth, a fourth part of the troops had not a scrip of anything but their ragged shirt flaps to cover their nakedness, and were obliged to remain so long after. I had picked up a few articles of light clothing during the past winter, while among the Pennsylvania farmers, or I should have been in the same predicament. "Rub and go" was always the Revolutionary soldier's motto.

As to provision of victuals, I have said a great deal already, but 10 times as much might be said and not get to the end of the chapter. When we engaged in the service we were promised the following articles for a ration: One pound of good and wholesome fresh or salt beef, or three fourths of a pound of good salt pork, a pound of good flour, soft or hard bread, a quart of salt to every hundred pounds of fresh beef, a quart of vinegar to a hundred rations, a gill of rum, brandy, or whiskey per day, some little soap and candles, I have forgot how much, for I had so little of these two articles that I never knew the quantity. And as to the article of vinegar, I do not recollect of ever having any except a spoonful at the famous rice and vinegar thanksgiving in Pennsylvania in the year 1777.

But we never received what was allowed us. Oftentimes have I gone one, two, three, and even four days without a morsel, unless the fields or forests might chance to afford enough to prevent absolute starvation. Often when I have picked the last grain from the bones of my scanty morsel, have I ate the very bones, as much of them as possibly could be eaten, and then have had to perform some hard and fatiguing duty when my stomach has been as craving as it was before I had eaten anything at all.... When General Washington told Congress, "The soldiers eat every kind of horse fodder but hay," he might have gone a little farther and told them that they eat considerable hog's fodder and not a trifle of dog's, when they could get it to eat.

We were also promised six dollars and two thirds a month, to be paid us monthly, and how did we fare in this particular? Why, as we did in every other. I received the six dollars and two thirds, till (if I remember rightly) the month of August, 1777, when paying ceased. And what was six dollars and sixty-seven cents of this "Continental currency," as it was called, worth? It was scarcely enough to procure a man a dinner. Government was ashamed to tantalize the soldiers any longer with such trash, and wisely gave it up for its own credit. I received one month's pay in specie while on the march to Virginia, in the year 1781, and except that I never received any pay worth the name while I belonged to the army[5]. Had I been paid as I was promised to be at my engaging in the service, I needed not

[5]   When Martin first enlisted in 1776, he received the standard bounty of £3 plus a cash allotment to pay for his military accouterments, including his musket. His monthly wages for 1776 were finally forthcoming in August 1777. At this juncture, Continental dollars were still holding some of their face value, but their plunge toward worthlessness was already well under way. During the spring of 1779 the Connecticut Assembly, in response to the near mutiny in January of the states's two Continental brigades, came up with funds to help offset arrearages in back pay. These paper notes were collapsing in value even as the soldiers received them. Whether Martin ever collected any other wages due him, except for his month's payment in specie, remains unclear. If he and his comrades did, such payments would have been in essentially worthless paper currency anyway.

to have suffered as I did, nor would I have done it; there was enough in the country, and money would have procured it if I had had it. It is provoking to think of it. The country was rigorous in exacting my compliance to *my* engagements to a punctilio, but equally careless in performing her contracts with me; and why so? One reason was because she had all the power in her own hands, and I had none. Such things ought not to be.

The poor soldiers had hardships enough to endure without having to starve; the least that could be done was to give them something to eat. "The laborer is worthy of his meat" at least,[6] and he ought to have it for his employer's interest, if nothing more. But as I said, there were other hardships to grapple with. How many times have I had to lie down like a dumb animal in the field and bear "the pelting of the pitiless storm,"[7] cruel enough in warm weather, but how much more so in the heart of winter. Could I have had the benefit of a little fire, it would have been deemed a luxury. But when snow or rain would fall so heavy that it was impossible to keep a spark of fire alive, to have to weather out a long, wet, cold, tedious night in the depth of winter with scarcely clothes enough to keep one from freezing instantly, how discouraging it must be I leave to my reader to judge.

It is fatiguing, almost beyond belief, to those that never experienced it, to be obliged to march 24 to 48 hours (as very many times I have had to) and often more, night and day without rest or sleep, wishing and hoping that some wood or village I could see ahead might prove a short resting place, when, alas, I came to it almost tired off my legs, it proved no resting place for me. How often have I envied the very swine their happiness, when I have heard them quarreling in their warm dry sties, when I was wet to the skin and wished in vain for that indulgence. And even in dry, warm weather, I have often been so beat out with long and tedious marching that I have fallen asleep while walking the road, and not been sensible of it till I have jostled against someone in the same situation; and when permitted to stop and have the superlative happiness to roll myself in my blanket and drop down on the ground in the bushes, briars, thorns, or thistles, and get an hour or two's sleep, O! how exhilarating.

Fighting the enemy is the great scarecrow to people unacquainted with the duties of an army. To see the fire and smoke, to hear the

---

[6]   Matthew 10:10, quoting the words of Jesus to his 12 disciples.
[7]   William Shakespeare's *King Lear*, Act 3, Scene 4.

din of cannon and musketry and the whistling of shot; they cannot bear the sight or hearing of this. They would like the service in an army tolerably well but for the fighting part of it. I never was killed in the army; I never was wounded but once; I never was a prisoner with the enemy; but I have seen many that have undergone all these; and I have many times run the risk of all of them myself. But, reader, believe me, for I tell a solemn truth, that I have felt more anxiety, undergone more fatigue and hardships, suffered more every way, in performing one of those tedious marches than ever I did in fighting the hottest battle I was ever engaged in, with the anticipation of all the other calamities I have mentioned added to it.

It has been said by some that ought to have been better employed that the Revolutionary army was needless; that the militia were competent for all that the crisis required. That there was then and now is in the militia as brave and as good men as were ever in any army since the creation, I am ready and willing to allow, but there are many among them too, I hope the citizen soldiers will be as ready to allow, who are not so good as regulars, and I affirm that the militia would not have answered so well as standing troops for the following reason among many others. They would not have endured the sufferings the army did; they would have considered themselves (as in reality they were and are) free citizens, not bound by any cords that were not of their own manufacturing, and when the hardships of fatigue, starvation, cold, and nakedness, which I have just mentioned, begun to seize upon them in such awful array as they did on us, they would have instantly quitted the service in disgust, and who would blame them? I am sure I could hardly find it in my heart to do it.

That the militia did good and great service in that war, as well as in the last, on particular occasions, I well know, for I have fought by their side, but still I insist that they would not have answered the end so well as regular soldiers, unless they were very different people from what I believe and know them to be, as well as I wish to know. Upon every exigency they would have been to be collected, and what would the enemy have been doing in the meantime? The regulars were there, and there obliged to be; we could not go away when we pleased without exposing ourselves to military punishment; and we had trouble enough to undergo without that.

It was likewise said at that time that the army was idle, did nothing but lounge about from one station to another, eating the country's bread and wearing her clothing without rendering her any essential service (and I wonder they did not add spending the country's money, too, it would have been quite as consistent as the other charges). You ought to drive on, said they, you are competent for the business; rid the country at once of her invaders. Poor simple souls! It was very easy for them to build castles in the air, but they had not felt the difficulty of making them stand there. It was easier with them taking whole armies in a warm room and by a good fire than enduring the hardships of one cold winter's night upon a bleak hill without clothing or victuals.

If the Revolutionary army was really such an useless appendage to the cause, such a nuisance as it was then and has since been said to be, why was it not broken up at once; why were we not sent off home and obliged to maintain ourselves? Surely it would have been as well for us soldiers, and, according to the reckoning of those wiseacres, it would have been *much* better for the country to have done it than for us to have been eating so much provisions, and wearing out so much clothing, when our services were worse than useless. We could have made as good militia men as though we had never seen an army at all. We should, in case we had been discharged from the army, have saved the country a world of expense, as they said; and I say, we should have saved ourselves a world of trouble in having our constitutions broken down and our joints dislocated by trotting after Bellona's car.[8]

But the poor old decrepit soldiers, after all that has been said to discourage them, have found friends in the community, and I trust there are many, very many, that are sensible of the usefulness of that suffering army, although perhaps all their voices have not been so loud in its praise as the voice of slander has been against it. President Monroe was the first of all our presidents, except President Washington, who ever uttered a syllable in the "old soldiers'" favor. President Washington urged the country to do something for them and not to forget their hard services, but President Monroe[9] told

---

[8]   Bellona was the goddess of war in Roman mythology. The car refers to Bellona's chariot.

[9]   James Monroe of Virginia, the nation's fifth president (1817–25), had initially enlisted as a company-grade officer in Virginia's 3rd regiment during September 1775. He was wounded at Trenton but went on to fight in several major battles before retiring from the service in November 1778. He became a law student of Thomas Jefferson and later held a number of prominent diplomatic and cabinet-level posts before acceding to the presidency. Monroe championed the adoption of pension legislation to assist aging, poverty-stricken veterans, and he gladly signed the Revolutionary War Pension Act of 1818 into law. To be eligible, claimants had to have served in the Continental army for at least nine months, and they also had to demonstrate their straitened financial circumstances. Rank-and-file soldiers were to receive $96 and officers $240 per year.

them how to act; he had been a soldier himself in the darkest period of the war, that point of it that emphatically "tried men's souls," was wounded, and knew what soldiers suffered. His good intentions being seconded by some Revolutionary officers then in Congress, brought about a system by which, aided by our present worthy Vice President,[10] then Secretary at War, heaven bless him, many of the poor men who had spent their youthful, and, consequently, their best days in the hard service of their country, have been enabled to eke out the fag end [last part] of their lives a little too high for the groveling hand of envy or the long arm of poverty to reach.

Many murmur now at the apparent good fortune of the poor soldiers. Many I have myself seen, vile enough to say that they never deserved such favor from the country. The only wish I would bestow upon such hardhearted wretches is, that they might be compelled to go through just such sufferings and privations as that army did; and then if they did not sing a different tune, I should miss my guess.

But I really hope these people will not go beside themselves. Those men whom they wish to die on a dunghill, men who if they had not ventured their lives in battle and faced poverty, disease, and death for their country to gain and maintain that Independence and liberty, in the sunny beams of which they, like reptiles, are basking, they would, many or the most of them, be this moment in as much need of help and succor as ever the most indigent soldier was before he experienced his country's beneficence.

The soldiers consider it cruel to be thus vilified, and it is cruel as the grave to any man, when he knows his own rectitude of conduct,

---

In Monroe's mind the country owed such compensation to soldiers and officers who had suffered and endured so much in the making of the nation. Martin certainly thought so. He quickly applied for a pension, declaring that he had virtually nothing in the way of an estate or income. Martin began receiving payments of $8 a month in April 1818. From his perspective he was at last obtaining the pay so long due him as a Continental soldier.

[10]   John C. Calhoun of South Carolina was Vice President under Andrew Jackson in 1830, the year in which Martin's narrative first appeared in print. Calhoun earlier had served as Secretary of War (1817–25) in the cabinet of James Monroe. An ardent nationalist at this time, he was a firm supporter of the Pension Act of 1818, and he also staunchly advocated a central role for professionally-trained soldiers, as opposed to militia, in providing for the nation's defense. Calhoun's position particularly appealed to Martin, who felt indignation whenever friends and neighbors claimed that the Revolution could have been won by militia troops alone. Calhoun in his subsequent political career became the South's leading proponent of states' rights in defense of the institution of slavery.

to have his hard services not only debased and underrated, but scandalized and vilified. But the Revolutionary soldiers are not the only people that endure obloquy; others as meritorious and perhaps more deserving than they are forced to submit to ungenerous treatment.

But if the old Revolutionary Pensioners are really an eyesore, a grief of mind, to any man or set of men (and I know they are), let me tell them that if they will exercise a very little patience, a few years longer will put all of them beyond the power of troubling them, for they will soon be "where the wicked cease from troubling and the weary are at rest."[11]

And now I think it is time to draw to a close (and so say I, says the reader). In truth, when I began this narrative, I thought a very few pages would contain it, but as occurrences returned to my memory and one thing brought another to mind I could not stop, for as soon as I had let one thought through my mind, another would step up and ask for admittance. And now, dear reader, if any such should be found, I will come to a close and trespass upon your time no longer.... But if you have been really desirous to hear a part, and a part only of the hardships of some of that army that achieved our Independence, I can say I am sorry you have not had an abler pen than mine to give you the requisite information.

To conclude. Whoever has the patience to follow me to the end of this rhapsody, I will confess that I think he must have almost as great a share of perseverance in reading it as I had to go through the hardships and dangers it records. And now, kind reader, I bid you a cordial and long farewell.

> Through much fatigue and many dangers past,
> The warworn soldier's braved his way at last.

THE END

---

[11] Job 3:17, in referencing Job's plea to find an end to his sufferings.

Suggestions for Additional Reading

General histories that focus on the American Revolution abound. For a crisp, brief introduction, none is easier to read than Edmund S. Morgan, *The Birth of the Republic, 1763–1789*, 3rd edition (Chicago, 1993). A much fuller exploration of major events and personalities may be found in Robert Middlekauff, *The Glorious Cause: The American Revolution, 1763–1789*, revised edition (New York, 2007). Exemplary of volumes that place more emphasis on ordinary persons and popular participation in the Revolution are Edward Countryman, *The American Revolution*, revised edition (New York, 2003); Gary B. Nash, *The Unknown American Revolution* (New York, 2005); and Ray Raphael, *A People's History of the American Revolution* (New York, 2001).

Studies of the Revolutionary War assume a variety of forms. Those taking a "guns and battles" approach, with much emphasis on combat as waged from the armchair general's point of view, include John Richard Alden, *The American Revolution, 1775–1783* (New York, 1954); Howard H. Peckham, *The War for Independence: A Military History*, reprint edition (Chicago, 1979); and Willard M. Wallace, *Appeal to Arms: A Military History of the American Revolution* (Chicago, 1951). R. Ernest Dupuy, et al., *The American Revolution: A Global War* (New York, 1977), looks at the martial contest in worldwide perspective. British scholars have offered a similarly broadened dimension, often from the point of view of determining why Britain failed to achieve victory over its erstwhile colonists. Good examples include Jeremy Black, *War for America: The Fight of Independence, 1775–1783* (New York, 1991); Stephen Conway, *The War of American Independence, 1775–1783* (London, 1995); and Piers Mackesy, *The War for America, 1775–1783*, reprint edition (Lincoln, Neb., 1993). By comparison, John Ferling carefully considers why Americans ultimately succeeded in *Almost a Miracle: The American Victory in the War of Independence* (New York, 2007).

In his memoir Martin challenged the notion that American colonists willingly sacrificed their all during eight long years of warfare. He found it galling to hear those persons who had served in militia units, but had hardly spent any time in the field, taking so much credit for winning the war. As a "duration" Continental soldier, Martin considered such claims to be little more than airy fluff from those who had lacked the courage to stay in the field over several years. The debate over the martial contributions of short-term militia in comparison to those of long-term regulars has pervaded studies not only about the Revolutionary War but also about American military history more generally. Valuable insights may be found in Marcus Cunliffe, *Soldiers and Civilians: The Martial Spirit in America, 1765–1865*, 2nd edition (New York, 1973), which investigates the early evolution of the "professional" and "antiprofessional" traditions from the Revolution to the Civil War, and Richard H. Kohn, *Eagle and Sword: The Federalists and the Creation of the Military Establishment in America, 1783–1802* (New York, 1975), which evaluates conflicting attitudes and military policy formulations after the war. Lawrence Delbert Cress, *Citizens in Arms: The Army and Military in American Society to the War of 1812* (Chapel Hill, NC, 1982), considers how an ideological tradition laden with fear about long-term soldiers in standing armies affected military decision making during the Revolution. Don Higginbotham, "The American Militia: A Traditional Institution with Revolutionary Responsibilities," in Higginbotham, ed., *Reconsiderations on the Revolutionary War: Selected Essays* (Westport, Conn., 1978), pp. 83–103, views the militia as a source of significant contributions to overall victory, an argument amplified in Mark V. Kwasny, *Washington's Partisan War, 1775–1783* (Kent, Ohio, 1996), which sees Washington often structuring strategy around available militia units. By comparison, James Kirby Martin, "The Continental Army and the American Victory," in John Ferling, ed., *The World Turned Upside Down: The American Victory in the War of Independence* (Westport, Conn., 1988), pp. 19–34, portrays militia as necessary auxiliary troops with little to brag about in regard to actual battlefield accomplishments.

In relation to the militia–regular debate, images of freedom-loving, landholding farmers shouldering their muskets and going off to defend their communities against a tyrannical enemy used to dominate historical commentary about who actually fought for American independence. Certainly at the outset, freehold farmers, many of them serving in selected Minutemen (ready-to-fight militia) units, were dominant in the first wave of combat. Two valuable studies touching upon the experiences of these citizen-soldiers are Robert A. Gross, *The Minutemen and Their World* (New York, 1976), and David Hackett Fischer, *Paul Revere's Ride* (New York, 1994).

In recent years a number of historians have investigated the question of what economic, social, ethnic, and racial groups actually sustained the long-term fight, ultimately making victory possible for all Americans. These studies have shown that downtrodden and poorer persons, including women with little or no property, indentured servants, African American slaves, and captured British (many of them Irish) and Hessian soldiers, came to make up the hard core of Washington's long-term Continentals. In many ways, then, Martin was among the more privileged of persons serving in the Continental army. For a summary of these findings, see James Kirby Martin and Mark Edward Lender, *A Respectable Army: The Military Origins of the Republic, 1763–1789*, 2nd edition (Wheeling, Ill., 2006). Charles Patrick Neimeyer, *America Goes to War: A Social History of the Continental Army* (New York, 1996), adds important information about Irish and German colonists recruited into the ranks as well as African American soldiers and Indian auxiliaries. A sampling of other studies includes Gregory T. Knouff, *The Soldiers' Revolution: Pennsylvanians in Arms and the Forging of Early American Identity* (University Park, Pa., 2004); Mark E. Lender, "The Social Structure of the New Jersey Brigade," in Peter Karsten, ed., *The Military in America: From Colonial Times to the Present* (New York, 1980), pp. 27–44; Edward C. Papenfuse and Gregory A. Stiverson, "General Smallwood's Recruits: The Peacetime Career of the Revolutionary War Private," *William and Mary Quarterly*, 3rd series, 30 (1973): 117–32; and essays by Walter Sargent, John Resch, Michael A. McDonnell, and Judith L. Van Buskirk in John Resch and Walter Sargent, eds., *War and Society in the American Revolution* (DeKalb, Ill., 2007).

On women serving in and around the Continental ranks, see Holly A. Mayer, *Belonging to the Army: Camp Followers and Community during the American Revolution* (Columbia, SC, 1996); Alfred F. Young, *Masquerade: The Life and Times of Deborah Sampson, Continental Soldier* (New York, 2004); Linda Grant De Pauw, "Women in Combat: The Revolutionary War Experience," *Armed Forces and Society*, 7 (1981): 209–26; and John Todd White, "The Truth about Molly Pitcher," in James Kirby Martin and Karen R. Stubaus, eds., *The American Revolution: Whose Revolution?* (Huntington, NY, 1981), pp. 99–105. On African Americans under arms, see Benjamin Quarles, *The Negro in the American Revolution* (Chapel Hill, NC, 1961), with additional amplification in Sylvia R. Frey, *Water from the Rock: Black Resistance in a Revolutionary Age* (Princeton, NJ, 1991). An introduction to Native American service may be found in Joseph T. Glatthaar and James Kirby Martin, *Forgotten Allies: The Oneida Indians and the American Revolution* (New York, 2006). On enemy troops faced by Martin and his comrades, good introductions include Sylvia R. Frey, *The British Soldier in America: A Social History of Military Life in the Revolutionary Period* (Austin, Tx., 1981), and Rodney Atwood, *The Hessians: Mercenaries from Hessen-Kassel in the American Revolution* (New York, 1980).

Despite the absence of broad-based participation in actually fighting the war, some studies have argued that the general populace kept viewing itself as deeply attached to the ideals of the Revolution, which allowed thousands of persons to portray themselves as abiding patriots after the achievement of independence. On this theme, see Charles Royster, *A Revolutionary*

People at War: The Continental Army and American Character, 1775–1783 (Chapel Hill, NC, 1979), which also downplays the importance of material factors in convincing the likes of Martin and other soldiers to stay out for the long-term fight. E. Wayne Carp, *To Starve the Army at Pleasure: Continental Army Administration and American Political Culture, 1775–1783* (Chapel Hill, NC, 1984), argues that ideological considerations were paramount in explaining why otherwise liberty-loving civilians repeatedly failed to meet supply quotas for the Continental army. Acceding to demands of local Revolutionary leaders to support the army with material goods was akin to what colonists thought they were rebelling against—arbitrary, tyrannical attacks on their property. Meanwhile, Martin and his comrades endured supply shortages of all kinds. In Connecticut, by comparison, contends Richard Buel, Jr., *Dear Liberty: Connecticut's Mobilization for the Revolutionary War* (Middletown, Conn., 1980), civilians contributed so much that they had worn themselves out long before the war had ended, which resulted in long-term economic dislocation for several years thereafter.

Additional information about the campaigns and events to which Martin contributed may be found in such studies as David Hackett Fischer, *Washington's Crossing* (New York, 2004); Stephen R. Taaffe, *The Philadelphia Campaign, 1777–1778* (Lawrence, Kans., 2003); Wayne Bodle, *The Valley Forge Winter: Civilians and Soldiers in War* (University Park, Pa., 2002); Thomas Fleming, *Washington's Secret War: The Hidden History of Valley Forge* (New York, 2005); Judith L. Van Buskirk, *Generous Enemies: Patriots and Loyalists in Revolutionary New York* (Philadelphia, 2002); Adrian C. Leiby, *The Revolutionary War in the Hackensack Valley: The Jersey Dutch and the Neutral Ground, 1775–1783*, revised edition (New Brunswick, NJ, 1992); and Jerome A. Greene, *The Guns of Independence: The Siege of Yorktown, 1781* (New York, 2005).

At no point did Martin portray the civilian populace as having given its all in supporting Continental forces. Increasingly, the army grew restive, finally to the point of line mutinies, which still need greater historical explication than is currently available. Those interested in investigating the army's mounting anger over civilian indifference should look at Carl Van Doren, *Mutiny in January* (New York, 1943), which focuses on the major uprisings of the Pennsylvania and New Jersey lines in January 1781, and James Kirby Martin, "A 'Most Undisciplined, Profligate Crew': Protest and Defiance in the Continental Ranks, 1776–1783," in Ronald Hoffman and Peter J. Albert, eds., *Arms and Independence: The Military Character of the American Revolution* (Charlottesville, Va., 1984), pp. 119–40. In a similar vein, readers might consider comparing Martin's attitudes about continued self-sacrifice in the face of so many problems with the thoughts of other lesser-ranking soldiers and officers. See in particular the observations contained in John Shy, "Hearts and Minds in the American Revolution: The Case of 'Long Bill' Scott and Peterborough, New Hampshire," in *A People Numerous and Armed: Reflections on the Military Struggle for*

American Independence (New York, 1976), pp. 163–79, and John Shy, ed., *Winding Down: The Revolutionary War Letters of Lieutenant Benjamin Gilbert of Massachusetts, 1780–1783* (Ann Arbor, Mich., 1989).

Among other compilations relating to the wartime experiences of Continentals, none is better on army doctrine and organization than Robert K. Wright, Jr., *The Continental Army* (Washington, DC, 1983). On wartime casualties, Howard H. Peckham, ed., *The Toll of Independence: Engagements and Battle Casualties of the American Revolution* (Chicago, 1974), provides the most complete analysis. Similarly, Charles H. Lesser, ed., *The Sinews of Independence: Monthly Strength Reports of the Continental Army* (Chicago, 1976), reprints materials showing how small the army's troop strength was at critical points during the war. John C. Dann, ed., *The Revolution Remembered: Eyewitness Accounts of the War for Independence* (Chicago, 1980), offers an introduction to the pension claims of thousands of aging Revolutionary soldiers as well as examples of personal histories that can be gleaned from these records. J. Todd White and Charles H. Lesser, eds., *Fighters for Independence: A Guide to Sources of Biographical Information on Soldiers and Sailors of the American Revolution* (Chicago, 1977), provides a useful list of diaries, memoirs, and recollections.

John Resch, *Suffering Soldiers: Revolutionary War Veterans, Moral Sentiment, and Political Culture in the Early Republic* (Amherst, Mass., 1999), concludes that service pensions became possible for the likes of Martin because of revised public memories of the Revolution that acknowledged the central importance of Continentals in winning the War for Independence. Martin presented the issue differently. He believed that the populace of the early nineteenth century had come to belittle if not dismiss the sacrifices and sufferings that he and comrades had made to the American cause. One of the reasons that he wrote his memoir was to challenge this popular impression. On the formation of public memories and their development over time, worthy introductions include Sarah J. Purcell, *Sealed with Blood: War, Sacrifice, and Memory in Revolutionary America* (Philadelphia, 2002); Alfred F. Young, *The Shoemaker and the Tea Party: Memory and the American Revolution* (Boston, 1999); and the various essays contained in Alfred F. Young, *Liberty Tree: Ordinary People and the American Revolution* (New York, 2006).

Index